Legalines

Editorial Advisors:
Gloria A. Aluise
Attorney at Law
David H. Barber
Attorney at Law
Robert A. Wyler
Attorney at Law

Authors:
Gloria A. Aluise
Attorney at Law
David H. Barber
Attorney at Law
Daniel O. Bernstine
Attorney at Law
D. Steven Brewster
C.P.A.
Roy L. Brooks
Professor of Law
Frank L. Bruno
Attorney at Law
Scott M. Burbank
C.P.A.
Jonathan C. Carlson
Professor of Law
Charles N. Carnes
Professor of Law
Paul S. Dempsey
Professor of Law
Jerome A. Hoffman
Professor of Law
Mark R. Lee
Professor of Law
Jonathan Neville
Attorney at Law
Laurence C. Nolan
Professor of Law
Arpiar Saunders
Attorney at Law
Robert A. Wyler
Attorney at Law

TORTS

Adaptable to Tenth Edition of Prosser Casebook

By Jonathan Neville
Attorney at Law

THE barbri GROUP

A THOMSON COMPANY

EDITORIAL OFFICES: 111 W. Jackson Blvd., 7th Floor, Chicago, IL 60604
REGIONAL OFFICES: Chicago, Dallas, Los Angeles, New York, Washington, D.C.

SERIES EDITOR
Gail O'Gradney, J.D.
Attorney at Law

PRODUCTION MANAGER
Elizabeth G. Duke

SECOND PRINTING—2004

SHORT SUMMARY OF CONTENTS

TABLE OF CONTENTS AND SHORT REVIEW OUTLINE

I. INTRODUCTION TO TORT LIABILITY

A. DEFINITIONS AND DISTINCTIONS

The body of law known as Torts is concerned with the allocation of losses resulting from the activities of people; it is an attempt to balance the utility of a particular type of conduct against the harm that it may cause, judged by the prevailing social and economic attitudes of the time. The word "tort" was introduced from the French into the English language after the Norman Conquest; it has its roots in the Latin word "tortus," meaning twisted, and in French roughly corresponds to the English word "wrong." In a broad sense, a tort is a wrong, and a tortious act or omission is a wrongful act or omission. While no one definition satisfactorily defines "torts" generally, a tort usually arises through conduct, in the form of an act or omission, affecting a legally protected interest in person or property (or both), usually done with a certain state of mind (*e.g.*, intention, reckless disregard of the consequences, inadvertence, mistake), which causes damage.

1. **Tort vs. Crime.** A tort is distinguished from a crime in that the latter is a social harm defined and made punishable by the state. While the same act or omission may result in both a crime and a tort, a tort is a wrong to the individual, while a crime is a wrong against the public at large for which the state seeks redress. Torts may be committed by individuals, corporations, associations, and other entities. The party who commits a tort is commonly referred to as the tortfeasor.

2. **Damages.** If the elements of a tort are established by the plaintiff and if the defendant fails to raise an adequate defense, a court will award nominal damages if no injury has in fact been sustained, or damages in such amount as it deems reasonable to compensate the plaintiff for the loss suffered. No other special damages (*i.e.*, damages not generally resulting from the tort but suffered by the plaintiff because of his particular circumstances, condition, etc.) need be shown for tort liability to attach to the defendant. However, when liability does attach to the defendant, any special damages caused to the plaintiff as a result of the defendant's act or omission may also be recovered. Further, if it appears that the act or omission of the defendant that forms the basis of the liability was either motivated by an intention to injure or harm the plaintiff or constituted a willful and wanton, or gross, disregard of the consequences, the court may, in addition, award punitive ("exemplary") damages against the defendant. (See more detailed discussion, *infra*, under **Damages**.)

3. **The Policies of Tort Liability.** Judicial opinions resolve controversies between two parties. Thus, the premises underlying tort law are seldom discussed in depth. There are several, sometimes conflicting, values involved:

(i) Compensating individuals who have been injured;

(ii) Preserving individual choice; and

(iii) Determining the social cost-benefit of a given policy.

For example, should the legal system force all persons to be vaccinated for polio? Even if there is some chance that a few will die from the vaccination? Should individual choice be allowed if the benefit to society is greater than the cost of the loss of some individuals?

4. **Objectives of the Tort System.** There are many possible compensation systems: negligence; negligence plus liability insurance; strict liability; strict liability plus insurance, etc. Whatever system is employed, it should fulfill the following objectives:

(i) Be equitable (between those who receive benefits and those who bear the burden; among beneficiaries; among the cost-bearers);

(ii) Contribute to the wise allocation of human and economic resources;

(iii) Compensate promptly;

(iv) Be reliable;

(v) Distribute losses rather than leave them on single individuals;

(vi) Be efficient;

(vii) Deter risky conduct; and

(viii)Minimize fraud.

Each compensation system meets these objectives to some extent. For example, negligence law is founded on the notion of compensation based on fault. But fault is objective. Thus, the moral basis of liability is eroded. Objectification may be defended in that it reduces cost and the error in administering the system. Also, fault is supported by commonly shared values of people. Possibly the system deters risky conduct.

B. HISTORICAL DEVELOPMENT OF LIABILITY BASED ON FAULT

1. **Origins.** Historians have disagreed as to the origins of the law of torts. One theory holds that liability was originally grounded on actual intent or personal fault within a strong moral framework, moving gradually toward the formulation of standards of conduct that were less concerned with subjective fault and more concerned with evaluating the alleged tortfeasor's conduct on the basis of an objective standard. The other and more generally accepted theory is that liability originally was not based

upon the immoral conduct of the alleged tortfeasor but upon the causal connection between the conduct and the damage (*i.e.*, a person was deemed to act at his own peril) and gradually evolved to a position where moral standards became the basis of liability. Today, while liability is generally recognized as being based on fault (*e.g.*, where there is intent to injure another, or where there is a breach of a duty owed another), the "fault" is not necessarily moral fault on the part of the tortfeasor; *i.e.*, no personal immorality is required; liability may stem from "social fault." "Social fault" will be found where the consequences of the tortfeasor's conduct are deemed by society to be so undesirable that the state of mind of the tortfeasor is immaterial (*e.g.*, liability of the insane for injuries caused to others, strict liability on businesses for placing adulterated foods in the hands of human beings who then suffer food poisoning, etc.).

a. **Early English law.** In the common law courts of the 13th century, only two writs were available for redressing torts. These were the writ of trespass and the writ of trespass on the case.

   1) **Trespass.** The writ of trespass provided relief for all direct and immediate forcible injuries to person or property. It covered unintentional as well as intentional injuries, required no proof of actual damages, and did not require fault on the part of the defendant (*i.e.*, wrongful intent or negligence was not required).

   2) **Trespass on the case.** The writ of trespass on the case provided relief for injuries that were intended but were either not forcible or not direct. Usually, the plaintiff was required to show actual damages and wrongful intent or negligence on the part of the defendant.

b. **Present law.** Today, tort liability generally falls into three classes:

   1) Liability based on intent of the defendant;

   2) Liability based on the negligence of the defendant;

   3) Liability that attaches irrespective of the state of mind of the defendant; *i.e.*, strict liability.

2. **Case Development.**

   a. **Intent or fault immaterial.** The case of *Anonymous* (Kings Bench 1466), indicates that early English common law recognized liability for the consequences of one's actions, notwithstanding that the consequences were unintended. The case cites the example of the person who accidentally drops a timber on his neighbor's house while constructing his own home and states that such person would be liable for the damages caused notwithstanding that the "erection of [the tortfeasor's] house was lawful and that the timber fell without [the tortfeasor's] intent." The case also states that a person defending himself from an assault will be liable for damages if he injures third parties while effecting his own defense against the attacker. Innocent intent was immaterial; the important criteria were direct, immediate, and forcible injury to person or property.

Weaver v. Ward

b. **Intent or fault possibly material--Weaver v. Ward,** 80 Eng. Rep. 284 (K.B. 1616).

1) **Facts.** Weaver (P) and Ward (D) were soldiers. In the course of a military exercise, D's musket accidentally discharged, wounding P. P brought an action in trespass for damages for the injury.

2) **Issue.** To recover for assault and battery, must a plaintiff show intent or fault on the part of a defendant?

3) **Held.** No. Judgment for P.

a) In an action for trespass, damages are awarded for hurt or loss, not as a punishment for D's felonious mind. Even though D claims the injury was an accident, he may be held liable.

b) D would not be liable if he had been utterly without fault. For example, if P had run in front of D's musket as it was firing, D would not be liable.

4) **Comment.** The court indicated a move toward looking at the defendant's intent or negligence instead of the artificial classification of the injury as direct or indirect. The shift was finally completed in the late 19th century when it was recognized that no liability would lie for pure accident and that, for the defendant to be held responsible for injury to the person, there must be fault on his part; *i.e.*, wrongful intent or negligence.

Brown v. Kendall

c. **American evolution of negligence--Brown v. Kendall,** 60 Mass. (6 Cush.) 292 (1850).

1) **Facts.** Brown's (P's) and Kendall's (D's) dogs were fighting. While attempting to separate the dogs, D struck P (who was standing behind him) in the eye with a stick. The trial court placed the burden on D to show that he exercised extraordinary care because he was not engaged in a necessary act. D's objection to this requirement was overruled, and judgment was rendered for P. D appeals.

2) **Issue.** Does a person have a duty to exercise extraordinary care in performing an unnecessary act?

3) **Held.** No. Judgment reversed and new trial ordered.

a) It was error to overrule D's objection. When a defendant is engaged in a lawful act and injures a plaintiff, the plaintiff may not recover damages if:

(1) The plaintiff and the defendant both exercise ordinary care;

(2) The plaintiff and the defendant both fail to exercise ordinary care; or

(3) The plaintiff alone fails to exercise ordinary care.

b) If the injury to P was only accidental, meaning that D did not intend to hit him and did not act negligently or carelessly, then D is not liable.

4) **Comments.**

a) The standard of care referred to by the court was not the subjective standard (*i.e.*, dependent upon the individuals involved), but an objective standard related to the degree of care prudent and cautious persons under similar circumstances would exercise. Further, the court pointed out that the plaintiff, and not the defendant, has the burden of proof; *i.e.*, the plaintiff has the burden of proving negligence, or fault, on the part of the defendant.

b) The importance of this case is that it indicates the shift to finding liability on the part of a defendant only if he is legally at fault. The court stated that ". . . if it appears that the defendant was doing a lawful act, and unintentionally hit and hurt the plaintiff, then, unless it also appears to the satisfaction of the jury that the defendant is chargeable with some fault, negligence, carelessness, or want of prudence, the plaintiff fails to sustain the burden of proof, and is not entitled to recover."

d. **Negligence: unforeseeable circumstances--Cohen v. Petty,** 65 F.2d 820 (D.C. Cir. 1933). Cohen v. Petty

1) **Facts.** Cohen (P) was a guest in Petty's (D's) automobile when D suddenly passed out, lost control of the automobile, and then crashed it. P was injured. At trial, D testified that he had never fainted before and that as far as he knew, he was in good health. The trial judge directed a verdict for D and P appeals.

2) **Issue.** May a person be liable for an unforeseeable occurrence that rendered him unable to control his actions?

3) **Held.** No. Judgment affirmed.

a) D was not negligent. The sudden fainting spell was unforeseeable and D was therefore not liable for the injury to P. The accident was unavoidable. There was no evidence of unreasonable conduct or negligence on the part of D.

b) It is undoubtedly the law that one who is suddenly stricken by an illness, which he had no reason to anticipate, while driving an automobile, which renders it impossible for him to control the car, is not chargeable with negligence.

4) Comments.

a) D was entitled to a directed verdict because as a matter of law, not fact, he was not negligent. A defendant is entitled to a directed verdict only if reasonable persons could not possibly find for the plaintiff. Matters of questionable fact over which reasonable persons may disagree are subject to jury determination.

b) This case carries *Kendall* a step further by establishing that knowledge of a risk can constitute negligence if an injury results from that risk.

Spano v.
Perini Corp.

e. Strict liability--Spano v. Perini Corp., 250 N.E.2d 31 (N.Y. 1969).

1) Facts. Spano's (P's) garage and a car inside were wrecked when Perini Corp. (D) set off dynamite (194 sticks) while blasting at a construction site 125 feet away. No negligence on D's part could be shown. The trial court held for P; the Appellate Term reversed and the Appellate Division affirmed, hence this appeal.

2) Issue. May a defendant be liable for damages caused by its dangerous activities, notwithstanding the absence of negligence?

3) Held. Yes. Judgment reversed.

a) P relied on the principle of absolute liability and did not try to prove that D failed to exercise reasonable care or take appropriate precautions. Traditionally, proof of negligence is required to recover damages caused by blasting unless there is an actual physical invasion of the plaintiff's property, such as by rocks or other debris.

b) This traditional New York rule has been rejected in most other jurisdictions. It was based on a public policy to promote property improvement, which requires use of explosives. However, that rationale is faulty. The question is not whether blasting is a legal activity, but who should pay for the damages. Between the person engaged in the dangerous activity and the innocent neighbor who is injured, the former should pay, even without proof of negligence.

4) Comment. The scope and application of strict liability is discussed in greater detail *infra*.

II. INTENTIONAL INTERFERENCE WITH PERSON OR PROPERTY

A. INTENT

1. **Introduction.** One of the major classifications of tort liability is liability based on the intent of the defendant. It is the intent to bring about certain consequences that is important, not merely the intent to do an act. Intent includes not only the desire to bring about the physical results, but also the knowledge or belief that certain results are substantially certain to follow from the actor's conduct.

   a. **Need not be malicious.** The intent forming the basis of tort liability need not be immoral, malicious, or hostile; instead, it need only be an intent to affect a legally protected interest in a way that will not be permitted by law.

   b. **Objective standard.** The actor's subjective knowledge or belief that certain results are substantially certain to follow from his conduct is determined on an objective rather than a subjective basis. That is, actual knowledge or belief, or lack thereof, on the part of the defendant is immaterial if a reasonable person in the position of the defendant would have believed that certain results were substantially certain to follow from the conduct of the defendant. Of course, the external, objective standard must have certain subjective inputs based upon the position of the defendant (*e.g.*, age, physical abilities, mental capacity, special skills). It is on the basis of the theoretical reasonable person who possesses these same characteristics as the defendant that knowledge or belief for purposes of tort liability is determined.

   c. **Intentional acts by children.** Children are charged with what is expected of them considering age, experience, intelligence, etc. They are liable only for what they are capable of, considering the foregoing factors. If they are capable of knowledge of the consequences of an act, they may be liable for these consequences.

2. **Substantial Certainty--Garratt v. Dailey,** 279 P.2d 1091 (Wash. 1955). Garratt v. Dailey

   a. **Facts.** Garratt (P) alleged that Dailey (D) had ***deliberately*** pulled a chair out from under her as she was sitting down, causing her to fall and fracture her hip. D, five years old, claimed that he had moved the chair so that he could sit in it himself, and, upon noticing that P was about to sit down, tried in vain to move the chair back in time. On remand, the court found that when D moved the chair, he knew with substantial certainty that P would attempt to sit down where the chair had been. P appeals from a decision denying P recovery of damages for an alleged assault and battery.

b. **Issue.** In an action for assault and battery, may the defendant be held liable if he did not subjectively intend to cause the resultant harm but knew with substantial certainty that his actions would likely cause it?

c. **Held.** Yes. Judgment reversed and remanded for clarification.

1) Battery is the intentional infliction of a harmful or offensive bodily contact upon another.

2) An "act" is deemed to be intentional if it is done either with the subjective purpose of causing the contact or the apprehension thereof, or with the knowledge that such contact or apprehension is ***substantially certain to result*** therefrom.

3) When a minor has committed a tort with force, he is just as subject to suit as any other person would be.

d. **Remand.** On remand, the court found that D knew with substantial certainty that P would attempt to sit where the chair had been located. Based on this finding that D had the requisite intent to be liable for battery, the court awarded P $11,000. This verdict was upheld on appeal. [Garratt v. Dailey, 304 P.2d 681 (Wash. 1956)]

e. **Comment.** Intentional conduct is an act that a reasonable person in the defendant's position would know is substantially certain to lead to the damage of another's legally protected interests.

Spivey v Battaglia

3. **Distinguishing Intent from Negligence--Spivey v. Battaglia,** 258 So. 2d 815 (Fla. 1972).

a. **Facts.** Spivey (P) and Battaglia (D) worked for the Battaglia Fruit Co. During a lunch break, D teased P by putting his arm around her and pulling her head toward him. The movement caused a sharp pain in P's neck and paralyzed her on the left side of her face and mouth. More than two years later, P sued for negligence and assault and battery. The trial court granted D summary judgment on the assault and battery allegation because the two-year statute of limitations for intentional torts had run. The trial court also granted summary judgment on the negligence allegation on the ground that D's conduct constituted assault and battery, which is not negligence. P appeals.

b. **Issue.** If a person intends to do an act that produces harm, but does not intend to cause the harm, may the person be liable for negligence?

c. **Held.** Yes. Judgment reversed.

1) Liability for intentional torts does not necessarily rest on a hostile intent or a desire to do harm. It is sufficient if a reasonable person

would believe that a particular result was substantially certain to follow. Knowledge and appreciation of a risk short of substantial certainty, however, is not equivalent to intent.

2) The line between negligence and intent is drawn where the known danger ceases to be only a foreseeable risk that a reasonable person would avoid, and becomes a substantial certainty. In this case, the harm suffered by P was not substantially certain to follow from D's conduct. D did not have the intent to cause P's paralysis and thus did not act intentionally for purposes of tort liability.

3) D may be liable for the unanticipated injury to P if he was negligent. This depends on whether the consequences of his acts were reasonably foreseeable, even though the exact result was not contemplated. The jury should decide this case after being instructed on the elements of negligence.

d. **Comment.** The court contrasted a case in which the defendant had embraced and kissed the plaintiff. During the plaintiff's struggle to resist, she struck her face on an object and suffered injury. That case was an assault and battery and not negligence, because the injury was substantially certain to follow from the defendant's conduct. In this case, by contrast, the injury was a bizarre result.

4. **Mistake.**

a. **Good faith mistake--Ranson v. Kitner,** 31 Ill. App. 241 (1888). Ranson v. Kitner

1) **Facts.** The defendants (Ds), while hunting wolves, shot the plaintiff's (P's) dog, mistaking it for a wolf. Ds acted in good faith, believing the dog to be a wolf. The jury gave a verdict to P for damages equal to the value of the dog.

2) **Issue.** Is a good faith mistake a defense to an intentional tort?

3) **Held.** No. Judgment affirmed.

a) While it was not Ds' intent to kill a dog, it was their intent to cause the result; *i.e.*, to kill the animal thinking it was a wolf. Ds' good faith mistake is not a defense.

4) **Comment.** Normally, good faith mistake is not a defense to a tort suit. Under certain circumstances, however, it may justify assertion of privilege, as when a defendant acted out of a mistaken but reasonable belief that he was being attacked when he injured the plaintiff in self-defense.

b. **Unavoidable mistake.** An unavoidable mistake is generally no defense to an intentional tort. The rationale is that when two parties are free from fault, the one causing the loss through her mistake should bear the consequences.

c. **Mistaken appropriation of property.** There is no defense for a mistaken appropriation of property. Even though a defendant may be innocent of blame or moral fault because she is acting under mistake, if her intentional act causes damage or harm to another's person or property, liability will attach. (However, *see* **Privilege**, *infra*.) "Fault" must be distinguished from "moral blame."

5. **Insanity.**

McGuire v. Almy

a. **General rule--McGuire v. Almy,** 8 N.E.2d 760 (Mass. 1937).

1) **Facts.** Almy (D), an insane person, was wrecking her room and threatened to kill anyone coming into the room. McGuire (P), D's nurse, entered the room and tried to take a table leg away from D and was struck over the head with the table leg by D. The jury returned a verdict for P and D appeals.

2) **Issue.** Can an insane person have the requisite intent for assault and battery?

3) **Held.** Yes. Judgment affirmed.

a) When an insane person, by her own action, does intentional damage to person or property, she is liable to the same degree that a sane person would be. Here, D is not morally to blame, but legally at fault.

b. **Policy.** A truly insane person cannot legally "act," since an act is an external manifestation of an inward will—a volitional movement. However, such persons are held liable for their actions as a matter of public policy. Why?

1) People legally charged with the care of incompetents will be more aware and watchful.

2) The insane must pay their way (support) if able and should pay for damages.

3) An innocent victim should not have to bear the damages caused by an insane person when the insane person is able to make restitution.

4) The difficulty of determining mental capacity should not be imposed in cases involving civil, rather than criminal, liability of the insane.

c. **Exception.** Mental incapacity has been held a bar to liability for certain torts, such as deceit, where it is necessary to show that the defendant had actual knowledge of the falsity of his statement.

6. **Transferred Intent.**

a. **General rule.** The old common law form of action called "trespass" gave rise to five modern actions: battery, assault, false imprisonment, trespass to land, and trespass to chattels. Under the doctrine of transferred intent, if D acts intending to cause one of these harms to X, D will be liable on an intentional tort theory if any of the five harms occurs to X, or even to P. This is true even though P is unexpected and the harm is unexpected.

b. **Example: intentionally throwing stick--Talmage v. Smith,** 59 N.W. 656 (Mich. 1894). Talmage v. Smith

1) **Facts.** Smith (D) threw a stick of wood at two boys who were on the roof of one of his sheds and the stick hit a third boy, Talmage (P), in the eye, causing him to lose sight in that eye. D could not see P but was held liable on an intentional tort theory. D appeals.

2) **Issue.** If D, intending to strike one party, instead strikes and injures P, who he could not see, is D liable for an intentional tort?

3) **Held.** Yes. Judgment affirmed.

a) The trial court instructed the jury that if D threw the stick intending to hit one of the boys, and if the force was unreasonable, under all the circumstances, then D would be doing an unlawful act and would be liable for the injury done to the boy hit by the stick. This instruction is a proper statement of the law in this case.

B. BATTERY

1. **Prima Facie Case.** A "battery" is the intentional, unprivileged harmful or offensive contact by the defendant with the person of another. The elements necessary to establish the tort of battery are as follows:

a. **Act.** There must be a volitional act by the defendant that causes the contact with the plaintiff.

b. **Intent.** The defendant must have intended the touching.

c. **Harmful or offensive touching.** The touching must have been harmful or offensive.

d. **Causation.** The defendant's act must have caused the touching.

2. **The Act.** The defendant's act must be an external manifestation of his will. It must be a volitional movement. For example, if the defendant was pushed into the plaintiff by a third person, the defendant would not be liable for battery (even though the third person may be).

3. **Defendant's Intent.** The general test used to determine intent is whether the defendant acted with the desire to cause, or substantially knew that her actions would cause, harm or offense, including either the actual contact or apprehension thereof. Since this test is founded on the defendant's desire or what she believed would be the consequences of her actions, the test is entirely subjective. The defendant need not have acted with a hostile or malicious intent.

4. **Causation.** The contact with the plaintiff's person must have been caused by the defendant's affirmative act. The action of the defendant must be the legal cause of or be the force that puts in motion the force that results in the plaintiff's injury. It is sufficient if it is a substantial factor in bringing about the harmful or offensive contact. Under the old common law, the defendant's act had to be the direct cause of the contact. The modern approach examines the results of the force that the defendant's act set in motion. For example, in the *Garratt* case, *supra*, the defendant's removal of the chair caused the injury.

5. **Harmful or Offensive Touching.** The action of the defendant must result in the infliction of a harmful or offensive touching to the plaintiff or something that is so closely associated with the plaintiff as to be tantamount to a touching of the plaintiff. A harmful touching is one that inflicts any pain or injury, while an offensive touching is one that offends a reasonable person's sense of personal dignity.

   a. **Nature of the contact.** *Cole v. Turner*, 90 Eng. Rep. 958 (N.P. 1704), distinguished between hostile touching and touching without any violence or design of harm, holding that the least touching of another in anger is a battery, while the gentle touching of another in a narrow passageway without a hostile intent is not a battery.

   b. **Physical harm unnecessary.** The contact of the defendant with the plaintiff need not cause actual physical harm (*i.e.*, pain, injury, disfigurement, etc., to the person). It is sufficient that the contact be offensive or insulting. The legally protected interest is the plaintiff's right to be free from being touched without consent. However, as *Cole* recognized, certain contact between individuals will result from the normal activities of people; consent will be implied if a touching would not be offensive to a reasonable person (*e.g.*, unavoidable but not deliberate jostling in a crowded subway car or passageway).

c. **Harmful because of condition of plaintiff.** While a polite touching, as to attract attention, is generally permitted, a defendant will be liable for any aggravation of the plaintiff's injury resulting from such touching, notwithstanding the defendant's ignorance of the plaintiff's condition; *e.g.*, the defendant opens stitches in hidden injury of the plaintiff, causing aggravation of injury.

d. **Plaintiff's knowledge.** The plaintiff need not know of the offensive touching at the time of contact. For example, if the plaintiff is kissed by the defendant while he sleeps and would otherwise have been offended by such an act if he had been awake, there is a battery.

e. **Plaintiff's person: body and things closely attached thereto--Fisher v. Carrousel Motor Hotel, Inc.,** 424 S.W.2d 627 (Tex. 1967).

Fisher v. Carrousel Motor Hotel, Inc.

1) **Facts.** Fisher (P), a black man, attended a dinner at the Carrousel Motor Hotel's (D's) club. D's manager approached P while he was in a food line for a buffet meal and grabbed a plate from P's hand. The manager shouted that P could not be served because of his race. P was not actually touched nor put in fear of physical injury, but was embarrassed severely. The jury verdict held for P, also giving punitive damages, but the trial court entered a judgment notwithstanding the verdict for D and P appeals.

2) **Issue.** Is actual contact with the plaintiff's body necessary to have a battery?

3) **Held.** No. Judgment reversed.

a) Contact with clothing or an object touching a plaintiff is sufficient to provide the contact necessary for a battery. A person's interest in bodily integrity includes things connected or in contact with his person.

b) If an employee is acting within the scope of his employment, in a managerial capacity, a plaintiff can recover punitive damages even though the act of the employee was not authorized or approved of by the employer.

c) The essence of battery is personal indignity. Thus, forcefully removing the plate from P's hand constitutes a battery. P is entitled to damages for mental suffering.

4) **Comment.** D had a rule of not serving blacks; this probably helped support the argument that D should be held liable because the act was within the scope of the manager's employment (enforcing rule of employer that blacks not be served) and to the holding of punitive damages.

f. **Relation to assault.** A battery usually consists of an assault (placing the plaintiff in fear or apprehension of an immediate harmful or offensive touching, without consent or privilege) and actual contact. However, there can be a battery (for purposes of tort liability) without an assault. Compare this with criminal liability, where assault is generally viewed as a lesser included offense in a battery.

6. **Consent or Privilege.** Facts that would otherwise give rise to liability for battery will be insufficient for such a finding if the plaintiff has consented to the harmful or offensive contact (*e.g.*, fraternity initiations, prize fights, and other contact sports) or if the defendant is otherwise privileged to so act. (*See infra* for a detailed discussion of **Consent** and **Privilege**.)

C. ASSAULT

1. **Prima Facie Case.** An assault is an act, other than the mere speaking of words, that directly is a legal cause of placing the plaintiff in fear or apprehension of immediate harmful or offensive contact without consent or privilege. The elements of assault that make up a plaintiff's prima facie case are:

   (i) Act by the defendant;

   (ii) Intent of the defendant;

   (iii) Fear or apprehension of the plaintiff; and

   (iv) Causal relationship.

   For liability to attach, there must be an absence of consent and privilege (discussed *infra*).

2. **Actual Physical Invasion of Plaintiff Unnecessary.** In *I. De S. Et Ux. v. W. De S.* (Eng. 1348), W came to I's tavern and wanted I to open and sell some wine. M told W to stop pounding on the door with his hatchet, then W struck at, but missed, M. The court awarded damages for an assault even though there was no other harm. The case stands for the principle that there need not be actual damage to support a recovery for assault—apprehension of a harmful or offensive contact is sufficient.

Western Union Telegraph Co. v. Hill

3. **Present Ability to Cause Damage Unnecessary--Western Union Telegraph Co. v. Hill,** 150 So. 709 (Ala. 1933).

   a. **Facts.** Hill (P) had gone to Western Union's (D's) place of business to ask D's agent to fix her clock. The agent had been drinking. He made improper advances toward P and reached out across a counter at her, intentionally and unlawfully attempting to put his hand on her. He never touched P. The counter was of such height that it would have been difficult for him to do so. On a judgment for P, D appeals, in part claiming that there was not an assault sufficient to justify an action for damages.

b. **Issue.** May there be an assault if there is no actual ability to do the threatened touching?

c. **Held.** Yes. Judgment for P affirmed on sufficiency of assault but reversed on appeal on other grounds.

   1) An offer to touch in a rude and angry manner so as to cause a well-founded fear of a disagreeable bodily contact is an assault. Here, the employee's apparent present ability to complete the threatened act was sufficient.

d. **Comment.** The threat of force must be immediate. Preparation is not sufficient. Thus one probably cannot assault another over the telephone as there would either be no present ability or no immediate threat of force. However, consider the following telephone message: "If you go outside this week, I'll kill you as your home is being constantly watched by a gunman."

4. **Words Alone.** Words alone usually are insufficient to create an assault. However, words may give a hostile character to an otherwise harmless act. For example, verbal threats by a defendant immediately followed by the defendant reaching into her pocket may create apprehension in the plaintiff (*e.g.*, that the defendant is reaching for a gun or knife), which might not be reasonable absent the verbal threats.

5. **Intent of Defendant.** The defendant must desire to inflict harmful or offensive contact, or apprehension thereof, on either the plaintiff or another, or have knowledge or belief that such results are substantially certain to follow from her acts. The doctrine of transferred intent applies in assault as in battery.

6. **Causal Relationship.** The defendant's act must be the cause of the plaintiff's apprehension of harmful or offensive contact. The standard for apprehension is objective; *i.e.*, would a reasonable person in the plaintiff's circumstances have been apprehensive?

7. **Consent or Privilege.** The defendant's act that causes the plaintiff to be apprehensive of harmful or offensive contact must be without consent or privilege for liability to attach. (*See* **Consent** and **Privilege**, *infra*, for a detailed discussion.)

8. **Damages.** Apprehension is all that the plaintiff need show, although special damages are recoverable if sustained.

D. FALSE IMPRISONMENT

1. **Prima Facie Case.** False imprisonment is the total obstruction and detention of the plaintiff, of which he is aware, within boundaries and for any length of time, with intent by the defendant to obstruct or detain the plaintiff or another, and without privilege or consent. The plaintiff's prima facie case includes the following elements:

    a. An act by the defendant;

    b. Obstruction or detention of the plaintiff;

    c. Intent; and

    d. Causal relationship.

2. **Obstruction or Detention.** The obstruction or detention element may be satisfied even if the person is not totally imprisoned.

    a. No reasonable exit. False imprisonment occurs if the plaintiff is in a place where there is no reasonable avenue of exit. An exit is not reasonable if it: (i) is unknown to the plaintiff, or (ii) requires the plaintiff to take risks to escape, is dangerous, or is simply uncomfortable.

    b. Restriction. Generally it is not sufficient that the plaintiff is not allowed to go where he wishes if he can go somewhere else. Under certain circumstances, exclusion, such as from one's home, may suffice. It is also sufficient that the plaintiff, even though allowed to move about several rooms in a building, is restrained from leaving the building.

Big Town Nursing Home, Inc. v. Newman

    c. Example: restraining plaintiff in nursing home--Big Town Nursing Home, Inc. v. Newman, 461 S.W.2d 195 (Tex. 1970).

        1) Facts. Newman (P), a retired single man with Parkinson's disease and other physical ailments, was taken to the Big Town Nursing Home, Inc. (D), by his nephew, who paid for one month's care in advance. Although P had been treated for alcoholism, he did not drink for a week before being admitted to D. After a few days, P tried to leave but was caught by D's employees and placed in a wing with senile, alcoholic, and mentally disturbed patients. P was caught trying to escape five or six additional times and was taped to a restraint chair. He was not seen by a doctor for over a week. About seven weeks after his admission, P finally escaped. He lost 30 pounds during his stay with D. P sued for false imprisonment. P won actual and exemplary damages and D appeals.

2) **Issue.** May a nursing home force a patient to stay when there is no compelling reason to do so?

3) **Held.** No. Judgment affirmed.

a) A person who directly restrains the physical liberty of another without adequate legal justification may be liable for false imprisonment.

b) D put P in a wing in which he did not belong. D locked P up and taped him in a restraint chair, prevented him from making a telephone call, and kept him for 51 days despite his demands and attempts to escape. As there was no court order for commitment, and the admission agreement provided that P was not to be kept against his will, the judgment is supported by the evidence.

c) D could be responsible for exemplary damages if its acts were done intentionally in violation of P's rights. However, the judgment was excessive and a remittitur is appropriate.

3. **Knowledge of the Obstruction or Detention.**

a. **Submission of will.** Obstruction or detention for purposes of false imprisonment must be against the will of the one restrained. Therefore, the majority holds that if there is no knowledge on the part of the plaintiff at the time of his detention, there can be no submission of his will and hence no false imprisonment. The fact that the plaintiff makes no resistance does not necessarily negate the element of submission against his will.

b. **Awareness required--Parvi v. City of Kingston,** 362 N.E.2d 960 (N.Y. 1977).

Parvi v. City of Kingston

1) **Facts.** Parvi (P) was drunk in the city of Kingston (D) and was picked up by the police. Rather than arrest him, they took him to an area out of town. P sued for false imprisonment. At trial, the evidence was unclear as to whether P went willingly with the police or wanted to be let out elsewhere. P could not recall what happened. The trial court dismissed the action and the appellate court affirmed. P appeals.

2) **Issue.** Must P have an awareness of confinement in order to recover for false imprisonment?

3) **Held.** Yes. Judgment reversed, however.

a) False imprisonment is a dignitary tort and only exists when the victim is aware of the invasion of his rights.

b) The trial court erred because although P may not recall whether he felt confined at the time, other evidence indicates that he did at the time feel confined. A jury should hear the evidence and determine whether P was aware of the confinement.

4) **Dissent.** P has not made a prima facie case because his only knowledge of how he felt comes from what others have suggested to him.

4. **Means of Obstruction or Detention.** The means of obstructing or detaining the plaintiff may be by conduct, words, force, or threats, as long as the act is against the plaintiff's will. The difficult cases arise when words alone are used. Words can restrain a person who fears disregarding them, even if there is no physical restraint. An arrest made with apparent but not actual legal authority constitutes false imprisonment even though no actual force is used. The fact that a person remains in a place solely because of what another says does not necessarily mean that the person remained against his will, however.

Hardy v. LaBelle's Distributing Co.

a. **Use of false pretenses to obtain plaintiff's consent--Hardy v. LaBelle's Distributing Co.,** 661 P.2d 35 (Mont. 1983).

1) **Facts.** Hardy (P) was hired by LaBelle's Distributing Co. (D) as a temporary employee. A week later, one of D's other employees thought she saw P steal a watch from inventory. The next day, D's assistant manager told P that he would give her a tour of the store. Instead, he took her to the manager's office and left her there. The showroom manager, the loss prevention manager, and a police officer were in the room. Confronted with the accusation, P denied it and agreed to take a lie detector test. The test showed that P was truthful. The next morning the manager apologized to P, but P left the store and sued, claiming that D wrongfully detained her. The jury found for D and P appeals.

2) **Issue.** If a person is willingly led to a location under false pretenses, is she a victim of false imprisonment?

3) **Held.** No. Judgment affirmed.

a) False imprisonment consists of (i) the restraint of an individual against her will and (ii) the unlawfulness of the restraint. Acts may produce the restraint as well as words that the victim fears to disregard.

b) In this case, P admitted that she wanted to stay in the manager's office and clear up the problem. She did not ask to leave and was not told she could not leave. She was led to the office under the pretense of a tour, but she testified that she would have gone anyway if she knew the true purpose for the meeting and that a police officer would be present.

b. **False arrest--Enright v. Groves,** 560 P.2d 851 (Colo. 1977).

Enright v. Groves

1) **Facts.** Groves (D), a police officer, saw a dog running loose in violation of a dog leash ordinance. He followed the dog to its apparent home, and encountered Enright (P), who had been identified as its owner. D asked P for her driver's license. P would not give it but gave her name and address. D arrested P for refusing to produce her driver's license and took her to the police station where she was charged with violation of the leash law. She was convicted of the violation, but brought suit for false arrest. P recovered damages and D appeals.

2) **Issue.** Is an officer liable for false arrest when he arrests someone for an improper reason but charges that person with an offense of which she is later convicted?

3) **Held.** Yes. Judgment affirmed.

a) D's demand for P's driver's license was improper and P committed no offense in refusing to comply. Therefore, there was no legal authority for the arrest. The subsequent conviction on a separate charge is irrelevant.

c. **Refusal to permit egress--Whittaker v. Sandford,** 85 A. 399 (Me. 1912).

Whittaker v. Sandford

1) **Facts.** Sandford (D), head of a religious sect, agreed to transport Whittaker (P), one of his members, back from Syria to the United States, after P had decided to abandon the movement. When they reached port, D would not allow P to use the only means to go ashore, the rowboat, and thus detained her for nearly one month until P obtained a writ of habeas corpus. P then sued D for false imprisonment and won $1,100. D appeals.

2) **Issue.** Does the refusal to allow the plaintiff to use the rowboat, the only means of conveyance between the ship and the shore, constitute false imprisonment?

3) **Held.** Yes. Judgment affirmed.

a) The physical restraint required for false imprisonment need not be physical force on the person. Restriction of a person to a confined area may suffice.

b) P had a personal right to go ashore. D denied her this privilege by refusing to allow her to use the rowboat, and thus falsely imprisoned her as much as if he had locked her in a room.

4) **Comment.** Inaction can result in false imprisonment. In this case there was an understood duty to take P ashore.

5. **Escape.** It is generally held that false imprisonment invites escape and that the plaintiff may recover for any injuries sustained in an escape attempt.

6. **Intent.** Intent of the defendant to obstruct or detain the plaintiff or another is a required element of false imprisonment. However, as noted, omission to carry out one's duty thereby causing confinement, as in *Whittaker*, will give rise to false imprisonment. Hostile or malicious intent is not required. Also, the doctrine of transferred intent applies; *e.g.*, if the defendant intends to detain butcher A in a frozen food locker, and thinking A is inside, shuts the door on B, the defendant is subject to an action by B for false imprisonment.

7. **Causal Relationship.** There must be a causal relationship between the act or omission of the defendant and the obstruction or detention of the plaintiff.

8. **Consent or Privilege.** The defendant's act that was the legal cause of the false imprisonment of the plaintiff must have been without consent or privilege in order for liability to attach (*see infra*).

9. **Damages.** When liability is established, the plaintiff may recover damages from the defendant even though no special damages (*e.g.*, injuries, loss of earnings) are proved. If special damages are proved, they are of course recoverable. Also note that any injuries sustained in an escape attempt are recoverable.

E. INTENTIONAL INFLICTION OF MENTAL DISTRESS

1. **Introduction.** Mental distress is characterized by physical injury or severe mental suffering of the plaintiff resulting from emotional disturbance, without physical impact, caused by highly aggravated words or acts of the defendant, done with intent to cause mental suffering or with knowledge or belief on the part of the defendant that such is substantially certain to result from such words or acts, and without consent or privilege.

   a. The words or acts must be severe, exceeding all socially acceptable standards, and must cause injury of a serious kind to the plaintiff.

   b. Today, however, there seems to be a move away from the requirement that there must be some physical injury manifestations from the emotional disturbance caused by the defendant. On the other hand, the law recognizes that humans must occasionally "blow off steam," and ordinarily defendants are not liable for mere insults that may cause emotional disturbance.

c. Intentional infliction of mental distress differs from negligent infliction of mental disturbance in that it is done with a more culpable state of mind.

2. **Traditional Objections to Mental Distress as a Basis of Tort Liability.**

a. **Early cases.** Mental distress was recognized as an element of damages in early assault cases. However, it was not until the early part of the 20th Century that the intentional infliction of mental distress, without any other accompanying tort, gained recognition as a separate basis for finding tort liability. The relatively slow development of the law to recognize the plaintiff's peace of mind as a legally protected interest has been due to the following objections traditionally voiced against its recognition.

1) The character of the injury suffered in mental distress is difficult to determine; *i.e.*, it is difficult to see mental anguish whereas it is easy to see a broken arm, an unlawful restraint, etc.

2) The damages resulting from mental distress are of a subtle and speculative nature (peculiar, variable, hard to assess, etc.).

3) Mental distress lends itself to fictitious claims.

4) Recognition of the basis of liability will open up floods of litigation.

5) Permitting recovery for mental distress will encourage perjury, either through overstating the facts or fabrication.

b. **Expansion of liability.** Notwithstanding the objections cited above, the law seems to be moving toward an expansion of the circumstances under which liability for the infliction of mental distress will be found.

3. **Extortion--State Rubbish Collectors Association v. Siliznoff,** 240 P.2d 282 (Cal. 1952).

State Rubbish Collectors Association v. Siliznoff

a. **Facts.** The State Rubbish Collectors Association (P) threatened to beat Siliznoff (D), destroy his truck, and put him out of business unless he gave P proceeds from a territory that P had allocated to someone in their membership. D signed a note for the amount he had earned from the disputed area. P sued D for payment of the note. D cross-complained to cancel the note claiming he signed under duress. D also sought punitive damages for assault and destruction of business, causing severe mental distress. The jury found for D on the complaint and the cross-complaint; P appeals.

b. **Issue.** May a plaintiff recover for intentional infliction of mental distress even when there is no actual assault?

c. **Held.** Yes. Judgment affirmed.

1) The 1934 Restatement did not permit recovery for mental and emotional distress in the absence of bodily harm. The 1947 Restatement permitted recovery for severe emotional distress by itself if it was intentionally caused. The new approach recognizes that there is no public policy reason for protecting antisocial behavior that causes such distress.

2) Often, the major element of damages in cases of assault, battery, false imprisonment, and defamation is mental suffering. There is no good reason to require physical injury before permitting recovery for mental distress.

3) This new rule is not intended to permit recovery for unfounded injuries. A jury must find that serious mental distress actually occurred.

d. **Comment.** Under the Restatement view, if there is no physical illness, there must be outrageous and extreme conduct.

Slocum v. Food Fair Stores of Florida

4. **Insults and Abusive Language--Slocum v. Food Fair Stores of Florida,** 100 So. 2d 396 (Fla. 1958).

a. **Facts.** Slocum (P), while shopping in a store owned by Food Fair Stores (D), asked the price of an item being marked by D's employee. The employee replied, "If you want to know the price, you'll have to find out the best way you can . . . you stink to me." P subsequently suffered a heart attack and alleged that the statements of the employee were intended to inflict, and did cause, great mental disturbance, resulting in the heart attack. The trial court dismissed the action and P appeals.

b. **Issue.** Does deliberate disturbance of a particular plaintiff's emotional equanimity constitute an actionable invasion of a legally protected right?

c. **Held.** No. Judgment affirmed.

1) Regardless of the fact that P suffered a heart attack allegedly as a result of her emotional state, the law employs an objective rather than a subjective test, so that the unwarranted intrusion must be calculated to cause severe emotional distress to a person of ordinary sensibilities, in the absence of special knowledge or notice that the one distressed is of less than normal sensibilities.

2) D's employee's acts were not totally intolerable, but were more in the nature of a common insult. A person has a right to express his feelings; there is no recovery for hurt feelings.

3) Trivial abrasive or abusive comments will not be actionable.

d. **Comments.**

1) The employer is responsible for the acts of its employees, acting on company business, in the scope of their employment, and had there been sufficiently aggravated words, D could have been liable for the employee's acts. There is no assault here since the employee did not create the apprehension of an immediate, harmful, or offensive contact.

2) Note that common carriers and innkeepers have a special obligation to the public and cannot insult customers.

5. **Severity of Conduct and Injury Caused.**

a. **Distress must be severe--Harris v. Jones,** 380 A.2d 611 (Md. 1977). Harris v. Jones

1) **Facts.** Harris (P) had a speech impediment, which caused him to stutter. P was sensitive about the impediment. Jones (D), P's supervisor at work, continually ridiculed P about his stuttering. P claimed that D's actions caused his condition to worsen and heightened his nervousness. P sued for intentional infliction of emotional distress. The trial court allowed the claim and the jury awarded damages. On appeal, the court held that the cause of action was proper but that P failed to adequately prove severe emotional distress and reversed. P appeals.

2) **Issue.** Must a plaintiff prove he suffered a severely disabling emotional response to D's conduct in order to recover for intentional infliction of emotional distress?

3) **Held.** Yes. Judgment affirmed.

a) The tort of intentional infliction of emotional distress is actionable standing alone if the following elements are satisfied: (i) the conduct must be intentional or reckless; (ii) the conduct must be extreme and outrageous; (iii) there must be a causal connection between the conduct and the distress; and (iv) the emotional distress must be severe.

4) **Comments.**

a) In this case, the first element was clearly satisfied. The second element may have been, given P's sensibilities, D's knowledge thereof, and D's position of authority.

b) However, P failed to prove that the distress was severe. Something more than mere exacerbation of a nervous condition must be proved. P's humiliation was not so severe as to be recognized as actionable by itself.

b. **Soliciting intercourse.** In *Samms v. Eccles*, 11 Utah 2d 289 (1961), the defendant repeatedly phoned the plaintiff, a respectable married woman, soliciting illicit relations. Once the defendant came to the plaintiff's home and indecently exposed himself. The trial court granted the defendant's summary judgment motion, but the decision was reversed on appeal. Although mere insults are insufficient, persistent and aggravated conduct of this type is extremely outrageous, going beyond all reasonable bounds tolerated by civilized society.

c. **Persistent and intolerable conduct.** Persistent and intolerable conduct not generally acceptable to normal standards of decency requires no physical damage to the plaintiff.

d. **Practical joke.** A practical joke may be sufficient; *e.g.*, calling on the phone and telling the plaintiff her husband is injured or dead.

e. **Known vulnerability.** A known vulnerability of the plaintiff, *e.g.*, age, sex, illness, pregnancy, will be considered by the court. Known vulnerability may supply outrage, notwithstanding an absence of intent, if there is wanton and willful infliction of mental distress in disregard of a high degree of probability of the consequences. In *Korbin v. Berlin*, 177 So. 2d 551 (Fla. 1965), the defendant told a six-year-old girl her mother was an adulteress and would be punished by God. On appeal the court reversed an order dismissing the complaint. The court said mere negligence is not sufficient but this was true malice and great indifference to the child's rights, going beyond all acceptable standards of society. The act was intended, or reasonably calculated, to cause "severe emotional distress."

6. **Acts Directed Against Third Parties.** Extremely outrageous conduct directed against third parties, intentionally or with reckless disregard of the consequences, that causes severe emotional distress in the plaintiff, may be enough to hold defendant liable if such distress is accompanied by bodily harm.

Taylor v. Vallelunga

a. **Family member--Taylor v. Vallelunga,** 339 P.2d 910 (Cal. 1959).

1) **Facts.** Vallelunga (D) and others severely beat Taylor's (P's) father. P witnessed the beating and as a result suffered fright and severe emotional distress. No physical injury was alleged. The court sustained D's demurrer and P appeals.

2) **Issue.** Does transferred intent apply to infliction of emotional distress?

3) **Held.** No. Judgment affirmed.

a) To recover for his own emotional distress, a plaintiff must show that the defendant could reasonably foresee the plaintiff's presence. An intent to injure a third party (P's father) is insufficient.

b) The doctrine of transferred intent, as developed in battery, generally has not been applied to mental distress, probably for the reason that emotional distress did not fall within the common law action of trespass.

b. **Others.** Most of the cases finding liability for mental distress caused to a party other than the one against whom the defendant's actions were directed involve a "close relative" relationship between the plaintiff and the defendant's target. However, there is no reason why the action should be limited to circumstances involving relatives, friends, or close associates if the mental distress is in fact the result of the defendant's acts.

F. TRESPASS TO LAND

Every unauthorized entry of a person or thing on land in the possession of another is a trespass. The basis of the tort is the right of another to the exclusive possession of land.

1. **Prima Facie Case.** The plaintiff's prima facie case consists of the following elements:

a. An act by the defendant;

b. Invasion of land in possession of the plaintiff;

c. Intent of the defendant; and

d. Causal relationship.

2. **Possession.** For purposes of trespass to land, possession means occupancy of the land with intent to control it and exclude others. The possession that is sufficient to entitle the plaintiff to bring an action for trespass may be actual or constructive (land in the custody of person responsible to the plaintiff, *e.g.*, employee, agent, etc.). It has been argued that one who has immediate right to possession, although never having made ac-

tual entry on the land, has a right to maintain an action for trespass if the act of trespass occurs after creation of the right to possession. Note that an owner of land may commit a trespass on her own land if the right to exclusive possession has been transferred to another (as under a lease).

3. Intent and Damages.

a. **Common law.** At common law, the important factor in determining liability was an unauthorized entry on the land of another. The plaintiff did not need to prove damages. However, the defendant's intent to commit the trespass was determined only on the basis of whether the act forming the basis of liability was voluntary. For example, if, without his consent, the defendant is pushed by a third party into the plaintiff's store, and causes damage, he will not be held liable for a trespass since he did not voluntarily act. As with other intentional torts, there was no requirement that the defendant's "intent" be malicious or intentionally harmful.

b. **Present authority.** Under the majority rule, if the defendant intends to be on the plaintiff's land (whether the defendant's presence is based upon mistake, ignorance as to the ownership or boundary of the land, claim of right, or some other matter) he is liable for trespass. The common law rule that the plaintiff need not prove damages or actual harm to the land continues to apply. Since the gist of the tort is interference with the right to possession, it is considered immaterial that the defendant's acts actually were intended but did benefit the land (*i.e.*, the defendant entered and constructed fences and made other improvements). In addition to liability for intentional trespass, present authority recognizes liability for harm done to the land of another that results from negligence or an ultrahazardous activity, such as blasting, even though unintentional. However, such actions are prosecuted on the basis of negligence or strict liability and not under the guise of an intentional tort, and, unlike intentional trespass, require proof of some actual damages.

Dougherty v. Stepp

c. **Subjective intent to violate plaintiff's rights unnecessary--Dougherty v. Stepp,** 18 N.C. 371 (1835).

1) **Facts.** Stepp (D), with surveyors and chains, etc., went onto the unenclosed land of Dougherty (P) without knowledge that it was P's land. D surveyed part of the land and claimed it as his own. The land was not posted. P sued for trespass. From a directed verdict for D, P appeals.

2) **Issue.** Must defendant have a subjective intent to violate the plaintiff's rights to exclusive possession for liability to attach for unauthorized entry?

3) **Held.** No. Judgment reversed.

a) An unauthorized entry onto the land of another is a trespass notwithstanding that the defendant had no subjective intent to violate the plaintiff's rights. The crucial questions are whether the entry was unauthorized and whether the defendant intended to enter the land. There need be no proof of actual damages in intentional trespass.

d. **Damages.** As *Dougherty* points out, actual damages need not be proved in intentional trespass. The law infers some damage simply from the fact that entry was unauthorized and, if there is no proof of actual damages, will award nominal damages. The reason that courts will entertain actions for trespass even though no damages are proved is that the action often is brought for the purpose of reinforcing the plaintiff's right to exclusive possession, which right could be lost in part if the conduct by the defendant were allowed to continue for the prescriptive period; *i.e.*, by using land of another in a manner adverse to the rights of the one entitled to such use, the adverse user may acquire a right to continue such use, free of interference from the party entitled to possession of the land, if the adverse use continues for a period of time (the prescriptive period) established by law as the minimum time required for the interest to gain recognition.

4. **Invasion by Gas and Particulates--Bradley v. American Smelting and Refining Co.,** 709 P.2d 782 (Wash. 1985).

Bradley v. American Smelting & Refining Co.

a. **Facts.** The American Smelting and Refining Co. (D) operated a copper smelter in Tacoma, Washington, for almost 100 years. The smelter emitted gases such as sulfur dioxide and particulates such as arsenic and cadmium. Particulates are distinct particles of matter that cannot be detected by human senses. Bradley (P) owned property four miles north of D's smelter. P sued for trespass based on the emissions from D's smelter. The district court certified the issue involved to the Washington Supreme Court.

b. **Issue.** May invasion by gas and particulate emissions constitute a trespass?

c. **Held.** Yes.

1) Traditionally, a trespass involved only an invasion by a thing or object. However, the doctrine of trespass was expanded to gaseous and particulate emissions in a 1959 Oregon case in recognition of modern scientific developments that make detection more precise. A chemical force may be just as real as a physical force.

2) Trespass and private nuisance are separate torts; a trespass is an invasion of a possessor's interest in the exclusive possession of his land, while a nuisance is an invasion of a possessor's interest in the use and enjoyment of his land. These theories are not inconsistent; they may be applied concurrently.

3) The difference between trespass and nuisance depends not on whether the intrusion is tangible or intangible, but whether the interest interfered with is the right to exclusive possession or the right to the use and enjoyment of property. A trespass requires proof of: (i) an invasion affecting an interest in the exclusive possession of property; (ii) an intentional doing of the act which results in the invasion; (iii) reasonable foreseeability that the act done could result in the invasion; and (iv) substantial damages to the property.

4) If airborne particles are transitory or quickly dissipate, they may present a nuisance but not a trespass because they do not interfere with possessory rights. If the particles accumulate, however, they may present a trespass.

5) The common law provided for nominal or punitive damages for any trespass, but this rule is impractical in the context of landowners surrounding a manufacturing plant. In this type of case, the plaintiff must prove actual and substantial damages or his claim is subject to summary judgment.

5. Above and Below the Surface. According to common law theory (ad coelum), a landowner was deemed to own a column of property that extended from the center of the earth to infinity in space, defined in terms of the cross-section on the earth's surface that he legally owned. Violation of the air space above an owner's parcel was deemed to be as much a trespass as entry upon the land or invasion of the earth below by tunneling. Of course, coincident with the right of ownership was the right to exclusive possession of that which was considered "owned."

a. Above the surface.

Herrin v. Sutherland

1) Shooting--Herrin v. Sutherland, 241 P. 328 (Mont. 1925).

a) Facts. Sutherland (D), while shooting fowl, repeatedly shot from another's land over Herrin's (P's) dwelling. P claimed that this disturbed his cattle and interfered with his enjoyment of the land. D's demurrer was overruled and P was awarded judgment when D failed to answer. D appeals.

b) Issue. Can trespass be based merely on violation of the air space above the plaintiff's land?

c) **Held.** Yes. Judgment affirmed.

(1) Violation of airspace over land is a trespass. Land includes not only surface but also space upward and downward. The airspace near the ground and that which is obviously within the range of the shotgun is as inviolate as the soil itself. Such space is important to the use and enjoyment of the land.

(2) There are nominal damages for a technical trespass even if no actual damages are shown. P has a right to full use and enjoyment of exclusive possession of the land.

(3) Shooting an animal on the plaintiff's roof is entry of the bullet into the protected airspace of the plaintiff. Similarly, sticking an arm over a fence between the plaintiff's and the defendant's adjoining land is technically a trespass.

2) **Airplanes.** State courts have rationalized trespass by airplanes on the basis of one of the four following theories.

a) **Actual use.** The property owner has the right to prevent third parties from using or trespassing the airspace above his parcel only to the extent that such airspace is actually used by him.

b) **Zone.** The property owner has a right to the airspace in his effective possession, which includes the space actually used plus that which could effectively be used in the future.

c) **Nuisance.** Under this theory, the third party using the airspace is not a trespasser, but may be prevented from continuing such use and be subject to damages when such use unreasonably interferes with the land use below.

d) **Privileged trespass.** The property owner is considered to have rights to the airspace above his parcel in accordance with the ad coelum theory, subject to the privilege of third parties to reasonable flights thereover.

b. **Below the surface.** Under the common law ad coelum theory, any invasion of the subsurface is a trespass. However, as with invasions of airspace above land, the literal application proved burdensome on certain activities deemed of societal benefit, and the law developed special rules in the area of mining (one may follow a "vein" even though it extends under the land of another) and oil exploration (slant drilling). The view favored today is that an interference with the subsurface of another will result in a trespass only if it causes physical damage to the surface or if it is an invasion at a depth that is within the zone of conceivable use by the owner of the surface, even though there is no damage to the surface.

6. **Physical Entry Required.** Under the general rule, physical entry is required for a trespass. When a defendant has engaged in an ultrahazardous activity, *e.g.*, blasting, liability is founded not on the basis of an intentional trespass, but on strict liability because of the danger involved in the activity. The requirement of physical entry has been carried to extremes. Lights reflecting on the plaintiff's land and interfering with his business have been held not to be a trespass because of the lack of a physical entry, whereas microscopic particles deposited on the plaintiff's land have been held to constitute a sufficient entry. Note, however, that invasions by such intangibles as noise and light may be so unreasonable as to give rise to an actionable nuisance.

   a. **Persons and things.** Entry need not be by the person. The unauthorized entry may be effected by throwing something onto the land of another or causing something that is tangible to invade the property of the plaintiff.

   b. **Agents.** The trespass may be effected through an agent. One who authorizes an illegal trespass is as much liable for the trespass as the trespasser. One who trespasses on the land of another incurs the risk of being liable for any bodily harm caused to the possessor of the land.

   c. **Continuing trespass.** When one enters the land of another rightfully, but then refuses to leave, he is a trespasser. Similarly, a trespass results when one who has placed a structure on land with privilege fails to remove it when the privilege has terminated. In both cases there is an interference with the right of another to the exclusive possession of the land.

Rogers v. Board of Road Commissioners

      1) **Failure to remove object--Rogers v. Board of Road Commissioners,** 30 N.W.2d 358 (Mich. 1948).

         a) **Facts.** The Board of Road Commissioners (D) had a license from Rogers (P) to place a snow fence on P's land with the understanding that D would remove it in the spring. D failed to remove one of the anchor posts and P's husband was killed in an accident caused when his mowing machine hit the post. P's cause of action was dismissed, the court finding (i) no trespass, and (ii) governmental immunity protecting D from any charge of negligence. P appeals.

         b) **Issue.** Does continued presence of D's structure on P's land after P withdraws consent constitute trespass?

         c) **Held.** Yes. Judgment reversed.

            (1) A trespass is committed by continued presence on land, whether person or object, after consent is terminated. Here, leaving the anchor post was a continuing trespass.

d. **Liability.** A trespasser is liable for the consequences of his acts. If physical harm is caused to either person or property on the land invaded as a result of an unauthorized entry, including the continuing trespass, liability will attach. The cases indicate that liability in trespass situations has been found for injury to the person in possession and also for injury to members of her family.

G. TRESPASS TO CHATTELS

1. **Introduction.** Trespass to chattels (trespass de bonis asportatis) results from intentional interference with possession or physical condition of a chattel in the possession of another, without consent of the person entitled thereto and without privilege, which interference causes actual damage. The gist of the tort is physical interference with the exclusive right of another to use and possess a chattel.

2. **Harmless Intermeddling--Glidden v. Szybiak,** 63 A.2d 233 (N.H. 1949). Glidden v. Szybiak

   a. **Facts.** Glidden (P), a four-year-old girl, was bitten and injured while playing with Szybiak's (D's) dog. P had climbed on the dog's back and pulled its ears. P brought suit under a statute that exempted D from liability for his dog's act if the damage was done while P was committing a trespass or other tort. The jury found for P and D appeals.

   b. **Issue.** Does harmless intermeddling with another's chattel, here the dog, constitute a trespass?

   c. **Held.** No. Judgment affirmed.

      1) Intentional intermeddling with a chattel constitutes a trespass only if the chattel is thereby harmed, or the possessor is deprived of the use of the chattel, or the possessor suffers bodily harm. Harmless intermeddling with a chattel is not a trespass.

      2) D did not allege that his dog was injured by P. P did not commit a trespass, and the statutory defense does not protect D.

3. **Intentional Intermeddling.** Intentional intermeddling with a chattel without consent or privilege to do so makes one liable for the harm caused to the possessor or his legally protected interest under the following conditions: (i) the condition, quality or value of the chattel is impaired; and (ii) the possessor is deprived of use of the chattel for a substantial period of time.

4. **Trespass Must Be Intentional**. The trespass must be intentional—negligence is not enough. However, as with trespass to land, mistake is no defense.

5. **Actual Damages Required.** Actual damages are required to sustain an action for trespass to chattels. Nominal damages are not awarded. There must be more than an interference with the "dignitary interest" of the person with the right to possession.

6. **Possessor's Use of Reasonable Force.** The person entitled to possession of the chattel has the privilege to use reasonable force to protect his possession against harmful interference.

7. **Modern Trend.** This tort is of diminishing importance as it is being substantially replaced by the tort of conversion. Trespass to chattels now is generally found applicable to interferences that are insufficient to sustain a claim of conversion, but are more than harmless intermeddling.

CompuServe Inc. v. Cyber Promotions, Inc.

8. **Unsolicited E-mail--CompuServe Inc. v. Cyber Promotions, Inc.,** 962 F. Supp. 1015 (S.D. Ohio 1997).

   a. **Facts.** CompuServe Inc. (P) is a commercial online computer service that gives its customers access to the Internet, including E-mail. Cyber Promotions, Inc. (D) is in the business of sending unsolicited E-mail ads ("spam") to hundreds of thousands of Internet users, including P's subscribers. P received complaints from its subscribers threatening to discontinue their subscriptions unless P prevented the spam. P notified D that it could not use P's equipment to process and store the unsolicited E-mail and asked D to stop sending it. P developed software to block D's spam, but D avoided the blocking software by concealing the domain names of its computers. When P was unable to block D's E-mail, P sought a temporary restraining order to prevent D's conduct. The court granted P relief. P now seeks a preliminary injunction.

   b. **Issue.** May the sending of unsolicited, unwanted E-mail advertisements be considered a trespass to chattel owned by the Internet service provider whose system receives the E-mails?

   c. **Held.** Yes. Injunction granted.

      1) The original common law trespass to chattels involved the asportation of another's tangible property. Eventually it also covered the unauthorized use of personal property, and now provides for recovery for interferences with the possession of chattels that are not sufficiently important to be classed as conversion.

      2) P notes that under the Restatement (Second) of Torts, section 217(b), a trespass to chattel may be committed by intentionally using or intermeddling with the chattel in possession of another. Intermeddling may include intentionally bringing about a physical contact with the chattel. Electronic signals generated and sent by computer

have been held to be sufficiently physically tangible to support a trespass cause of action.

3) Section 218(b) recognizes a trespass to chattel if the tortfeasor impairs the chattel as to its condition, quality, or value. Here, D's voluminous E-mail messages demand disk space and processing power of P's computer equipment. This diminishes the value of the equipment to P, even though it is not physically damaged by D's conduct.

4) Section 218(d) recognizes another basis for a trespass to a chattel, here there is harm caused to some person in which the possessor has a legally protected interest. D's unwanted messages cause damage to P's customers, who pay incrementally to access their E-mail, read it, and discard it. P's customers also have to sift through all of D's unwanted messages to find the ones that they want. The inconvenience caused by D's spam has caused some of P's customers to terminate their accounts.

H. CONVERSION

1. **Introduction.** Conversion is the intentional, wrongful, acquiring, altering, damaging, transferring, using, or withholding of the personal property of another. The interest protected is that of possession, control, or right to control of a chattel. There must be more than a mere intermeddling for a conversion to lie.

2. **History.** After the actions of trespass and trespass on the case, English law developed the actions of debt, detinue, and replevin. Debt was the action for recovery of a specific and identical sum of money, but in spite of its recuperative effect, it died with the person. The actions of detinue and replevin were both for the recovery of specific chattels; the former for chattels rightfully obtained but wrongfully detained and the latter for chattels wrongfully obtained and wrongfully detained. However, late in the 15th Century, another branch of trespass on the case emerged in the name of "trover." This became the action for recovery of damages for wrongful interference with chattels of another, but like debt, trover died with the person. Notwithstanding this infirmity, it had certain procedural advantages and evolved into the modern action for conversion.

3. **More than Intermeddling Required.**

   a. **Restatement (Second) of Torts, section 222A.** This section provides that a conversion is an intentional exercise of dominion or control over a chattel that so seriously interferes with the right of another to control it that the one interfering with it is justly liable to the other for the full value of the chattel. The following factors are to be considered in determining whether the interference is serious enough to require full compensation:

1) Extent of dominion.

2) Duration of the interference.

3) Harm done to the chattel.

4) Inconvenience and expense to the one entitled to possession.

5) Good faith of the person exercising control.

Pearson v. Dodd

b. Intermeddling short of conversion--Pearson v. Dodd, 410 F.2d 701 (D.C. Cir.), *cert. denied*, 395 U.S. 947 (1969).

1) Facts. Certain staff members of Senator Thomas Dodd (P) entered P's office at night, removed and copied documents from P's files, then replaced them before the office opened the next morning. They then gave the information to Pearson (D), a newspaper columnist, who knew how the information was obtained. D published the information in a column. P sued for conversion. The trial court granted partial summary judgment on a theory of conversion. D appeals.

2) Issue. Does a person who photocopies documents convert those documents?

3) Held. No. Judgment reversed.

a) The tort of conversion protects the owner's interest in his property. The measure of damages is the value of the goods converted, because the plaintiff could ask the court to treat the conversion as a sale by the plaintiff to the defendant.

b) Not every wrongful interference with another's personal property is a conversion; otherwise the measure of damages could be excessive. If the intermeddling does not at least substantially deprive the owner of his possessory rights, it is not conversion but trespass to chattels. The measure of damages for trespass to chattels is the actual diminution in the value of the property caused by the interference.

c) P was never deprived of the use of his documents. Normally, information alone is not subject to conversion. The exception is when the information is gathered and sold as a commodity, such as literary works or commercial information. The information D obtained does not fall within this protected category of information.

4) **Comment.** The privacy aspects of this case are discussed in the privacy section, *infra*.

4. **What May Be Converted.** At common law, only property that could be lost could be the subject of an action for trover. This limited the action to ***tangible*** personal property. However, because of the need to protect intangible rights evidenced by commercial paper, the action for conversion was extended so that intangible rights merged with an instrument; *e.g.*, checks, notes, bonds, stock certificates, etc., were considered converted when the instrument evidencing such rights was converted. Today, some jurisdictions permit recovery for conversion of an intangible right (if it is of the type considered merged with an instrument) even though the instrument itself has not been converted (*e.g.*, refusal to transfer stock by a corporation). Under the general rule, intangible rights not considered merged with an instrument are not recognized as capable of being converted (*e.g.*, ideas, goodwill, etc.).

5. **Parties Plaintiff.** Conversion is a tort against possession. Anyone entitled to possession at the time of conversion has a cause of action, even if that possession is wrongful or arises through finding the chattel. However, wrongful possession must be under color of lawful claim—not theft.

   a. At common law, an owner of a chattel who had given up the immediate right to possession (*e.g.*, as through a bailment for a term) could not maintain an action for conversion until he had the right to possession.

   b. Today, courts have recognized a present right of action in those not entitled to immediate possession, probably to foreclose a multiplicity of action. Those holding future rights to possession have been permitted to enter into actions against converters brought by those entitled to immediate possession. In such cases, however, the future interest holder has been limited to the damages apportionable to his interest.

6. **Other Types of Conversion.** Besides dispossession and destruction of another's chattel, the following situations give rise to a claim for conversion.

   a. **Unauthorized use by bailee.** When a defendant receives possession of the chattel as bailee, and uses it in such a manner as to constitute a material breach of her authority, there is a conversion.

   b. **Stolen property.** Even though done in good faith, buying or receiving stolen property still involves the requisite intent to assert ownership rights and to deal with the chattel in a manner inconsistent with the rights of the true owner therein; hence, a conversion. [Restatement (Second) §229] This rule does not apply if the defendant did not intend to acquire ownership rights—as when she receives possession of the chattel solely for storage or safekeeping, or for transportation to another. In such cases, the defendant is not liable for conversion as long as she was acting in good faith. Also, selling or otherwise disposing of stolen property, even though in good faith, constitutes conversion.

c. **Misdelivering a chattel.** This covers the situation where a bailee, acting under an innocent mistake, or in good faith, delivers the chattel to the wrong person; or where she violates some condition in delivering it, even though she did deliver to the right person. For example, if a bailor says, "Give this ring to X if he pays you $10" and the bailee delivers the ring without receiving $10, there is a conversion.

d. **Refusing to surrender a chattel on demand.** If the acquisition itself was not wrongful, there must be a demand for return of the chattel before there can be a conversion. [Restatement (Second) §237] However, a carrier or bailee (*e.g.*, a finder) in possession of the chattel is privileged to make a qualified refusal to deliver, for the purpose of investigating the claimant's right to the chattel.

e. **Multiple acts of conversion.** The defendant's conduct may result in several distinct invasions of the plaintiff's interest—*i.e.*, several different acts of conversion. For example, if the defendant steals the chattel, sells it to an innocent purchaser, later buys it back and then refuses to give it to the plaintiff upon demand, the defendant has committed four separate acts of conversion.

7. **Good Faith and Mistake.** Generally neither good faith nor mistake will constitute a defense to conversion.

8. **Remedies.** If the defendant's conduct amounts to a "dispossession" (*i.e.*, an assertion of ownership rights in the chattel inconsistent with the rights of the true owner), the plaintiff will often have a choice of actions:

a. **Replevin, detinue, or claim and delivery.** The plaintiff may obtain return of the chattel and damages for its detention.

b. **Trespass to chattels.** The plaintiff can recover damages for the dispossession, but does not concern himself with the location of the chattel. (He either has it himself, or the chattel is completely destroyed, etc.).

c. **Conversion.** The plaintiff can recover the value of the chattel plus damages for the dispossession. Hence, satisfaction (*i.e.*, payment) of the judgment operates as an enforced sale of the chattel to the defendant.

1) **Measure of value.** The measure of recovery is ordinarily the market value of the goods at the time of the conversion (plus interest to date of suit). And, if the defendant is liable for several different acts of conversion (*e.g.*, the defendant steals the plaintiff's chattel, sells it to another, etc.), the plaintiff can choose the value at the time of any of the acts in order to obtain maximum recovery. If the property

has a fluctuating value, some courts allow the plaintiff to recover the highest value between the time of the conversion and the time of trial.

2) **Effect of offer to return.** An offer by the defendant to return the chattel does not affect her basic liability, but will mitigate damages recoverable if the defendant acquired the property innocently and in good faith—provided she made the offer to return promptly after learning that the plaintiff was the rightful owner, and provided the chattel was not impaired in value or condition since originally converted. [Restatement (Second) §922]

III. PRIVILEGE

A. CONSENT

1. **Introduction.** Consent of the plaintiff or the existence of a privilege in the defendant will exonerate the defendant from liability for an act that, on its face, would otherwise give rise to tort liability. Of course, the burden is on the defendant to plead and prove the existence of a privilege or consent. Under the general rule, consent by the plaintiff to an act that would otherwise give rise to tort liability will act as a bar to an action based on such act. However, the consent must be effective to act as a bar. Problems often arise as to whether the plaintiff has in fact given consent and whether the plaintiff has the capacity to give consent.

2. **Manifestation of Consent.** Consent may be express or implied. When the plaintiff, by words or conduct, intentionally indicates that she is willing to permit an invasion of her rights by the defendant, there is express consent. Implied consent, on the other hand, may be either implied-in-fact, as where the plaintiff acts in such a way as would be understood by a reasonable person to be consent to invasion of the plaintiff's rights by the defendant, or implied-in-law, as where circumstances are such as to create the privilege in the defendant to invade the plaintiff's rights without liability (*e.g.*, doctor rendering emergency medical care to unconscious person).

O'Brien v. Cunard Steamship Co.

a. **Conduct as consent--O'Brien v. Cunard Steamship Co.,** 28 N.E. 266 (Mass. 1891).

1) **Facts.** O'Brien (P) was a steerage passenger on Cunard's (D's) ship and was vaccinated along with other passengers by the ship's physician. P did not object verbally or by conduct to the vaccination, but raised her arm. P sued for assault. From a directed verdict for D, P appeals.

2) **Issues.** May a party reasonably rely on another's conduct showing consent, even if that person subjectively does not consent?

3) **Held.** Yes. Judgment affirmed.

a) P did not verbally object. The act of raising her arm was conduct that indicated consent to what would otherwise have been a tort.

b) All the passengers, including P, knew that the vaccination was required by immigration officials.

c) There was no evidence that the act was unlawful or negligent.

4) **Comment.** P's actual state of mind was immaterial, as a reasonable person would have concluded from P's act of raising her arm that she consented to the vaccination.

b. **Silence or inaction as consent.** Silence or inaction may or may not be consent, depending upon what a reasonable person under like circumstances would think. While it is unreasonable to think that silence in the face of a threatened beating is an implied consent thereto, it might not be unreasonable to assume that silence in response to an offered hug from a friend is consent.

c. **Participation in professional sports--Hackbart v. Cincinnati Bengals, Inc.,** 601 F.2d 516 (10th Cir.), *cert. denied*, 444 U.S. 931 (1979).

Hackbart v. Cincinnati Bengals, Inc.

1) **Facts.** During a professional football game, Hackbart (P) was intentionally struck by a member of the opposing Cincinnati Bengals (D). The blow was illegal under the rules of the game, but no action was taken by the officials or the players during the game. Later, P sued D for injuries suffered. The trial court determined that the available sanctions were provided by the game's rules, not by tort law, and entered judgment for D. P appeals.

2) **Issue.** May a professional football player recover in tort for injuries intentionally inflicted during a game in violation of the rules of the game?

3) **Held.** Yes. Judgment reversed.

a) The rules of football do not sanction the intentional punching of others. The rules are designed to establish reasonable boundaries to avoid intentional infliction of serious personal injuries. P is entitled to a trial to determine the extent of his rights and whether they were violated.

d. **Failure to press a right as consent.** In *Marsh v. Colby*, 39 Mich. 626 (1878), the defendant fished in an unposted pond on the plaintiff's land and the plaintiff brought an action for trespass. The appellate court reversed for the defendant, holding in effect that the plaintiff's failure to press his right to control the land acted as a consent to the trespass.

e. **Mistake of fact.** The plaintiff's mistake as to the nature of the defendant's conduct will vitiate the plaintiff's apparent consent. For example, if the plaintiff submits to a body massage under the mistaken belief that the defendant is treating an illness and that the massage is a necessary part of the treatment, the plaintiff will not be deemed to have consented to the defendant's offered indecent familiarities. Similarly, a person who accepts and eats candy poisoned by the defendant, without knowledge of the poison, does not consent to be poisoned by the defendant.

f. **Mistake of law.** Consent is ineffective if given under a mistake of law; *e.g.*, submitting to arrest under the belief that an arrest warrant is valid, when in fact it is not.

g. **Fraud.** Consent procured by fraud is ineffective, *e.g.*, the body massage example, above. However, fraud as to a collateral matter does not vitiate consent; *e.g.*, when the plaintiff consents to sexual intercourse with the defendant in return for a $10 bill offered by the defendant, the fact that the plaintiff did not know that the bill was counterfeit will not negate the consent if it is otherwise effective.

h. **Duress.** Consent given in response to physical force or threats thereof against the plaintiff or a member of the plaintiff's family will be ineffective.

3. **Surgical Operations and Emergency.** While a doctor is generally subject to the same rules with respect to invasion of another's rights, the law has developed certain exceptions. If, during an operation, a doctor discovers a condition in the plaintiff that requires immediate attention, consent to the additional surgical procedure is deemed implied-in-law, unless the patient specifically limited the authority of the doctor prior to the operation. With respect to emergencies, the victim is assumed to consent to acts by a doctor consistent with what a reasonable person would desire under the same circumstances.

Mohr v. Williams

a. **Action for assault and battery--Mohr v. Williams,** 104 N.W. 12 (Minn. 1905).

1) **Facts.** Mohr (P) went to Williams (D), an ear specialist, to have an operation on her right ear. While P was under anesthesia, D found a more serious condition in her left ear, ultimately dangerous, but not immediately critical, and operated on it instead. P sued. The jury awarded P $14,322.50. D moved for judgment n.o.v., which the judge denied, but he did grant a new trial because he found the damages excessive. P and D both appeal.

2) **Issue.** Does beneficial surgery performed without the patient's prior knowledge and consent amount to assault and battery?

3) **Held.** Yes. Judgment affirmed.

a) Although the method of treatment is generally up to the doctor due to his skill, the doctor does not have a free license to perform whatever procedures he desires. He must first consult the patient. The exception would be in an emergency or a life-threatening situation. Neither was present here.

b) The fact that D acted without wrongful intent and was not guilty of negligence does not relieve D from the charge of assault and battery. He wrongfully, and hence unlawfully, operated on P.

c) The amount of damages depends on P's actual injury, in light of the benefit conferred as well as D's good faith.

4) **Comment.** P ultimately recovered only $39 in damages for assault and battery.

b. **Beyond the scope of consent.** If a patient specifically tells the doctor before the operation to do X and no more, the doctor may be liable if she does Y, even if she feels that Y is necessary and it in fact benefits the patient.

c. **Parental consent.** Generally, consent of a parent is necessary to operate on a minor, except in an emergency. This raises the issue of how extreme an emergency is necessary. Some cases have permitted minors to consent to operations minor in scope.

d. **Incapacity.** In personal injury cases, when a person is unable to give consent and no one with authority to consent is available, sound professional judgment can be exercised.

4. **Informed Consent.** It is generally held that consent must be informed and that mistake in the factum will vitiate apparent consent.

a. **Ignorance of true circumstances--DeMay v. Roberts,** 9 N.W. 146 (Mich. 1881).

DeMay v. Roberts

1) **Facts.** DeMay (D), a surgeon, asked a young unmarried man to assist him in delivering Roberts' (P's) child. P thought D's assistant was also a physician and made no objection to his presence. Upon finding out that he was not, P brought suit for invasion of privacy and assault, in that D's assistant had held her hands during the pain. P won at trial and D appeals.

2) **Issue.** Can one who gives implied consent to an invasion of privacy under a mistaken supposition later sue when a mistake is found?

3) **Held.** Yes. Judgment affirmed.

a) The doctor and his assistant deceived P by not disclosing the assistant's true identity. Consent given under faulty assumption or ignorance of the true facts does not preclude suit when the true circumstances are determined. Consent must be informed.

b) P could recover for the shame and mortification she suffered when she discovered the assistant's true identity.

b. **Absence of informed consent as basis for negligence action.** When an operation or treatment is unsuccessful, the patient may be able to sue the doctor on alternative theories of medical malpractice (based on negligence) or battery, if there has not been "informed consent." Modern courts generally use the former theory. [*See* Scott v. Bradford, *infra*]

5. **Unlawful Acts.** There is a split of authority concerning whether a voluntary participant to an unlawful act can be deemed to have "consented" thereto for the purpose of barring a subsequent action against a fellow participant for damages.

Hart v. Geysel

a. **General rule--Hart v. Geysel,** 294 P. 570 (Wash. 1930).

1) **Facts.** Cartwright and Geysel (D) engaged in an illegal prize fight, which resulted in Cartwright's death. Hart (P), Cartwright's administrator, seeks damages. From a dismissal, P appeals.

2) **Issue.** Are damages recoverable when two parties freely engage in an unlawful act and one injures or kills the other?

3) **Held.** No. Dismissal affirmed.

a) A party participating in an illegal act may not gain a right of action that he would not have had, had he not so participated. The rationale is that (i) the consent to invasion of a private right negates the cause of action therefor, and (ii) no person should be allowed to profit from his own wrongdoing.

4) **Comment.** Even in states following this case, the finding of effective consent applies only in civil actions for damages and not in criminal actions.

b. **Member of protected class.** A member of a class of persons protected under the law may not consent to an assumption of risk contrary to the intent of the law. In *Hudson v. Craft*, 204 P.2d 1 (Cal. 1949), Hudson successfully sued the promoter of an ***illegal*** boxing concession for assault and battery he suffered when he was induced to engage in a boxing match and was injured. The law was intended to protect participants in boxing contests from serious injury. This approach was adopted in section 892C of the Restatement (Second) of Torts.

B. SELF-DEFENSE

One may be privileged to use force in self-defense if such force appears reasonably necessary for the protection of the actor.

1. **Nondeadly Force.** Nondeadly force (not likely to cause death or serious bodily harm) may be used in self-defense when the actor reasonably believes she will be caused immediate harm by the other person's conduct. The force used by the actor must be reasonable under the circumstances, and cannot go beyond the necessity of the situation. There is generally no duty to retreat or comply with the demands of the aggressor.

2. **Deadly Force.** Deadly force (likely to cause death or serious bodily harm) may be used in self-defense when the actor reasonably believes that the other person's conduct will result in either death or serious bodily harm to the actor. Under the minority rule, the actor has a duty to retreat before using deadly force, except if (i) the actor is in her own home, or place of business (recognized only in a few of the minority jurisdictions), (ii) retreating would be dangerous, or (iii) the actor is attempting a valid arrest.

3. **Retaliation.** There is no right to retaliate. When the danger has passed, the privilege of self-defense expires.

4. **Excessive Force.** If an actor uses excessive force in asserting her privilege of self-defense, the other party then has the privilege of protecting himself against the degree of force being exerted by the actor.

5. **Reasonable Force.** Whether force is reasonable is determined on an objective basis; *i.e.*, what force would have been used by the average, reasonable person under the same or similar circumstances.

C. DEFENSE OF OTHERS

Under the ***majority view***, one may be privileged to use force in the defense of others if he reasonably believes that: (i) the other person would be privileged to defend himself, (ii) the force used is reasonable under the circumstances, and (iii) intervention is necessary to protect the other person. Under the ***minority view***, the actor steps into the shoes of the third person and may be liable if he defends a third person who is actually the aggressor, regardless of how reasonable such intervention may have appeared to him. At common law, one was privileged only to come to the aid of one's family or servants. Today, it is recognized as socially desirable to aid those in distress, even if they are strangers.

D. DEFENSE OF PROPERTY

One is privileged to use only that force reasonably necessary to defend one's property. Deadly force generally can only be used in defense of one's dwelling, and some courts further restrict its use to situations where the invasion appears to threaten death or serious bodily harm (*i.e.*, tying it into another privilege—self-defense or defense of others).

Katko v. Briney

1. **Mechanical Devices (Mantraps)--Katko v. Briney,** 183 N.W.2d 657 (Iowa 1971).

   a. **Facts.** Katko (P) entered the Brineys' (Ds') farmhouse, which was boarded up and posted with "no trespassing" signs, to look for and steal old bottles and jars. Ds lived far away and had set a shotgun in the bedroom to shoot whoever opened the door because Ds' farm building had been broken into before. There was no posted notice of the trap. P was shot as he entered the room and most of his leg was blown off. The jury awarded P actual and punitive damages. Ds appeal.

   b. **Issue.** May a landowner lawfully set a spring gun against possible trespassers?

   c. **Held.** No. Judgment affirmed.

      1) Landowners cannot mechanically do what they could not do in person. The value of life outweighs that of the interest of the landowners; they have no right to use force likely to kill or inflict serious harm, unless self-defense or another privilege is involved.

   d. **Dissent.** This principle may apply to mere trespassers but not to burglars.

   e. **Comments.**

      1) Even if the landowners post notices of traps, they are not privileged in using them to defend their property because one may not do indirectly what one cannot do directly. The same rule applies to vicious dogs.

      2) In this case, the judgment against Ds was so large that they had to sell most of their farm to pay it.

E. RECOVERY OF PROPERTY

1. **Recapture of Chattels.** Under the Restatement (Second) of Torts, sections 101-106, one is privileged to use reasonable force to recapture chattels if: (i) he is entitled to immediate possession; (ii) return has been demanded and refused; (iii) he is in "fresh pursuit" (*i.e.*, he has been reasonably diligent in discovering his loss and in attempting to recover the chattel); (iv) the person from whom the recapture is effected is the

wrongdoer or is not a bona fide purchaser from the wrongdoer; and (v) the force used is reasonable under the circumstances.

a. **Fresh pursuit--Hodgeden v. Hubbard,** 18 Vt. 504 (1846). Hodgeden v. Hubbard

1) **Facts.** P fraudulently induced D to sell him a stove on credit by misrepresenting his ability to pay for it. D learned of the fraud on the day of the sale. D and an employee pursued P to get back the stove. Upon being confronted, P drew a knife. D and the employee forcibly overpowered P and took back the stove. The jury found for P and D appeals.

2) **Issue.** May a person use reasonable force to recover chattels?

3) **Held.** Yes. Judgment reversed for D.

a) D had a right to retake the property since it was taken by fraud, his pursuit was diligent, and there was no use of unnecessary force in so doing. Here, P's force could be met with force.

b. **Detention to investigate--Bonkowski v. Arlan's Department Store,** 162 N.W.2d 347 (Mich. 1968). Bonkowski v. Arlan's Department Store

1) **Facts.** Bonkowski (P) was stopped in a store parking lot and accused by a private police officer of having stolen costume jewelry. P denied the allegation but the private officer told P he wanted to see the contents of her purse. She emptied the contents on the ground and showed the officer the sales slips for all the articles in her purse. P then sued Arlan's Department Store (D) for false arrest and slander. D appeals a judgment for P.

2) **Issue.** Does a merchant have a right to reasonably detain and search a person suspected of theft?

3) **Held.** Yes. Judgment reversed.

a) The right to make a reasonable limited investigation extends to the premises and to the immediate vicinity of the premises. D must have reasonable belief of the theft, and the detention and investigation must be reasonable in scope and duration.

c. **Conditional sales.** There is no right to use force to recapture a chattel if the chattel was obtained in a legal manner in the first instance. If a contract contains a clause allowing seller to repossess from buyer for failure of payment, seller can attempt repossession. But since there was no force or fraud on the part of the buyer (possession given to the buyer peacefully and voluntarily), the seller has no right to use any force in recapture of the chattel.

1) **Force defined.** Force is any intrusion into the premises of the plaintiff or use of force against the chattel or force against the possessor. Breaking into a car, garage, home, etc., using a skeleton key or master key, hot wiring, intruding, or any force against chattel or person is tortious. Watch for trespass to chattels or trespass to land, or false imprisonment or battery to the person, in recovery cases.

2) **No force allowed.** The defendant can peacefully repossess the chattel, but he cannot use any kind of force, even if the plaintiff resists the recapture. Also, consent to repossess is not necessary if no force is used.

3) **No right to self-help.** While the repossessor has a legal right, he must use the courts to enforce that right and has no right to take the law upon himself.

4) **Contract clause.** A contract with a clause permitting use of force in repossession is void as contrary to public policy.

5) **Damages.** Note that a repossessor may even be liable for conversion in some cases and may be subject to punitive damages.

d. **Damages by reason of the invasion of another's land to reclaim chattels.** If the defendant damages the plaintiff's land in recapturing his chattels, and the plaintiff wrongfully obtained the defendant's chattels, the defendant will not be liable for the damage, provided the entry and force used to recapture the chattels was reasonable. On the other hand, if the plaintiff was not a wrongdoer and the chattel is on the plaintiff's land through an act of God or an act of a third party, the defendant will be liable for any damage done in reclaiming the chattel, though he is not liable for damage caused by the chattel being deposited on the plaintiff's land. If the defendant's chattel is on the plaintiff's land through the fault of the defendant, the defendant has no privilege of any kind to go on the plaintiff's land and reclaim it.

2. **Reentry upon Real Property.** The statute of Richard II made it a criminal offense for one entitled to possession of land to reenter by force. Today, there is a split of authority as to the existence of a civil action.

a. **Minority view.** The minority position is that there is a privilege to use reasonable force in reentry, but (in the majority of these jurisdictions) the actor (i) may be subject to criminal prosecution if he harms the possessor, and (ii) must protect the property of the possesssor for a reasonable time, and (iii) cannot eject the possessor of land into a dangerous position.

b. **Majority view.** Under the majority position, there is no privilege to use force, and the legal owner must rely on legal processes to regain possession. Why?

1) There is a summary method to gain reentry.

2) In a modern society citizens should rely on the state to enforce their rights, not self-help.

3. **Removing Trespassing Chattels.** The person in possession of land or chattels is privileged to use reasonable force to remove chattels belonging to another in order to protect her interest in her own land or chattels. The "reasonableness" of the force applied to the trespassing chattels is in part determined by the relative value of the actor's property as opposed to the value of the trespassing chattels (*i.e.*, the actor is not privileged to totally destroy a valuable trespassing chattel in order to effect immediate removal when the damage caused to her property by a more time-consuming but orderly removal would be nominal).

F. NECESSITY

1. **Public Necessity.** One is privileged to enter land or interfere with chattels of another if it is reasonably necessary or if it reasonably appears necessary to avert a public disaster. To invoke the privilege, the following are required: (i) an immediate and imperative necessity and not just one that is expedient or utilitarian; and (ii) an act that is in good faith, for the public good. The privilege is conditional, and it disappears when the act becomes unreasonable under the existing circumstances. The rationale behind this privilege is that when peril threatens the whole community, or so many people that there is a public interest involved, one has a complete defense or privilege to act to protect the public interest.

a. **Extent of privilege.** This is a complete privilege. The defendant is not liable for any damage or destruction to the land or chattels involved, as long as this was done in the proper exercise of the privilege.

1) **Damage to improvements.** The defendant is also completely privileged to break and enter fences and any buildings, including dwellings.

2) **Force to the person.** If the property owner resists the defendant's attempt to enter the land or to deal with the chattels, the defendant may use whatever force is reasonably necessary to effect the privilege, including deadly force if necessary. When a public disaster is threatened, it may be appropriate to endanger one life to protect many lives.

b. **Who may claim privilege.** There is no distinction between public officers and private citizens in the exercise of this privilege.

Surocco v. Geary

c. **Right to destroy--Surocco v. Geary,** 3 Cal. 69 (1853).

1) **Facts.** A fire was burning in the city where Surocco (P) lived. Geary (D), a city official, determined that P's house had to be blown up to stop the fire from spreading. P was removing property from his house when D stopped him and blew up the house. P sued for damages and recovered. D appeals.

2) **Issue.** Is a person liable for damages to private property resulting from action taken to avert a public disaster?

3) **Held.** No. Judgment reversed.

a) In times of public necessity, the individual rights of property give way to the higher laws of necessity. A house that could serve to propel the fire is a nuisance, which D could abate. P's private rights must yield to the interests of society. D would be liable if his conduct were not justified, but here it was.

2. **Private Necessity.** When there is no public interest involved and the defendant acts to protect her own interest, she is not liable for the technical tort and the landowner has no privilege to expel her.

a. **Narrower privilege.** The private necessity privilege is narrower than the public one; the landowner may recover any damages caused by the exercise of the privilege.

Vincent v. Lake Erie Transportation Company

b. **Liable for property damage--Vincent v. Lake Erie Transportation Company,** 124 N.W. 221 (Minn. 1910).

1) **Facts.** Lake Erie (D), a transportation company, following Vincent's (P's) instruction, moored its boat to P's wharf so that P's cargo could be unloaded. During unloading, a violent storm arose that prevented the boat from leaving the wharf. Thereafter, the storm threw the boat against the wharf and damaged the wharf. P sued to recover for damages. D appeals an order denying the motion for judgment notwithstanding the verdict.

2) **Issue.** May one who is forced by necessity to use the property of another do so without liability for damage to the property caused by his use?

3) **Held.** No. Judgment affirmed.

a) The ship's master exercised ordinary prudence and care in keeping the ship moored to the wharf during the storm.

b) In so doing, he deliberately protected the ship at the expense of the wharf.

c) The damage to the wharf did not result from an act of God or unavoidable accident but from circumstances within D's control.

d) Having deliberately availed himself of P's property, as the storm gave D the right to do, D was liable for injury inflicted by his actions.

4) **Comment.** The invasion of the other person's property out of private necessity must protect an interest greater than the interest involved. If this is the case, the party whose interests are invaded will be liable if he tries to expel the invading party.

G. AUTHORITY OF LAW

1. **Trespass Ab Initio ("From the Beginning").** One who enters on the land of another by authority of law and abuses his power is a trespasser from the time that he entered upon the land. This doctrine applies only to acts done under legal authority. The doctrine is a legal fiction and is rarely used today. The rationale is that the original entry is a trespass because of subsequent wrongs committed (usually a trespass). The doctrine has been repudiated in the Restatement (Second) of Torts.

2. **Good Faith.** With respect to "discretionary" or "quasi-judicial" acts (those requiring some degree of personal judgment), "good faith" is generally a defense for those acting in their official capacity, even if they overstep the bounds of their authority. The "good faith" defense does not generally apply to "ministerial acts," which require little or no personal judgment.

H. DISCIPLINE

There is a limited right of discipline of captains over the crew and even passengers, of teachers over students, and of parents over children. The privilege extends only to acts that are reasonable under the circumstances.

I. JUSTIFICATION

Generally, restraint or detention that is reasonable under the circumstances and that is imposed for the purpose of preventing another from inflicting personal injuries or damaging or interfering with real or personal property in one's lawful possession or custody is not unlawful.

Sindle v. New York City Transit Authority

1. **False Imprisonment--Sindle v. New York City Transit Authority,** 307 N.E.2d 245 (N.Y. 1973).

a. **Facts.** Sindle (P), a fourteen-year-old schoolboy, boarded a bus with his classmates on the last day of school. The students began to vandalize the bus, and after several minutes, the bus driver informed the students that he was taking them to the police station. There was no evidence that P was involved in the vandalism. P sued the New York City Transit Authority (D) for negligence and false imprisonment. The negligence action was waived by P. The trial court refused to allow D to amend to include the defense of justification. D appeals.

b. **Issue.** Is reasonableness of restraint or detention used to prevent injury to people or interference with property a defense to a claim for false imprisonment?

c. **Held.** Yes. Order reversed and remanded for a new trial.

1) A bus driver is entrusted with the care and safety of the children and with the care of the bus. This duty allows the bus driver to use reasonable physical restraint to prevent injury to the children or property in his charge.

IV. NEGLIGENCE

A. INTRODUCTION

As indicated *supra*, liability based on the negligence of the defendant is another of the major classifications of tort liability. The Restatement (Second) of Torts, section 282, defines negligence as "any conduct, except conduct recklessly disregardful of an interest of others, which falls below the standard established by law for the protection of others against unreasonable risk of harm."

B. ELEMENTS OF PLAINTIFF'S PRIMA FACIE CASE

The following are the elements of a plaintiff's prima facie case based on negligence of the defendant:

(i) Act or omission of the defendant;

(ii) Duty owed by the defendant to exercise due care;

(iii) Breach of duty by the defendant;

(iv) Causal relationship between the defendant's conduct and the harm (both actual and proximate cause) to the plaintiff;

(v) Damages.

1. **Burden of Proof.** Each of the above elements must be alleged by the plaintiff, who has the burden of proving the allegations by a preponderance of the evidence.

2. **Act or Omission.** As in intentional torts, the act of the defendant must be the external manifestation of his will, (*i.e.*, volitional movement) in order to support a cause of action based on negligence. However, liability in negligence can also be based on the failure or omission of the defendant to act if he is under an affirmative duty to act.

C. DETERMINATION OF RISK

1. **Unreasonable Risk.** A person is bound only to use care that is commensurate with the hazard involved. The risk reasonably perceived defines the duty owed.

   a. **Possibility versus probability--Lubitz v. Wells,** 113 A.2d 147 (Conn. Super. Ct. 1955). Lubitz v. Wells

      1) **Facts.** Wells (D), the owner of a golf club, left it in his backyard and his son picked it up and swung it at a stone on the

ground. In so doing, the son hit Lubitz (P) in the jaw with the club. P alleged that D knew that the club was there and should have known that children who played in his yard would play with the club and could be injured through its negligent use. D's demurrer was sustained.

2) **Issue.** Must an act present an unreasonable risk in order to constitute negligence?

3) **Held.** Yes. Judgment affirmed.

a) The act must be unreasonable. The mere possibility of injury is not sufficient. There must be a foreseeable, reasonable probability of injury. It is not a question of what might happen. The club was not so intrinsically dangerous that it was negligence to leave it in the yard.

b) Although D could have foreseen some possibility of injury, there must be sufficient probability to cause a reasonable person to take action against the appreciable risk.

Blyth v. Birmingham Waterworks Co.

b. **Unusual conditions--Blyth v. Birmingham Waterworks Co.,** 156 Eng. Rep. 1047 (Ct. Exch. 1856).

1) **Facts.** A water hydrant that Birmingham Waterworks Co. (D) had installed 25 years earlier sprung a leak in an extraordinary frost and water flooded Blyth's (P's) home, causing damage. In installing the water mains, D had taken precautions to make them safe against such frosts as experience indicated might occur. P sued.

2) **Issue.** Is a person liable for negligence if he takes all reasonable precautions against the foreseeable harms?

3) **Held.** No. Verdict for D.

a) D did all that a reasonable person under like circumstances would be expected to do. The result of the unusual conditions was an accident for which D cannot be held liable.

4) **Comment.** Negligence is an act or omission that falls below the care that a reasonable person would have shown under the same conditions. In this case, the conduct was not unreasonable in relation to the known foreseeable risks involved. A defendant can often rely on past history and experience as to what is foreseeable. Furthermore, some risks are too small to demand that a reasonable person take precautions; *e.g.*, extraordinary conditions.

c. **Foreseeability--Gulf Refining Co. v. Williams,** 185 So. 234 (Miss. 1938).

Gulf Refining Co. v. Williams

1) **Facts.** Williams (P), while using a drum of gasoline distributed by Gulf Refining Co. (D), was burned in a fire caused by a spark from defective threads of the bung cap. From a judgment for P, D appeals, claiming the incident was so unusual that it could not have been anticipated.

2) **Issue.** May a likelihood of injury short of a probability give rise to liability for negligence?

3) **Held.** Yes. Judgment affirmed.

a) Proof of a disputed fact must establish a probability of that fact, not just a possibility of that fact. Foreseeability does not require such a high standard, however.

b) It is only necessary to show that an injury was likely to occur, not that injury was highly probable. The test of foreseeability is not a balance of the probabilities, but is a question of whether the likelihood of harm would cause a reasonably prudent person to guard against it.

2. **Justified Risk.** Tort law does not require elimination of all risk. Life cannot be made absolutely safe. The utility of a product must be balanced against the risk it presents.

a. **Utility versus harm--Chicago Burlington & Quincy Railroad Co. v. Krayenbuhl,** 91 N.W. 880 (Neb. 1902).

Chicago Burlington & Quincy Railroad Co. v. Krayenbuhl

1) **Facts.** An employee of the Chicago Burlington & Quincy Railroad Co. (D) failed to lock a turntable and Krayenbuhl (P), a trespassing four-year-old child, was seriously injured while playing on it. From a judgment for P, D appeals.

2) **Issue.** Does the operator of inherently dangerous equipment have a duty to take reasonable precautions to make the equipment safe?

3) **Held.** Yes. Judgment reversed on other grounds.

a) The social utility in the use of dangerous machinery outweighs the danger of possible injury, thus justifying the risks involved in use of the machinery. However, the burden of locking such machinery was slight and the gravity of possible harm large.

b) Not locking the machinery under such circumstances was an omission a reasonable person of ordinary prudence would not allow. The Restatement (Second) of Torts, section 291, states that a risk is unreasonable and an act negligent if the risk is of such magnitude as to outweigh the utility of the act.

4) **Comment.** *See* discussion *infra* under **Trespassing Children**.

Davison v. Snohomish County

b. **Knowledge--Davison v. Snohomish County,** 270 P. 422 (Wash. 1928).

1) **Facts.** Davison (P) was injured when his car skidded on dirt on the road and crashed through a wooden bridge guard rail. P contended that Snohomish County (D) negligently constructed and maintained the bridge. From a judgment for P for $2,500, D appeals.

2) **Issue.** Did D owe a duty to provide guard rails sufficient to keep autos from skidding off the approach?

3) **Held.** No. Judgment reversed.

a) Maintenance of all country roads to meet the needs of modern vehicles may be too large a burden, even considering the possible injuries.

4) **Comment.** The decision may have been different if the town maintaining the road had had notice of the danger.

c. **Possible harm great.** When the risk is serious (possible harm great), the possibility that the injury will occur need not be high for the duty to guard against it to arise.

United States v. Carroll Towing Co.

d. **The Hand Formula--United States v. Carroll Towing Co.,** 159 F.2d 169 (2d Cir. 1947).

1) **Facts.** The United States Government's (P's) barge broke from its moorings and sank, allegedly because of Carroll Towing Co.'s (D's) negligence in handling the barge's mooring lines. P's employee, who was in charge of the barge, was not on the barge when it broke loose, and had been ashore for 21 hours. The accident occurred in the full tide of war activity when barges were constantly being towed in and out of the harbor. P sued for damages. D contended that P was also negligent in that its employee was not on the barge when it broke loose. P appeals a verdict for D.

2) **Issue.** If the possible harm is great, is there a duty to guard against it even if the probability of its occurring is small?

3) **Held.** Yes. Judgment affirmed.

a) The barge owner's liability depends upon whether its burden (B) of adequate precautions is less than (<) the probability (P) that the barge will break away multiplied by the gravity of resulting injury if it does (L). If B<PL, the barge owner is negligent.

b) The harbor was crowded; it was not beyond reasonable expectation that work might not be done carefully. Under such conditions, it is a fair requirement that the barge owner have a bargee aboard during working hours.

4) **Comment.** The main question in a negligence case is whether a reasonable person would have realized the risk involved in a course of action but still would not have changed his conduct; in that case, no negligence can be inferred. Because of the balancing of specific factors in the *Carroll Towing* case, analysis of the opinion has frequently centered on economics. The balancing of burdens against risks to be avoided translates easily into a cost-benefit analysis.

D. STANDARD OF CARE

In general, the standard of care that must be exercised is that conduct that the average reasonable person of ordinary prudence would follow under the same or similar circumstances. The standard of conduct is an external and objective one, and has nothing to do with individual judgment, although higher duties may be imposed by specific statutory provisions or by reason of special knowledge or skill on the part of the actor. Since the standard is an external one, being a fool is no excuse; likewise, being an expert is no excuse if a reasonable person of ordinary prudence would do otherwise. The reasonable person standard takes no account of the personality of the particular person involved.

1. The Reasonable Prudent Person.

a. **Best judgment immaterial--Vaughan v. Menlove,** 132 Eng. Rep. 490 (1837).

Vaughan v. Menlove

1) **Facts.** D built a hay rick, *i.e.*, haystack, on his premises near the boundary adjacent to P's barn, stables, and cottages. D was repeatedly warned of the danger of spontaneous combustion but ignored the warnings. The hay rick eventually caught fire and the fire spread to P's barn, stables, and then to P's cottages, destroying the entire structures.

2) **Issue.** Is D liable to P even though in his own judgment he acted reasonably?

3) **Held.** Yes. Judgment for P affirmed.

a) The question of whether D acted honestly and to the best of his judgment is immaterial. The rule by which D's conduct is measured requires in all cases a regard for caution such as a person of ordinary prudence would observe.

b. **General knowledge and skills.** All persons are deemed to possess certain minimum levels of knowledge and skills, and as a consequence, are held to certain minimum standards of care in their activities.

Delair v. McAdoo

1) **Actual knowledge not required--Delair v. McAdoo,** 188 A. 181 (Pa. 1936).

a) **Facts.** McAdoo (D) failed to replace threadbare tires on his car. D had no actual knowledge of the danger involved. When D was passing Delair (P) on the road, one of the tires blew out and D's car collided with P's. The jury found for P. D appeals the trial court's refusal to grant a judgment n.o.v.

b) **Issue.** Is actual knowledge of the danger necessary to support a finding of negligence?

c) **Held.** No. Judgment affirmed.

(1) An ordinary person of reasonable prudence has a duty to know some things of general knowledge and must be aware of things reasonably ascertainable upon inspection.

(2) The danger associated with threadbare tires is so great that drivers must be held to a knowledge of the facts. This is the same principle that makes a loaded gun dangerous, regardless of the owner's ignorance that the gun is dangerous when loaded.

d) **Comment.** Recall that it was negligent not to know of spontaneous combustion in the burning hay rick case (*Vaughan*, *supra*).

2) **Duty to discover.** There is a duty to find out what one does not know. A city dweller in the country has a duty to find out what she does not know, *e.g.*, where lightning is likely to strike.

3) **Common facts.** There are some facts in the community such as gravity, leverage, that fire burns, etc., that a person must know at his peril.

4) **Experts.** The reasonable person can rely upon others, *e.g.*, experts or those reasonably deemed to possess superior knowledge.

c. **Custom.** Following custom in the community is not conclusive that the conduct is reasonable or that the proper standard of care has been met. Custom is merely evidence of the standard of care owed. The test still is whether the average reasonable person would have so acted under the same or similar circumstances. Many customs may be considered to be negligent (initiations and other forms of hazing, etc.) when viewed from the reasonable person standard.

1) **Evidence of custom to prove reasonableness--Trimarco v. Klein,** 436 N.E. 2d 502 (N.Y. 1982).

Trimarco v. Klein

a) **Facts.** Trimarco (P) rented an apartment from Klein (D). One day while P was sliding the glass door to get out of the bathtub, the door shattered and P was severely injured by the glass. The door was made of ordinary, not tempered, glass, although both types of glass have the same appearance. P sued for negligence. At trial, P produced expert testimony showing that for over 20 years, tempered safety glass had been used for bathroom enclosures. By the time of the accident in 1976, regular glass in this application did not conform to accepted safety standards. The state business law outlawed the use of other than safety glazing material in bathroom enclosures. Although this statute did not apply to D's installation, the court instructed the jury that the statute could be considered as a standard by which to measure D's conduct. The jury awarded P $240,000. The appellate court reversed on the ground that D had no duty to replace the glass unless D had received prior notice of the danger from P or from a similar accident, and alternatively noted that the instructions based on the inapplicable state law were erroneous. P appeals.

b) **Issue.** May evidence of custom be used to prove that a defendant had a duty of care?

c) **Held.** Yes. Judgment reversed.

(1) Evidence of a customary way of doing things safely that eliminates certain dangers may be used to show that one who did not comply with the custom fell below the required standard. Proof that D did not comply with a common practice thus may establish liability.

(2) Custom and usage reflects the judgment, experience, and conduct of others in the given situation. It also shows feasibility and the opportunity to learn the safe way. The custom need not be universal, so long as it is sufficiently known to charge the actor with knowledge or negligent ignorance.

(3) Evidence of a custom is not conclusive; it is merely evidence that is subject to the test of reasonableness. Custom shows what perhaps should be done, but the standard of care is what prudence requires whether it is usually followed or not.

(4) The evidence in this case supports the jury's verdict. The jury could decide that due to the low cost and availability of safety glass, com-

bined with the custom of using it, the glass door that was safe when installed was no longer safe. The jury was properly instructed to evaluate the reasonableness of D's conduct under all the circumstances.

(5) A new trial is necessary, however, because it was error to instruct as to the inapplicable state law.

d) **Comment.** There is a definite movement toward imposing a higher standard of care when the defendant knows of inherent dangers in an industry-wide custom. To decide otherwise would allow an entire industry to keep its safety standards artificially low just by refusing to raise the industry-wide standards.

d. Emergency. The reasonable person confronted with an emergency may act differently than he would if there were no emergency. This does not mean that there is a different standard applied; it only indicates that the emergency conditions are added to the circumstances that are taken into consideration in determining how a reasonable person would act when confronted with the situation.

Cordas v. Peerless Transportation Co.

1) **No liability for quick response--Cordas v. Peerless Transportation Co.,** 27 N.Y.S. 2d 198 (1941).

a) **Facts.** A man who had just committed a robbery jumped into Peerless Transportation Co.'s (D's) taxi and ordered the driver to drive away. After a short distance, the driver suddenly jammed on the brakes and jumped out of the car. The car kept going, jumped over a curb, and injured Cordas and her children (Ps). The trial court dismissed the complaint. Ps appeal.

b) **Issue.** May a person who acts quickly and without considering all the consequences, but in response to a sudden emergency, be held liable for negligence?

c) **Held.** No. Judgment affirmed.

(1) Negligence is always determined in relation to the circumstances. The standard is still that of the reasonable person but less is expected of a reasonable person under such circumstances; *i.e.*, even a reasonable person reacts without long reflection when his life is in jeopardy.

(2) In this case, the driver acted in response to a sudden and frightening emergency. He cannot be held liable.

2) **Caveat.** The emergency doctrine is limited. It does not apply when the defendant creates the emergency himself or when he should have anticipated it.

e. **Physical attributes.** The physical attributes of the reasonable person are deemed to be identical to those of the actor.

1) **Blindness--Roberts v. State of Louisiana,** 396 So.2d 566 (La. 1981).

Roberts v. State of Louisiana

a) **Facts.** Roberts (P), a 75-year-old man, was walking in the hall of the United States Post Office building when he was bumped and knocked to the floor by Burson, a blind man who operated a concession stand in the building. Burson was not using his cane at the time because he was familiar with the building. He was relying on his facial sense as he usually did for short trips in the building, although he did use his cane to get to and from work. Burson was operating the concession pursuant to a program operated by the state of Louisiana (D). P sued, claiming that Burson was negligent and that D negligently supervised him. The trial court dismissed P's suit and P appeals.

b) **Issue.** Is a disabled person held to the same standard of care as a nondisabled person?

c) **Held.** No. Judgment affirmed.

(1) A disabled person must take the precautions that the ordinary reasonable person would take if he were blind. This does not necessarily mean that a disabled person must use a greater degree of care than one who is not disabled.

(2) In this case, Burson admitted he did not use his cane for short trips within the building because his facial sense was adequate for such trips. It is not uncommon for blind persons to rely on techniques other than a cane when moving in familiar settings. In fact, some evidence indicated that a cane can be more of a hazard than a help in a busy area.

(3) P's only testimony that Burson was negligent was P's expert witness. This witness did not examine Burson's particular skills, however. This evidence was not sufficient to show that Burson was negligent.

d) **Comment.** In *Hill v. City of Glenwood*, 124 Iowa 479 (1904), a blind man was injured while walking on a public street. In holding for the man, the court pointed out that a blind man is not required to use extraordinary care, as the city contended, but only that care that a reasonable person under similar circumstances with the same disability would use. Note, however, that a disabled person who engages in an activity that a reasonable person with such disability would not have attempted may be found negligent.

f. **Children.** The usual, objective standard of care has been somewhat modified in the case of children. The majority view is that the standard is based on what may be expected of children of like age, intelligence, and experience. At common law, a child under age seven was presumed to be incapable of negligence, between the ages of seven and 14 rebuttably presumed incapable, and over 14 presumed capable. A minority of the jurisdictions still have arbitrary age limits. Some jurisdictions still make the age/intelligence/experience allowance when a child is driving a car or engaging in other "adult" activity, but the better reasoned cases hold children to an adult standard in such situations. [*Accord*, Restatement (Second) of Torts, §283A]

Robinson v. Lindsay

1) **Inherently dangerous activity--Robinson v. Lindsay,** 598 P.2d 392 (Wash. 1979).

a) **Facts.** Anderson (D), a 13-year-old boy, was driving a snowmobile on which Robinson (P), an 11-year-old girl, was a passenger. P was injured in an accident while they were riding, and suit was bought on her behalf. The jury was instructed that the duty of care for children is that which a reasonably careful child of the same age and experience would exercise. The jury found for D. The court ordered a new trial and D appeals.

b) **Issue.** When a child engages in an inherently dangerous activity, should he be held to an adult standard of care?

c) **Held.** Yes. Judgment affirmed.

(1) Courts excepted children from the reasonable person standard in recognition of their need to pursue childhood activities without the same responsibilities adults have. Therefore, children are generally held to a reasonable child standard of care, considering the age, experience, intelligence, etc., of the child.

(2) When children are engaged in an inherently dangerous activity, however, the rationale for the exception does not apply. Holding children to an adult standard of care in such situations recognizes the hazard presented by children involved in such activity. At the same time, it discourages children from participating in such activity.

(3) Snowmobiles are inherently dangerous vehicles. The one D was operating here was very powerful. Therefore, the adult standard of care should apply.

g. **Mental capacity.** A person with a mental incapacity is held to the same standard of care as a person of ordinary intelligence because of the difficulties that would occasion determining the degree of disability. Restatement (Second) of

Torts, section 283B, states that insane persons are held in all respects to the reasonable person standard of a sane person, the only exception being where malice or intent is necessary for the cause of action (not applicable to negligence, however).

1) **Insanity--Breunig v. American Family Insurance Co.,** 173 N.W.2d 619 (Wis. 1970).

Breunig v. American Family Insurance Co.

a) **Facts.** American Family Insurance Co.'s (D's) insured (Veith), suffering an insane delusion, believed God was operating her car. She saw Breunig's (P's) truck coming and stepped on the gas to become airborne, but crashed into P's truck, injuring P. From a judgment for P, D appeals, arguing that there was no negligence by Veith because there was no evidence that she had known or had warning that she would experience the delusion.

b) **Issue.** Are some forms of insanity a defense to a negligence action?

c) **Held.** Yes. But judgment for P is affirmed here.

(1) Although there is no negligence when one is afflicted with a ***sudden unforeseeable delusion*** that blurs understanding (the delusion being similar to a heart attack, stroke, etc.), here, Veith had a history of delusions. So the insanity defense does not apply.

d) **Comment.** When the defendant's insanity prevents the plaintiff from understanding the danger and taking action, the defendant will not be permitted to assert contributory negligence as a defense.

2) **Decreased capacity.** In *Lynch v. Rosenthal*, 396 S.W.2d 272 (Mo. App. 1965), Lynch, a 22-year-old man with the mental capacity of a 10-year old, brought suit for injuries he received from a mechanical corn picker. The defendant raised the defense of contributory negligence. The court found for Lynch and held that his decreased mental capacity could be considered in determining whether he was contributorily negligent.

h. Voluntary intoxication. The courts will not make an allowance for voluntary intoxication (alcohol, drugs, etc.) in determining the standard. However, the rule may differ if involuntary intoxication is involved. Note also that if the plaintiff is voluntarily drunk, the defendant may have the benefit of contributory negligence as a defense (*see* discussion of **Contributory Negligence**, *infra*).

2. **The Professional.** A doctor or other professional is required to have the same skill and learning as average members of the profession and to apply that skill and learning with the same care as generally exercised by other members of the profession. Although the medical profession may ordinarily set its own standard by customary practice, if a practice appears unreasonable even to lay people, a higher standard may be set.

Heath v. Swift Wings, Inc.

a. **Pilot's standard of care--Heath v. Swift Wings, Inc.,** 252 S.E.2d 526 (N.C. 1979).

1) **Facts.** Fred Heath piloted an airplane owned by Swift Wings, Inc. (D). His wife and son were among the passengers. Shortly after takeoff, the plane crashed, and the passengers died. There was testimony that a reasonably prudent pilot could have avoided the deaths by landing in a field after experiencing difficulty. Heath (P), the administrator for the wife and son, brought suit alleging negligence. The trial court instructed the jury that aviation negligence could be defined as "the failure to exercise that degree of ordinary care and caution which an ordinary prudent pilot, having the same training and experience as Fred Heath, would have used in the same or similar circumstances." The jury found that the pilot was not negligent and P appeals.

2) **Issue.** Does negligence on the part of a professional depend on the professional's personal training and experience?

3) **Held.** No. Judgment reversed for a new trial.

a) The standard of care of a reasonably prudent person remains constant but the degree of care required varies with the attendant circumstances.

b) A greater standard of care than that of the ordinary prudent person may apply for persons shown to possess special skill. Thus, a professional must exercise the requisite degree of learning, skill, and ability of the profession with reasonable and ordinary care.

c) The professional standard remains objective, however. The person must meet the standard of care applicable to all professionals in his field, which is the minimum standard for the profession. The instruction was erroneous because it made Fred Heath's subjective training determinative.

Hodges v. Carter

b. **Attorney's error in judgment--Hodges v. Carter,** 80 S.E.2d 144 (N.C. 1954).

1) **Facts.** Hodges (P) sued Carter (D), his former attorney, for negligence in failing to use the proper procedure for serving process on fire insurance companies. Process was served in accordance with the statute and a 20-year custom. The trial court in the insurance case sustained the service, but the appeals court reversed. In this case the trial court granted an involuntary nonsuit and P appeals.

2) **Issue.** Is the standard of care for an attorney that he will use reasonable care and diligence in applying requisite skills and knowledge to his client's cause?

3) **Held.** Yes. Judgment affirmed for involuntary nonsuit.

   a) Ordinarily, when an attorney engages in the practice of the law and contracts to prosecute an action on behalf of his client, he impliedly represents that (i) he possesses the requisite degree of learning, skill, and ability necessary to the practice of his profession and which others similarly situated ordinarily possess; (ii) he will exert his best judgment in the prosecution of the litigation entrusted to him; and (iii) he will exercise reasonable and ordinary care and diligence in the use of his skill and in the application of his knowledge to his client's cause.

   b) An attorney who acts in good faith and in an honest belief that his advice and acts are well founded and in the best interest of his client is not answerable for a mere error of judgment, or for a mistake in a point of law that has not been settled by the court of last resort in his state and on which reasonable doubt may be entertained by well-informed lawyers.

   c) Conversely, he is answerable in damages for any loss to his client that proximately results from a want of that degree of knowledge and skill ordinarily possessed by others of his profession similarly situated, or from the omission to use reasonable care and diligence, or from the failure to exercise in good faith his best judgment in attending to the litigation committed to his care.

   d) Here, the attorney had reasonable cause to believe that the statute was valid. A long-standing practice and statute was reversed by the Supreme Court, which indicated the closeness of the question and therefore the reasonableness of the attorney's reliance on the service of process selected.

c. **Locality rule for medical malpractice--Boyce v. Brown,** 77 P.2d 455 (Ariz. 1938). Boyce v. Brown

1) **Facts.** Boyce (P) was treated for a bone fracture by Brown (D), a surgeon. Seven years later, P returned complaining of pain in the bone. D

examined it visually, but did not take an X-ray. P continued to have pain and went to another physician who X-rayed the bone and operated to remove a metal screw that had been inserted by D and was now aggravating P's arthritis. P sued D for malpractice for omitting to X-ray the bone. The trial court directed a verdict for D and P appeals.

2) **Issue.** May the standard of care for a physician be based on a lay person's testimony of the standards of medical practice in the community?

3) **Held.** No. Directed verdict for D affirmed.

   a) The general rules of law governing actions of medical malpractice, which are almost universally accepted by the courts, are as follows:

      (1) One licensed to practice medicine is presumed to possess the degree of skill and learning that is possessed by the average member of the medical profession in good standing in the community in which he practices, and to apply that skill and learning, with ordinary and reasonable care, to cases that come to him for treatment. If he does not possess the requisite skill and learning, or if he does not apply it, he is guilty of malpractice.

      (2) Before a physician or surgeon can be held liable for malpractice, he must have done something in his treatment of his patient that the recognized standard of good medical practice in the community in which he is practicing forbids in such cases, or he must have neglected to do something that such standard requires.

      (3) To sustain a verdict for the plaintiff in an action for malpractice, the standard of medical practice in the community must be shown by affirmative evidence, and, unless there is evidence of such a standard, a jury may not be permitted to speculate as to what the required standard is, or whether the defendant has departed therefrom.

      (4) Negligence on the part of a physician or surgeon in the treatment of a case is never presumed, but must be affirmatively proven, and no presumption of negligence nor want of skill arises from the mere fact that a treatment was unsuccessful or failed to bring the best results, or that the patient died.

      (5) The accepted rule is that negligence on the part of a physician or surgeon, by reason of his departure from the proper standard of practice, must be established by expert medical testimony, unless the negligence is so grossly apparent that a lay person would have no difficulty in recognizing it.

      (6) The testimony of other physicians that they would have followed a course of treatment different from that followed by the defendant is

not sufficient to establish malpractice, unless it also appears that the course of treatment followed deviated from one of the methods of treatment approved by the standard in that community.

(7) X-ray is only one tool of diagnosis and only an expert witness can testify as to the standards in the community on the use of this technique.

b) Here there was no testimony that the treatment given was a deviation from the proper standard of treatment.

4) Comment. Most courts have modified the locality rule, allowing evidence of the standard of care in ***similar*** communities. Other courts apply a national standard, especially where specialists are concerned.

d. National standard of care--Morrison v. MacNamara, 407 A.2d 555 (D.C. 1979). Morrison v. MacNamara

1) Facts. Morrison (P) submitted to a urethral smear test at a Washington, D.C., medical laboratory. MacNamara (D) administered the test while P was standing. P fainted and hit his head when he fell, permanently losing his sense of smell and taste. P sued for medical malpractice, relying on an expert witness from Michigan who explained that the national standard of care requires patients to sit or lie down because the test often makes patients feel faint. However, the trial court excluded this testimony on the ground that in medical malpractice cases, the expert witnesses must come from the defendant's community. D's expert witnesses from D.C. all gave the test to a standing patient. The jury found for D and P appeals.

2) Issue. In a medical malpractice case, is the standard of care measured only by the standard of conduct prevalent among the medical profession in the defendant's community?

3) Held. No. Judgment reversed.

a) The locality rule followed by the trial court was created in response to the dichotomy between rural and urban medical practice in the late 19th century. At that time, rural doctors could not be expected to have the same skill and care as urban doctors. The locality rule has not been specifically challenged in this jurisdiction, however.

b) The policy behind the locality rule has no relevance to medical practice in the District of Columbia, which is one of the leading medical centers in the nation. Medical education has become standardized throughout the nation, and medical information is widely accessible due to modern developments in transportation and communication.

c) The locality rule also tends to protect doctors in communities where medical practice is substandard. This has the effect of fostering substandard care. In addition, the rule is only applied to medical malpractice, not to malpractice claims against other professionals.

d) The best approach is to apply a national standard of care. The standard applies to a clinical laboratory as well as to physicians, especially here, where D is a nationally certified medical laboratory. Because the jury was instructed to compare D's conduct with the standard of care in the District of Columbia, P is entitled to a new trial.

Scott v. Bradford

e. **Informed consent--Scott v. Bradford,** 606 P.2d 554 (Okla. 1979).

1) **Facts.** Scott (P) consented to a hysterectomy to be performed by Bradford (D). After the operation, complications arose which required three subsequent surgeries to correct. P sued for malpractice, claiming that D did not advise her of the risks and alternatives. The jury found for D and P appeals.

2) **Issue.** Does a doctor have a duty to fully inform his patient of her options and their attendant risks?

3) **Held.** Yes, but judgment affirmed because this duty is prospective only.

a) Each person is considered as his own master, and a physician cannot substitute his own judgment for that of the patient. Therefore, a doctor has a duty to inform the patient of the risks of the medical procedure and available alternatives. The patient must give informed consent; if the patient is not adequately informed, the physician may be liable for negligence, even though not negligent in the actual performance of the procedure.

b) In the present case, the jury instructions were adequate, so there is no error. However, the rule must be clarified for causes of action arising prospectively.

c) In a medical malpractice action, the patient must prove that:

(1) The physician failed to inform her adequately of a material risk before securing her consent to the proposed treatment;

(2) If the patient had been informed of the risks, she would not have consented to the treatment (this is a subjective test, not a reasonable patient standard);

(3) The adverse consequences that were not made known did in fact occur, and the patient was injured as a result of submitting to the treatment.

d) The physician may defend by proving that the patient knew of the risks, that full disclosure would be detrimental to the patient's best interest, or that an emergency existed that required prompt treatment and the patient could not decide for herself.

4) **Concurrence and dissent.** I would apply a reasonable person test rather than the subjective test.

f. **Breach of fiduciary duty--Moore v. Regents of the University of California,** 793 P.2d 479 (Cal. 1990).

Moore v. Regents of the University of California

1) **Facts.** Moore (P), shortly after being diagnosed with hairy-cell leukemia, was treated by Golde, a physician at UCLA Medical Center, which was operated by The Regents of the University of California (D). After withdrawing blood, bone marrow, and other bodily substances, Golde represented that removal of P's spleen would slow the progress of the disease. Golde, however, without informing P, used P's cells to develop and patent a cell line that Golde and his colleagues licensed for commercial development to two biotech firms (also named as defendants). P's complaint contained 13 causes of action, including conversion, lack of informed consent, and breach of fiduciary duty for failing to disclose Golde's financial interest. After sustaining a demurrer to the conversion count, the trial court dismissed the entire complaint on the basis that the other counts simply repeated the conversion count's inadequate allegations. The court of appeals reversed and D appeals to the California Supreme Court.

2) **Issue.** Does failure to disclose personal interests unrelated to a patient's health vitiate the patient's consent and constitute a breach of fiduciary duty?

3) **Held.** Yes. Judgment affirmed in part and reversed in part.

a) The law recognizes several well-established principles in connection with the providing of medical treatment.

(1) An adult of sound mind has the right to determine whether to submit to lawful medical treatment;

(2) A patient's consent to treatment, to be effective, must be an informed consent; and

(3) In soliciting the patient's consent, a physician has a fiduciary duty to disclose all information material to the patient's decision.

b) Thus, a physician must disclose personal interests unrelated to the patient's health, whether research or economic, that may affect the physician's professional judgment. Failure to so disclose such interests may give rise to a cause of action for performing medical procedures without informed consent or for breach of fiduciary duty. The possibility that an interest extraneous to the patient's health has affected the physician's judgment is something that a reasonable patient would want to know in deciding whether to consent to a proposed course of treatment. Since such disclosure is material to the patient's decision, it is a prerequisite to informed consent.

c) A physician acting solely in the best interests of the patient is permitted to consider whether excessive disclosure will harm the patient. However, when there is a conflict of interest (*e.g.*, a procedure is ordered partly to further a research interest unrelated to the patient's health), such argument cannot be used to avoid disclosure.

3. Aggravated Negligence.

a. **"Degrees of care or negligence."** The care that the reasonable person must exercise will vary according to the risk involved; *e.g.*, more care must be used when handling explosives than when handling lumber; common carriers must exercise "high degree of care" with regard to their passengers. Although some cases and authors have taken a different approach and emphasized the "degree of negligence" concept, the other view is that there are no different "degrees of negligence," just circumstances requiring more or less care.

b. **Gross negligence.** Statutes speaking of gross negligence or recklessness are usually interpreted to mean something equivalent to conscious and deliberate disregard of a high degree of probability—a state of mind between negligence and intention. One author has likened the difference to that between "a fool, a damned fool, and a God-damned fool."

c. **Guest statutes.** A few states have auto guest statutes providing that a driver is liable to his guest passenger (one not paying part or all of the fare) only for injuries resulting from aggravated misconduct; *e.g.*, gross negligence, or something between intention and inadvertence.

1) Most jurisdictions calling for more than simple negligence have some such standard as conduct that is willful, wanton, or reckless—an intentional act that would lead a reasonable person to know that his conduct will probably result in substantial harm. Some jurisdictions use the "gross negligence" standard.

E. RULES OF LAW

1. **Introduction.** Rules of law are standards of care acknowledged by courts and given the effect of law. Duty depends upon the circumstances.

2. **Effect of Circumstances--Pokora v. Wabash Railway Co.,** 292 U.S. 98 (1934). Pokora v. Wabash Railway Co.

   a. **Facts.** Pokora (P) approached a railroad crossing in his truck, stopped, looked, and listened as well as possible but did not get out of his truck, which would have been necessary to see sufficiently both ways as the view was partially blocked by parked box cars. As P proceeded across the tracks, he was struck by a train coming from the direction where his view was partially impaired. The trial court directed a verdict for the railway (D), holding that P was contributorily negligent. P appeals.

   b. **Issue.** Was P negligent as a matter of law?

   c. **Held.** No. Judgment reversed.

      1) Dictum from an earlier opinion implied that one must always get out and look down the tracks if the view is obstructed. This rule is too rigid.

      2) The better approach finds a duty to stop depending on the particular circumstances. The reasonableness of P's conduct is a fact question that should be left to the jury.

   d. **Comment.** The case points out that there are no ironclad rules as to what is negligent conduct—the duty varies with the circumstances. It is usually negligence as a matter of law not to stop, look, and listen, but not always.

F. VIOLATION OF STATUTE

Statutes that affect a defendant's conduct may be either civil or criminal. If the plaintiff is provided a civil remedy under a statute, she will not have to be concerned with establishing negligence. If the defendant's conduct violates a criminal statute that does not provide a civil remedy, the plaintiff may still obtain a remedy through a negligence action. When a court adopts a standard of care embodied in a criminal statute, the rationale is that a reasonable person always obeys the criminal law. However, for the plaintiff to support a claim that the violation of the criminal statute by the defendant was negligence, the statute must have clearly defined the conduct or duty required and the class or individual to whom it applies. Failure of the defendant to act as required will constitute a breach of the duty. However, for the plaintiff to establish liability, she must show that she is in the class protected by the statute and that the statute was enacted to protect members of the class from the type of injury she suffered. Depending on the jurisdiction, violation of a statute can have several effects. The ***majority view*** finds violation of a statute to give rise to a conclusive presumption of negligence; *i.e.*, negligence per se. In California, violation is deemed to give rise to a ***rebuttable presumption*** of negligence. In still other jurisdictions, violation is deemed to be ***merely evidence of negligence***. However, when the plaintiff's claim is based on violation of the statute as negligence, the defendant generally has available to him the defenses of contributory negligence and assumption of risk.

1. Violation by Defendant.

Osborne v. McMasters

a. Negligence--Osborne v. McMasters, 41 N.W. 543 (Minn. 1889).

1) **Facts.** A drugstore clerk employed by McMasters (D) sold to Osborne's (P's) decedent poison without a "poison" label. The label was required by law. The decedent later took the poison and died. A verdict was returned against D and D appeals.

2) **Issue.** Does a statutory right of action exist?

3) **Held.** Yes. Judgment affirmed.

a) The statute created a duty in D to use reasonable care to protect customers from taking the wrong drug. D failed to use reasonable care and is therefore chargeable with negligence on the theory of respondeat superior (*see infra*). There was no common law right of action; the statute created such a right. There was a breach of a statutory duty meant to protect this class of people from this type of injury. The injury was the proximate cause of death.

Stachniewicz v. Mar-Cam Corp.

b. Class protected--Stachniewicz v. Mar-Cam Corp., 488 P.2d 436 (Or. 1971).

1) **Facts.** Stachniewicz (P) was injured in a brawl that occurred in Mar-Cam Corp.'s (D's) bar. The other participants had been drinking in the bar for two and a half hours and were visibly intoxicated. An Oregon statute provides that "No person shall give or otherwise make available any alcoholic liquor to a person visibly intoxicated." Regulations also provide that no licensee shall permit disorderly or boisterous conduct or permit any visibly intoxicated person to enter or remain upon licensed premises. Before the brawl, D's bartender warned P's friends not to start any trouble with the customers who later started the brawl and injured P. The trial court rendered judgment for D and P appeals.

2) **Issue.** When a statute imposes a duty, will a civil cause of action be implied for a person of the intended protected class of the statute?

3) **Held.** Yes. Judgment reversed and remanded.

   a) The statute is an inappropriate basis for a civil action because of the extreme difficulty, if not impossibility, of determining whether a third party's injuries would have been caused in any event by the already inebriated person. However, the liquor commission regulation was intended to protect patrons, such as P, from abusive conduct and personal injuries caused by drunk and disorderly clientele and thereby can be the basis of civil suit for damages as a result of its breach by D.

c. **Relation of injury to violation--Ney v. Yellow Cab Co.,** 117 N.E.2d 74 (Ill. 1954).

Ney v. Yellow Cab Co.

1) **Facts.** A cab driver employed by Yellow Cab Co. (D) left his cab unattended without stopping the engine or removing the key. A thief stole the cab and ran into Ney's (P's) car. A traffic statute required all drivers to stop their engines and remove the key before leaving their car unattended. P sued for damages on the theory that the violation of the statute was negligence and the proximate cause of the damage. The lower courts held for P and D appeals.

2) **Issue.** May special circumstances surround a violation of a statute and make the violation the proximate cause of an injury, although the specific injury was not that clearly protected against by the statute?

3) **Held.** Yes. Judgment affirmed.

   a) The inquiry requires consideration of three questions:

      (1) What was the legislative intention in enacting the statute?

      (2) Was the violation of the statute the proximate cause of the injury?

      (3) Does the intervention of a third party break the causal connection between the violation and the injury?

   b) The statute here appears to be intended to assure the public safety. It was not an antitheft statute. However, some act must have been foreseen by the legislature because no harm to the public could result by having a vehicle left with the key in the ignition.

   c) The violation of the statute is prima facie evidence of negligence. Liability accrues only if it was also a proximate cause of the injury.

Here, there was an intervention by a third party. The intervention does not necessarily interrupt the relation of cause and effect, however.

d) The question of whether the intervening force is within the range of reasonable anticipation and probability was properly given to the jury, rather than ruled on as a matter of law.

4) Dissent. The majority finds that the legislative intent was not to deter theft, but then concludes that the statute was intended to prevent operation of the vehicle by an unauthorized person. The statute does not prevent the willful movement of the car by an unauthorized person. Therefore, violation of the statute cannot be the proximate cause of the injury.

d. Type of risk covered. There must be a causal relationship between the breach of statute and the alleged wrong.

Perry v. S.N. and S.N.

1) Failure to report a crime--Perry v. S.N. and S.N., 973 S.W.2d 301 (Tex. 1998).

a) Facts. The Texas Family Code required any person having cause to believe a child is being abused to report the abuse to state authorities. The knowing failure to do so was a misdemeanor. S.N. and S.N. (Ps) left their children at a day care center operated by the Kellers. Ps claimed that Perry and other friends of the Kellers (Ds) were aware of physical and sexual abuse by the Kellers against Ps' children and other children. Ps sued Ds, claiming that Ds were negligent per se because they violated the Family Code by failing to report the abuse, and that Ds' negligence proximately caused them harm by permitting the day care center to remain open. Ds moved for summary judgment. The trial court granted Ds' motion on the basis that Ps failed to state a cause of action. The court of appeals affirmed regarding common law negligence, but reversed and remanded for trial on the issues of negligence per se and gross negligence. Ds appeal.

b) Issue. Is failure to report child abuse as required by law negligence per se?

c) Held. No. Judgment reversed.

(1) A prerequisite for any tort liability is the existence of a legally cognizable duty. Everyone has a duty to obey the criminal law in the sense that they may be prosecuted for failure to do so, but that does not necessarily create a tort duty. The doctrine of negligence per se should not be applied if the criminal statute does not provide an appropriate basis for civil liability.

(2) The statute does not specifically apply to the failure of an eyewitness to report the sexual molestation of preschool children, which is what Ps accuse Ds of doing in this case. The statute requires every person who "has cause to believe" that a child's physical or mental health has been or may be adversely affected by abuse or neglect to make a report.

(3) The element of duty for a negligence per se cause of action against Ds would arise solely from the Family Code, because at common law there was no duty to protect another from the criminal acts of a third party. In most negligence per se cases, the defendant already owes the plaintiff a preexisting common law duty to act as a reasonably prudent person, and the statute merely defines more precisely what conduct breaches that duty. A common example is a violation of traffic laws.

(4) In determining whether to apply negligence per se, the courts should consider whether the penal statute is too obscure to put the public on notice, whether it may impose liability without fault, or whether it may lead to ruinous monetary liability for relatively minor offenses.

(5) In this case, Ds clearly had cause to believe abuse was occurring because they allegedly saw it. In other cases, however, a person may hear second-hand reports, and it is unclear whether that circumstance would provide cause to believe that abuse may be taking place. The statute does not clearly define what conduct is required.

(6) The statute would not impose liability without fault, because it requires a knowing failure to report. This factor tends to favor imposing negligence per se liability.

(7) The statute in this case imposes a maximum penalty of six months in jail and a $2,000 fine, compared with the maximum penalty for child abuse itself of up to 99 years in prison and a $10,000 fine. The legislature thus intended to penalize non-reporters less severely, suggesting that a non-reporter should not be held civilly liable for the enormous damages that an abuser inflicts. The specter of disproportionate liability, especially where there is an indirect relationship between violation of the statute and the victim's ultimate injury, is a factor against imposing tort liability.

(8) Negligence per se under this statute would impose immense potential liability under an ill-defined standard on a broad class of individuals whose relationship to the abuse is indirect, so the statute should not be deemed as establishing a duty and standard of conduct in tort.

d) Comment. Violation of licensing statutes normally does not give rise to negligence per se. [Brown v. Shyne, 151 N.E. 197 (N.Y. 1926)]

2. **Violation by Plaintiff.** The effect of a plaintiff's violation of a statute can vary dramatically from one jurisdiction to another.

Martin v. Herzog

a. **Per se approach--Martin v. Herzog,** 126 N.E. 814 (N.Y. 1920).

1) **Facts.** Martin (P) sued for the death of her husband from a car accident. Herzog (D) negligently crossed the "white line" in negotiating a curve at night and hit P's buggy, which, in violation of statute, had no lights. The trial court refused to instruct that having no lights on the buggy was contributory negligence as a matter of law. The appellate court reversed a judgment for P and P appeals.

2) **Issue.** Is the unexcused violation of a safety statute contributory negligence per se?

3) **Held.** Yes. Judgment of appellate court affirmed.

a) D was within the class of persons protected by the statute, and P's failure to supply lights places the burden on P to show there was no contributory negligence. Absence of the lights is negligence, not merely evidence of negligence.

b) To omit safeguards prescribed by statute for the benefit of others is to fall short of the duty owed to the rest of society. The trial court erred in giving the jury the power to relax the duty that P's intestate owed to other travelers.

Zeni v. Anderson

b. **Rebuttable presumption approach--Zeni v. Anderson,** 243 N.W.2d 270 (Mich. 1976).

1) **Facts.** Zeni (P) was walking to work on a snowy, cold morning when she was hit from behind by a car driven by Anderson (D). P was not using the sidewalk provided on the other side of the street and was walking with the traffic coming at her back. A statute required use of a sidewalk if provided and walking facing traffic if practicable. Evidence indicated that the sidewalk was dangerous in snowy conditions and that the path P was following was well-used. P sued for damages and the jury gave a verdict for P. D appealed and the court of appeals reversed. P appeals.

2) **Issue.** Does violation of a statute create merely a rebuttable presumption of negligence?

3) **Held.** Yes. Judgment reversed.

a) Violation of a statute establishes a prima facie case of negligence, but the presumption may be rebutted by showing that the violation was excused under the facts and circumstances. This approach is fair and logical. The alternative would be liability without fault, which is not truly negligence.

b) Some cases seem to apply negligence per se, which is really strict liability. This rule should not be followed.

c) Some cases use violation of statutes only as evidence of negligence. This approach is not necessary where the presumption is easily rebutted.

d) Therefore, a penal statute may be adopted as the standard of care in an action for negligence. When it is, a violation constitutes a prima facie case of negligence, and the fact finder must determine whether there is a legally sufficient excuse for the violation. If there is, the standard of care becomes one established by the common law.

G. PROOF OF NEGLIGENCE

1. **Court and Jury—Circumstantial Evidence.** If people of reasonable intelligence may differ as to the conclusion to be drawn from facts in evidence, the issue must be left to the jury; if not, the court will decide. Generally, the burden of proof, *i.e.*, the risk of nonpersuasion, is on the plaintiff, and if the evidence he introduces is not greater, or more persuasive, than that of his adversary, he must lose. The burden of going forward, on the other hand, is established by presumptions, and the failure to rebut may result in a directed verdict.

a. **Circumstantial evidence.** Circumstantial evidence is the proof of one fact, or group of facts, that gives rise to an inference by reasoning that another fact must be true.

b. **Insufficient evidence--Goddard v. Boston & Maine Railroad Co.,** 60 N.E. 486 (Mass. 1901).

Goddard v. Boston & Maine Railroad Co.

1) **Facts.** Goddard (P) was a passenger on the Boston & Maine Railroad Company's (D's) train. After alighting from the train, P slipped on a banana peel and was injured. Many people were on the platform. The trial court directed a verdict for D and P appeals.

2) **Issue.** Must a court direct a verdict for the defendant when the evidence would not reasonably support a finding for the plaintiff?

3) **Held.** Yes. Judgment affirmed.

a) P has the burden to show (i) existence of negligence, and (ii) that D was the negligent actor. He simply failed to do so here because the peel could have been dropped by anyone who just left the train.

4) **Comment.** It is important to note that there was no evidence that D dropped the peel, knew of its presence, or should have known of its presence.

Anjou v. Boston Elevated Railway Co.

c. **Evidence sufficient to support inference of negligence--Anjou v. Boston Elevated Railway Co.,** 94 N.E. 386 (Mass. 1911).

1) **Facts.** Anjou (P) slipped on a banana peel at Boston Elevated Railway Company's (D's) railroad station. Witnesses claimed that the peel was black, flattened, and gritty. The verdict was directed for D and P appeals.

2) **Issue.** May a trial court direct a verdict for the defendant if the evidence supports a reasonable inference of negligence?

3) **Held.** No. Judgment for P ordered.

a) The issue of negligence should have been submitted to the jury.

b) *Goddard* is distinguishable, as there was no evidence in *Goddard* indicating that the peel was not dropped immediately before the accident. Here, there was evidence that the peel had been present long enough for an employee to have noticed and removed it; therefore, the jury could have found that D did not use reasonable care in protecting customers.

4) **Comment.** In tort, the plaintiff only need show that a preponderance of the affirmative evidence is in his favor (51%) to prevail.

Joye v. Great Atlantic and Pacific Tea Co.

d. **Constructive notice--Joye v. Great Atlantic and Pacific Tea Co.,** 405 F.2d 464 (4th Cir. 1968).

1) **Facts.** Joye (P) slipped on a banana in Great Atlantic and Pacific Tea Company's (D's) supermarket. There was no evidence showing that D put the banana on the floor or had actual notice that the banana was there. P attempted to show constructive notice by proving that the floor had not been swept for 35 minutes and that the banana was brown and covered with dirt after P slipped on it. The trial court entered judgment for P and D appeals denial for its motion for judgment n.o.v.

2) **Issue.** Must a court direct a verdict for the defendant if the evidence demonstrates a possibility of negligence, but not a sufficient probability?

3) **Held.** Yes. Judgment reversed and remanded with instructions to grant D's motion.

a) P's case was based on a theory that D had constructive notice of a dangerous condition. This requires proof that the condition existed for a sufficiently long time that D should have known about it.

b) The evidence here did not sufficiently prove how long the banana had been on the floor. The jury would not be able to decide if the banana had been there for an unreasonable period of time so that D would have been charged with constructive notice of the condition.

e. **Constructive notice arising from inherently dangerous activity-- Jasko v. F.W. Woolworth Co.,** 494 P.2d 839 (Colo. 1972).

Jasko v. F.W. Woolworth Co.

1) **Facts.** Jasko (P) slipped on a piece of pizza on the terrazzo floor near F.W. Woolworth Co.'s (D's) pizza hoagie counter. D's practice was to sell slices of pizza on wax paper to customers who would eat the pizza while standing there. P did not offer proof that the pizza was dropped there by D's employees or that D had actual notice of the pizza on the floor. The trial court held that P had not shown constructive notice and P appeals.

2) **Issue.** When a method of doing business is such that a dangerous condition is likely to arise, is constructive notice of the actual danger required?

3) **Held.** No. Judgment reversed and remanded for a new trial.

a) D's method of selling pizza inherently resulted in frequently spilled pizza. D also must have known that spilled pizza on its floor would be dangerous.

b) The requirement to prove notice applies when the dangerous condition is not normal. If the dangerous condition is continuous, proof of notice is not necessary.

2. **Res Ipsa Loquitur.** Res Ipsa Loquitur ("RIL") directly translated means "the thing speaks for itself." In situations where (i) it is highly probable that the injury would not have occurred in the absence of someone's negligence, (ii) the indicated source of the negligence is within the scope of a duty owed by the defendant to the plaintiff, and (iii) neither the plaintiff nor any third party appears to have contributed to the plaintiff's injuries, an inference is permitted that the defendant was negligent, without any direct proof. The defendant then has the burden of going forward and introducing evidence to overthrow the inference. The courts recognize RIL because of the existence of a necessitous plaintiff and a defendant with better access to the evidence concerning the cause of the injury.

Byrne v. Boadle

a. **Barrel rolling out of window--Byrne v. Boadle,** 159 Eng. Rep. 299 (1863).

1) **Facts.** P was walking on the street when a barrel rolled out of D's window, striking and injuring him. There was no other evidence. P was nonsuited by the trial court.

2) **Issue.** Can P get the case to the jury by showing only that there was an accident and it was caused by the barrel?

3) **Held.** Yes. Verdict for P.

a) All that is necessary is that a reasonable person would say that more likely than not there was negligence.

b. **Burden on defendant.** RIL puts the burden on the defendant to explain away the negligence. However, the doctrine does not apply if negligence by the defendant is no more likely than another explanation (*e.g.*, an automobile inexplicably runs off the road but is subsequently found to have a flat tire). There must be some evidence of negligence, but control of the instrumentality by the defendant gives rise to an inference that it happened from lack of care, if it would not ordinarily happen without a lack of care. The doctrine does not apply unless reasonable persons could not disagree that 51% percent of the probabilities point to the defendant's liability.

c. **Explanation of all possibilities.** The plaintiff need not explain away all possibilities as long as she shows that such an accident ordinarily does not occur without negligence.

McDougald v. Perry

1) **Spare tire coming loose on highway--McDougald v. Perry,** 716 So.2d 783 (Fla. 1998).

a) **Facts.** McDougald (P) was driving behind a tractor-trailer driven by Perry (D). D's employer had leased the trailer. When D crossed some railroad tracks, the spare tire fell out of its cradle under the trailer and bounced into the air, striking P's windshield. P sued for damages. At trial, D testified that he had inspected the trailer and had seen the chain that secured the tire. The chain was held with a nut and bolt instead of the original latch device. D speculated that one of the links of the chain had stretched and slipped from the nut. The trial judge instructed the jury on the doctrine of res ipsa loquitur. The jury found for P. D appealed, and the appellate court reversed with instructions to direct a verdict for D. P appeals.

b) **Issue.** Does the doctrine of res ipsa loquitur apply when a spare tire escapes from a cradle underneath its truck and crashes into the vehicle behind it?

c) **Held.** Yes. Judgment reversed.

(1) The appellate court held that P failed to prove that, in the ordinary course of events, this accident would not have occurred without negligence by D, and that the mere fact that an accident occurred does not support the application of the doctrine. This is too restrictive of an approach.

(2) Res ipsa loquitur is a rule of evidence that permits an inference of negligence when there is insufficient direct proof of negligence, but the plaintiff can show that (i) the instrumentality that caused the injury was under the exclusive control of the defendant and (ii) the accident is one that, in the ordinary course of events, would not have occurred without negligence on the part of the one in control. This requires more than mere proof of an accident, for an injury standing alone does not indicate negligence.

(3) Res ipsa loquitur should be applied only in rare instances, where there is a basis of past experience that reasonably permits the conclusion that the event causing the injury does not ordinarily occur unless someone has been negligent. For example, a tire blowing out by itself, without any further proof, is not sufficient to permit the conclusion that there was negligence in inspecting the tire.

(4) In this case, a spare tire falling out from under the trailer so that it bounced and hit P's windshield is, on the basis of common experience and as a matter of general knowledge, the type of accident that would not occur but for the failure to exercise reasonable care by the person who had control of the spare tire. The possibility of explanations other than negligence does not defeat application of res ipsa loquitur, so long as there is evidence from which reasonable persons can say that it is more likely than not that there was negligence associated with the cause of the event.

d) **Concurrence.** This is a classic case to apply the common law rule of res ipsa loquitur in *Byrne*, *supra*.

d. **Expert testimony.** In some medical malpractice cases, in order to gain the benefit of RIL, the plaintiff needs expert testimony to show that her injuries probably resulted from someone's negligence because it is not obvious to the jury that the injury would not have occurred but for negligence on the part of someone. Such testimony is not necessary if it is obvious to the jury; *e.g.*, hot water bottle burn on body. The big problem is what to do if the experts disagree. Should the court let the jury decide whom to believe?

e. **Control of instrumentality of injury.** In most cases, the injury must be caused by something that was in the exclusive control of the defendant. However, do not attempt to make a rule of RIL. Look at the facts and see what inferences can be drawn. RIL is just a way in which circumstantial evidence is applied to facts. While most cases involve defendants who have superior knowledge, this is not a necessary ingredient. In fact, it has been suggested that "exclusive control" is not a necessary element, the central question being whether the injury to the plaintiff was one the defendant owed a duty to guard against.

Larson v. St. Francis Hotel

1) **Exclusive control--Larson v. St. Francis Hotel,** 188 P.2d 513 (Cal. Dist. Ct. App. 1948).

a) **Facts.** Larson (P) was struck by a chair thrown from one of the hotel's (D's) windows on V-J Day. Someone either intentionally or negligently dropped the chair, but "who" is unknown. P relied on RIL, but the court granted D's motion for a nonsuit. P appeals.

b) **Issue.** Does RIL apply if the accident could have happened even if the defendant had used ordinary care?

c) **Held.** No. Judgment affirmed.

(1) The element of exclusive control on the part of D is missing. The act might just as easily have been done by a guest as by D.

(2) This accident is not one that would ordinarily not happen without D's negligence. In fact, it would ordinarily happen despite D's exercise of due care. Although the hotel has a duty to protect passersby, it is not required to put guards in every tenant's room.

d) **Comment.** The decision may have been different if D had notice of the possibility of such an occurrence.

2) **Multiple defendants.** RIL may be applied to two defendants in some circumstances, although neither has exclusive control. For example, tenant and a landlord both might have a duty to the plaintiff. Or, in the case of an elevator accident, the building owner and the elevator company both may be responsible for maintenance.

3) **Common carrier.** A collision of two or more autos does not necessarily give rise to an inference of negligence, but some jurisdictions hold that if the defendant is a common carrier, there is such an inference in regard to the passenger-plaintiffs because the defendant has a higher degree of care and must show it fulfilled its duty to the passenger-plaintiff. However, if a bus hits a truck, forcing the truck to hit a bystander, RIL does not apply. There is no special duty on the common carrier with respect to those outside the bus.

4) **Doctors--Ybarra v. Spangard,** 154 P.2d 687 (Cal. 1944). Ybarra v. Spangard

a) **Facts.** Ybarra (P), while unconscious and under anesthesia for an appendicitis operation, sustained injuries that caused his right arm and shoulder to develop paralysis and atrophy. P brought suit against the doctors and nurses attending him (Ds). The trial court entered a nonsuit as to all Ds and P appeals.

b) **Issue.** Does RIL apply absent exclusive control?

c) **Held.** Yes. Judgment reversed.

(1) RIL applies to all, as all were responsible for the patient's safety. There was an absence of exclusive control by any one defendant, but a burden was placed upon each of them who had "shared control" to exonerate themselves from fault. Since P was unconscious, it is unreasonable to put the burden of proof on him.

d) **Comment.** The public policy here is that doctors, like common carriers, have special responsibilities to the public who must accept their services and are in helpless situations while being served. Someone was negligent and it is more reasonable to shift the burden in such circumstances to the defendants to explain away the inference of their negligence.

5) **Products liability.** On similar reasoning, a bottler and/or a retailer may be liable to a consumer for an exploding soft drink bottle; or a dynamite manufacturer and/or cap maker may be held liable to an injured plaintiff. The rationale is that both defendants contribute to the final product.

6) **Exceptions to common carrier rule--Sullivan v. Crabtree,** 258 S.W.2d 782 (Tenn. Ct. App. 1953). Sullivan v. Crabtree

a) **Facts.** Sullivan was a guest passenger in a truck driven by Crabtree (D). D's truck swerved from the road after being passed by another truck, crashed, and Sullivan was killed. There was no explanation for the wreck, and D did not know what caused him to lose control of the truck. Sullivan's parents (Ps) sued. The jury found for D. Ps appeal.

b) **Issue.** Did the unexplained cause of the wreck require a finding of negligence by D?

c) **Held.** No. Judgment affirmed.

(1) The doctrine of RIL raises an inference that the jury may or may not adopt; here it chose not to.

f. **Three views of the effect of RIL.**

1) **Permissible inference.** Under the majority view, a permissible inference arises, the strength of which varies with the circumstances of the case. The jury may accept or reject the inference.

2) **Presumption of negligence.** Under another view, a presumption of negligence is raised and unless the defendant shows evidence to rebut, the court must find negligence as a matter of law.

3) **Shifting of burden of proof.** Under a third view, the burden of proof shifts to the defendant, making the defendant introduce evidence to support his defense. If the defendant's evidence is sufficient to support a finding of fact in his favor, the burden of proof shifts back to the plaintiff who then must prove the defendant's negligence.

g. **Additional comments on RIL.**

1) RIL is limited to inferences introduced by the evidence and the pleadings.

2) If nothing is left unknown, RIL is "proved away." If all the facts are known, there is nothing to infer.

3) If there are no general allegations of negligence, RIL may be applied only to the extent that it will support allegations in the pleadings.

V. CAUSATION IN FACT

A. INTRODUCTION

If the defendant did not cause the injury in fact, he is not liable, but even if the defendant caused the injury in fact, he is not liable if he was not the proximate cause of the injury or damage. This may be thought of in terms of the following diagram, with liability accruing to the defendant only if the circumstances are within both circles:

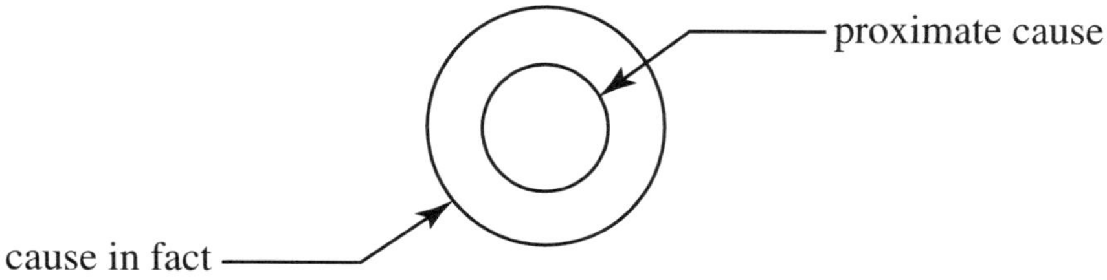

Causation is always a question of fact. The court enters only in deciding if reasonable people could find such a fact. Proximate cause is a question of law, not concerning facts; it involves conflicting considerations of policy and comes into consideration only after causation in fact is established. In order to recover, the plaintiff must sustain the burden of proof as to both.

B. SINE QUA NON ("BUT FOR" RULE)

1. **In General.** If the injury to the plaintiff would not have happened "but for" the act or omission of the defendant, such conduct of the defendant is the cause in fact of the plaintiff's injury. For example:

    a. The ***failure of one driver to give a turn signal*** is not a cause of an auto collision when the driver of the other auto was not looking and would not have seen the signal even if it had been given. In such a case, the defendant was negligent, but his negligence in not signaling his intention to turn was not the actual cause of the damage.

    b. Likewise, the ***failure to supply fire fighting equipment*** that could not have been used anyway because of no available water is not the actual cause of the plaintiff's loss when her building burns.

    c. ***When the defendant hits a child who darts out in front of his car*** being driven at 80 miles per hour but the child would have been killed even if the defendant had not been speeding, the defendant's speed is not the cause in fact of the child's death.

Perkins v. Texas and New Orleans Railway Co.

2. **Injury Would Have Occurred Even Without Defendant's Negligence --Perkins v. Texas and New Orleans Railway Co.,** 147 So.2d 646 (La. 1962).

   a. **Facts.** Perkins, whose widow (P) brought this action, was a passenger in a car driven by Foreman. The car approached a train crossing. The view between the road and the railroad track was obstructed by a warehouse, but the Texas and New Orleans Railway Co. (D) had installed a signal device, and stop signs were positioned at the crossing. The signal device was operating because a train was also approaching the intersection. The train was blowing its whistle. The car entered the intersection just in front of the train. The train, which was going 37 miles per hour, struck the car and killed both passengers. The train speed limit at the crossing was 25 miles per hour. The speed of the car could not be determined, but estimates ranged from 3 to 25 miles per hour. P sued for wrongful death, and the trial court awarded damages. The appellate court affirmed, and the Supreme Court of Louisiana granted certiorari.

   b. **Issue.** If an injury would have occurred even if the defendant had not been negligent, may the defendant be held liable for its negligence?

   c. **Held.** No. Judgment reversed.

      1) Negligence must be a cause in fact of the harm suffered in order to support a tort action. To be a cause in fact, the negligence must be a substantial factor in bringing about the harm. In this case, if the collision would have occurred regardless of D's negligence, that negligence was not a substantial factor.

      2) Even though D's train was exceeding its speed limit due to the negligence of D's employees, the evidence indicates that the train would not have been able to stop in time even if it had been going 25 miles per hour instead of 37 miles per hour.

      3) P claims that if the train had been going 12 miles per hour slower, the car containing her husband might have had enough time to clear the intersection. The evidence does not support this purely conjectural theory. Thus the speed of D's train was not a substantial factor in causing the accident.

C. PROOF OF CAUSATION

The plaintiff has the burden to prove that more likely than not, the defendant was a substantial factor in bringing about the result.

1. **Mere Possibility of Negligence Is Insufficient--Gentry v. Douglas Hereford Ranch, Inc.,** 962 P.2d 1205 (Mont. 1998). Gentry v. Douglas Hereford Ranch, Inc.

a. **Facts.** Gentry's (P's) wife was a guest of Bacon's wife, whose grandmother owned the Douglas Hereford Ranch, Inc. (D). Bacon was carrying a rifle when he stumbled either on or approaching some steps on a deck adjacent to the ranch house. The rifle discharged and a bullet struck P's wife in the head and she died several weeks later. P sued Bacon and D. Bacon sought bankruptcy protection and was dismissed from the case. The trial court entered summary judgment in favor of D. P appeals.

b. **Issue.** Is evidence of a possibility sufficient causation to overcome a motion for summary judgment based on failure to prove cause in fact?

c. **Held.** No. Judgment affirmed.

1) P claims that D was negligent because it failed to maintain the stairs in a reasonably safe condition: the bottom stair was unstable and the area around it was cluttered with debris. In his deposition, however, Bacon testified that he couldn't remember anything about the accident, whether he missed the step or tripped or hit it. He also testified that he had previously stumbled climbing those steps due to his own clumsiness, not because of the condition of the steps.

2) Bacon did make a statement to investigators that there was a rock underneath the step to keep it level, but that he did not think that was what caused the accident, that it was the step. But he also stated that he couldn't remember what he stumbled on.

3) This evidence supports at most an inference that Bacon was about to ascend the stairs when he stumbled and fell. Finding why he did so would require speculation, but speculation cannot defeat a motion for summary judgment. Speculative statements do not raise a genuine issue of material fact. P has failed to produce evidence from which it can be reasonably inferred that D was the proximate cause of P's injuries.

2. **Possibility of Plaintiff's Negligence--Reynolds v. Texas & Pacific Railway Co.,** 37 La. Ann. 694 (1885). Reynolds v. Texas & Pacific Railway Co.

a. **Facts.** Reynolds (P) and her husband were waiting at D's station at night for a train. When the train arrived, the passengers were told to "hurry up." P, who weighed 250-pounds, was injured while hurrying down some unlighted steps toward the train. P claims that D was negligent in not lighting the stairs. The trial court rendered a verdict for P and D appeals. D claims that P might have fallen in broad daylight and that the lack of lighting was not a cause of the injury.

b. **Issue.** Was the lack of lighting a cause in fact of the injury?

c. **Held.** Yes. Judgment affirmed.

1) D had a duty to safeguard customers. D was negligent in failing to light the stairway. When the defendant's negligence greatly multiplies the possibility of injury, the mere possibility of the plaintiff's negligence does not break the chain of causation.

Kramer Service, Inc. v. Wilkins

3. **Coexistence Does Not Prove Causation--Kramer Service, Inc. v. Wilkins,** 186 So. 625 (Miss. 1939).

a. **Facts.** Wilkins' (P's) forehead was cut when a piece of broken glass fell from a transom in a hotel operated by Kramer Service, Inc. (D). The wound would not heal and two years after the injury, P discovered that he had developed skin cancer in the area of the injury. The jury found for P. D appeals.

b. **Issue.** Did the fact that the cancer occurred at the place of P's injury indicate that D's negligence was the cause?

c. **Held.** No. Judgment reversed.

1) There was no proof of causation. It is not enough that negligence and injury are coexistent—there must be a causal link.

2) The medical testimony showed only that there was a possibility, not a probability, that the injury caused the skin cancer.

d. **Comment.** A mere possibility of the defendant's negligence is never sufficient. In this case, P might have prevailed if an expert had testified in his favor as to the fact that the skin cancer would not have developed but for the injury received from the broken glass.

Wilder v. Eberhart

4. **Expert Testimony to Rebut Plaintiff's Prima Facie Case--Wilder v. Eberhart,** 977 F.2d 673 (1st Cir. 1992).

a. **Facts.** Wilder (P) suffered serious complications from tears in her lower esophagus after surgery performed by Dr. Eberhart (D), which involved stapling her stomach to treat her obesity. P's expert testified that the sole cause of the injury to P's esophagus was D's negligence during surgery. P's counsel made a motion in limine to exclude the testimony of D's experts, who were prepared to testify that the least likely cause of P's injury was that offered by P's expert and that there were other possible causes. The trial judge granted the motion, thereby excluding the testimony of D's experts, because their opinions could only be expressed as "mere possibility" rather than "probability." After a judgment for P, D appeals.

b. **Issue.** After P offers expert testimony that it is more likely than not that her injury was caused by D's negligence, may D offer expert testimony in rebuttal that simply offers other possible causes of P's injury without specifying another cause?

c. **Held.** Yes. Judgment vacated and remanded.

1) The plaintiff in a negligence action bears the burden of producing evidence to prove that it is more likely than not that the plaintiff's injury was caused by the defendant's negligence. The defendant, however, need not prove another cause. The defendant need only convince the trier of fact that the alleged negligence was not the legal cause of the injury. This may be done by producing other "possible" causes of plaintiff's injury, which need not be proved with certainty or more probably than not. Thus, the granting of P's motion in limine (excluding the testimony of D's experts as to other possible causes of P's injury) was prejudicial to D and constituted reversible error.

5. **Decrease in Chance of Survival--Herskovits v. Group Health Cooperative of Puget Sound,** 664 P.2d 474 (Wash. 1983).

Herskovits v. Group Health Cooperative of Puget Sound

a. **Facts.** Group Health Cooperative of Puget Sound (D) treated Herskovits and allegedly negligently failed to diagnose his cancer on his first visit. Herskovits (P), the executor of her husband's estate, brought suit claiming that D's negligence proximately caused a 14% decrease in her husband's chances of survival, even though he had less than a 50% chance of survival anyway. The trial court granted D summary judgment. P appeals.

b. **Issue.** When a patient has less than a 50% chance of survival, is there a cause of action against the hospital that negligently failed to diagnose the patient's lung cancer and thereby reduced the patient's chance of survival by 14%?

c. **Held.** Yes. Judgment reversed.

1) Normally, a tort case involves a "but for" test, whereby the plaintiff must prove that the injury would not have occurred but for the negligence of the defendant. In this case, however, D allegedly failed to protect Herskovits against harm from another source.

2) The fact finder must consider what might have occurred as well as what did occur. Although this involves considerable uncertainty, the actor should not be immune merely because of this uncertainty. So long as D's acts or omissions increased the risk of harm to Herskovits, the jury may determine whether the increased risk was a substantial factor in the eventual harm.

3) The parties have agreed for this appeal that D's negligence was the proximate cause of reducing Herskovits's chances of survival by 14%. Even though he had less than a 50% chance of survival anyway, the reduced chance of survival is sufficient to present a jury question on the proximate cause issue.

4) Damages for loss of chance to recover must be limited to damages caused directly by premature death, such as lost earnings and increased medical expenses.

Daubert v. Merrell Dow Pharmaceuticals, Inc.

6. Statistically Significant Relationship--Daubert v. Merrell Dow Pharmaceuticals, Inc., 43 F.3d 1311 (9th Cir. 1995).

a. **Facts.** Ps are minors with serious birth defects allegedly caused by their mothers' ingestion during pregnancy of Bendectin, an anti-nausea drug marketed by Merrell Dow Pharmaceuticals (D). D moved for summary judgment on the basis that maternal use of the drug has not been shown to be a risk factor for human birth defects. Ps then attempted to introduce testimony from their experts reaching contrary conclusions. The district court granted D's motion for summary judgment, concluding that Ps' evidence was not based upon principles that were "generally accepted" in the field. The Ninth Circuit affirmed, citing *Frye v. United States*, 293 F. 1013 (1923), and stating that expert opinion based on a scientific technique is inadmissible unless the technique is "generally accepted" as reliable in the relevant scientific community. The court concluded that Ps' evidence was inadmissible, and, therefore Ps would be unable to prove causation at trial. The United States Supreme Court granted certiorari to consider the proper standard for admission of expert scientific testimony. The Court then remanded to the Ninth Circuit to determine if Ps' proposed expert testimony "both rests on a reliable foundation and is relevant to the task at hand."

b. **Issue.** Can Ps use their experts' scientific testimony to prove that Bendectin caused their birth defects?

c. **Held.** No. Judgment affirmed.

1) Scientists do not know exactly how birth defects occur, but this is not necessarily fatal to Ps' claim. Causation can be proved if there is compelling proof that the agent in question must have caused the damage somehow. For example, a plaintiff can offer statistical evidence. This is the method Ps attempt to use.

2) Under *Frye*, our task was simple: we just had to determine whether the methods used by Ps' experts are generally accepted in the scientific community. Now, we must use a two-part test: (i) whether the experts' testimony reflects "scientific knowledge," whether their find-

ings are "derived by the scientific method," and whether their work product amounts to "good science"; and (ii) whether the proposed testimony is "relevant to the task at hand."

3) As to (i), the proposed expert's testimony alone is not enough. There must be some objective validation of the expert's methodology. Here, none of Ps' experts studied the effect of Bendectin on birth defects independent of researching it for this or a related case. Furthermore, none of Ps' experts' findings has been published or subject to formal peer review.

4) The proposed testimony also fails to satisfy (ii) because Ps' experts' testimony is not relevant and would only confuse the jury. Ps must show that their mothers' ingestion of Bendectin ***more likely than not*** caused their injuries (*i.e.*, not just that it increased the likelihood of birth defects, but that it more than doubled it). None of Ps' experts makes this claim. A statistically significant relationship is not enough for legal causation.

D. CONCURRENT CAUSES

1. **Generally.** In the case of concurrent causes, strict application of the rule of sine qua non fails if each cause, by itself, would not have been sufficient to bring about the result or if each cause, by itself, would have been sufficient to bring about the result. Conduct then is considered a cause if it is a substantial factor in bringing about the harm. Thus, a streetcar driver is liable if he negligently stops suddenly to pick up a passenger who is negligently running across the street to catch the streetcar and the plaintiff runs into the streetcar to avoid hitting the passenger.

2. **Combined Causes--Hill v. Edmonds,** 270 N.Y.S.2d 1020 (1966).

Hill v. Edmonds

a. **Facts.** Bragoli had left his truck in the middle of the road without its lights on during a stormy night. Edmonds (D) was driving her car with Hill (P) as a passenger. D collided with the truck. She later claimed that she had seen the truck and tried to miss it, but she initially had said that she did not know what happened and had just awakened. The trial court found that D was solely negligent and dismissed P's claim against Bragoli. P appeals.

b. **Issue.** When separate acts of negligence combine to produce directly a single injury, is each tortfeasor responsible for the entire result, even though his act alone might not have caused the injury?

c. **Held.** Yes. Dismissal reversed.

1) When separate acts of negligence combine to cause one injury, each negligent actor is liable for the whole injury, as though he

alone had caused it, even though his act alone might not have caused the injury.

2) Although both are liable for all, P can only collect up to the amount of the judgment, whether in part from both (joint liability) or in total from one (several liability).

d. **Comment.** When a defendant's negligence results in injury that would not have otherwise occurred, the defendant is liable even though a third party's negligence also contributed to the injury.

Anderson v. Minneapolis, St. Paul & Saulte Sainte Marie Railroad Co.

3. **Substantial Factor--Anderson v. Minneapolis, St. Paul & Saulte Sainte Marie Railroad Co.,** 179 N.W. 45 (Minn. 1920).

a. **Facts.** One fire caused by the negligence of the railroad (D) combined with a fire of unknown origin and burned P's land. D claimed that the fire of unknown origin would have burned P's land anyway ("but for" rule). After a verdict for P, D's motion for judgment notwithstanding the verdict was denied. D appeals.

b. **Issue.** Is the "but for" rule applicable to concurrent causes?

c. **Held.** No. Judgment affirmed; "but for" is faulty logic here.

1) If both causes are substantial factors, both are responsible for P's loss. A tortfeasor is not excluded just because someone else is also liable. One hundred defendants may be liable if they are all tortfeasors.

2) The "substantial factor" rule rather than "but for" should be used when there are concurrent causes, each sufficient by itself, because:

a) The language is intelligible to regular jury members.

b) It eliminates the small number of cases where there is a trivial cause of insignificant contribution; *e.g.*, dropping a match after a forest fire has started. However, when there is a question as to whether a cause is a substantial factor, it is a question for the jury.

d. **Comment.** Except for cases like this one and ones with insignificant causes, the result is the same as the "but for" rule. The change of language is for freak cases. For example:

1) A wants to hang herself. Both B and C give her ropes. A uses B's rope. Is C liable?

2) Two motorcycles scare a horse, and either of them alone would have done the same—both are substantial factors.

3) A stabs B and C fractures B's skull with a rock; either act would kill. Who is liable? Both—the law cannot apportion death.

E. DETERMINING WHO CAUSED THE HARM

1. **Alternative Liability.** When there is undoubtedly fault and alternative liability, the rule of causation is relaxed.

a. **The landmark case--Summers v. Tice,** 199 P.2d 1 (Cal. 1948). Summers v. Tice

1) **Facts.** Tice and Simonson (Ds), hunting quail, shot in Summers' (P's) direction with their shotguns at the same time and a shot hit P in the eye. Obviously only one of the Ds shot P, but P could not tell which one. Ds argued that, therefore, P could not show which D was negligent (*i.e.*, that the "but for" test could not be satisfied). From judgment for P against both Ds, Ds appealed.

2) **Issue.** Has P shown causation?

3) **Held.** Yes. Judgment affirmed.

a) Ds' acts of shooting in P's direction were negligent and P's injury would not have resulted but for Ds' acts. Ds are joint tortfeasors and each is liable (joint and several liability), even though only one inflicted the injury. Ds brought about the harm, so they can untangle the facts.

4) **Comment.** The effect of this rule (alternative liability rule) is to shift the burden of causation on to the defendants; each must absolve himself. This is similar to *Ybarra, supra*, where each defendant was required to absolve himself from the breach of the duty. This shift of the burden is based on policy and justice, not logic.

b. **Examples where rule applies.**

1) Two defendants negligently sell bullets to boys and one bullet kills a boy. There is joint and several liability.

2) Two negligently driven cars, A and B, collide. Then a negligent third driver, C, runs into the wreck and a passenger in car A is hurt. The result is that all three drivers are liable (absent guest statute protection for driver A, etc.), but only because all

three were negligent and there is no evidence as to which driver caused the injury.

c. **Compare.** Distinguish the case where the plaintiff does not prove a case against one or more defendants from the alternative liability case where the plaintiff proves he was injured by ***one*** of several negligent defendants but does not know which one. The difference is that under the alternative liability rule, both defendants are negligent although only one caused the injury; whereas under the other rule, only one defendant was negligent. Both defendants must be negligent to apply *Summers v. Tice*.

2. **Apportioning Damages Where Actual Tortfeasor Is Unknown.**

a. **"Enterprise liability."** In *Hall v. E.I. DuPont de Nemours & Co.*, 345 F. Supp. 353 (E.D.N.Y. 1972), the plaintiffs were injured separately in numerous separate explosions of blasting caps. The blasting cap industry was concentrated among six manufacturers that collaborated through a trade association in designing the caps. The court concluded that all the defendants jointly controlled the risk and that if the plaintiffs could prove that the injurious caps were manufactured by one of the defendants, the burden of proof as to causation would shift to all the defendants.

Sindell v. Abbott Laboratories

b. **"Market shares liability"--Sindell v. Abbott Laboratories,** 607 P.2d 924 (Cal. 1980).

1) **Facts.** Sindell (P) sued several drug companies that had produced diethylstilbestrol ("DES"). P's mother had taken DES while pregnant and P consequently suffered a malignancy. Approximately 200 companies had produced DES, and P could not prove which one had produced the DES used by her mother. The lower court dismissed the complaint, and P appeals.

2) **Issue.** May P recover from the drug manufacturers that produced a drug identical to the one which injured P without identifying the manufacturer of the precise product that caused the injury?

3) **Held.** Yes. Judgment reversed.

a) The "alternative liability" theory of *Summers* cannot apply since P cannot identify the actual tortfeasor. Nor can the "enterprise liability" theory of *Hall* apply since that theory is appropriate only when a small number of manufacturers jointly control the risk and do not simply comply with governmental standards.

b) The rationale behind *Summers* applies here, however. Between an innocent plaintiff and negligent defendants, the latter should bear the cost of the injury when the nature of the product delays injury so as to make identification of the tortfeasor impossible.

c) It is reasonable to measure the likelihood that any of the defendants supplied the injurious product by the percentage of the entire production of DES attributable to each defendant. Thus, once P proves injury caused by DES, each DES manufacturer is liable to P in proportion to its individual share of the entire DES market, unless it can prove individually that it could not have produced the precise product that injured P.

d) To take advantage of this theory, P must join sufficient manufacturers of the product in order to prove that a substantial share of the market is represented.

VI. PROXIMATE CAUSE

A. INTRODUCTION

1. **Limit on Liability.** Proximate cause is the legal concept used to determine the extent of the defendant's liability after actual causation (causation in fact) is established. The "but for" test of causation must be limited in some way. As noted in *Atlantic Coast Line Railroad Co. v. Daniels*, 70 S.E. 203 (Ga. 1911), the "but for" argument could be extended to the point that "if the injured person had never been born, the injury would not have happened."

2. **Terminology.** "Proximate cause" is a potentially deceptive term because closeness in time and space are not determinative. The issue really is how far public policy will extend liability to the defendant for the consequences of his act. The Restatement uses the term "legal cause," but this term is no more descriptive and has not replaced the term "proximate cause" in the cases. Regardless of the term used, it is important to realize that the true test is one of public policy.

3. **Foreseeability.** One test of proximate cause is the foreseeability of the result, given the defendant's action. Foreseeability alone is not determinative, however, as the cases illustrate. Part of the reason is that virtually anything that happens is in some sense foreseeable. The problem is determining what is reasonably foreseeable.

4. **Direct and Indirect Results.** When there is no intervening force between the defendant's negligent act and the harm to the plaintiff, such harm is said to be the direct result of the defendant's act. For example, if the defendant negligently reaches for his cigarette lighter while driving his car, and the car hits a telephone pole, which falls onto the plaintiff's house, the damage to the plaintiff's house is the direct result of the defendant's negligence. Indirect results occur when there is an intervening force (or forces) between the defendant's act and harm to the plaintiff. Intervening causes present some of the most difficult causation problems.

B. UNFORESEEABLE CONSEQUENCES

1. **Foreseeability of Harm.** The harm caused to the plaintiff as a direct result of the defendant's acts may be either foreseeable (*e.g.*, it is foreseeable that pedestrians and other drivers may be injured if the defendant negligently runs a red traffic light) or unforeseeable (*e.g.*, it is unforeseeable in the preceding example that buildings in the neighborhood will have all their windows blown out by an explosion caused by the defendant running into another vehicle, which turns out to be a gasoline truck).

2. **The Opposing Views.** There are two opposing views on foreseeability of the consequences of the defendant's act. One view is that the defendant's acts will be considered the proximate cause of the plaintiff's injury only if such consequences, judged by time, place, and under the circumstances when the defendant acted, were reasonably foreseeable. Essentially, this view uses the same criteria for foreseeability to determine the extent of liability as is used to determine whether the defendant's act is negligent—is the injury reasonably foreseeable as something likely to happen? The other view, where the injury to the plaintiff is the direct result of the defendant's act, is that foreseeability is important only in determining whether there is negligence; if the injury follows in an unbroken sequence of events, the defendant will be liable for the consequences regardless of the remoteness of the injury.

3. **Unexpected Harm.** The defendant's act may be negligent. In addition, some harm may result. The harm, however, may be different than foreseen due to some preexisting condition or subsequent circumstances.

4. **Fire Cases.** The unpredictability of a spreading fire has produced difficult causation problems. The courts evaluate each case on the specific facts involved.

   a. **One house rule--Ryan v. New York Central Railroad Co.,** 35 N.Y. 210, 91 Am. Dec. 49 (1866).

   Ryan v. New York Central Railroad Co.

      1) **Facts.** An engine owned by the New York Central Railroad Co. (D) malfunctioned and negligently set fire to D's woodshed, which contained a lot of wood. The fire spread to several other houses, including one owned by Ryan (P). P's house was 130 feet from the shed. The trial court dismissed P's action against D and the appellate court affirmed. P appeals.

      2) **Issue.** Is the person who negligently starts a fire liable for all the damage directly caused by that fire?

      3) **Held.** No. Judgment affirmed.

         a) As a general rule, every person is liable for the consequences of his own acts. This extends only to proximate results, however, not to remote damages.

         b) Liability should not be extended to include consequences against which the negligent person could not have guarded. The damages would be too great for the negligent party to pay. In a society, each person runs the hazard of his neighbor's conduct, and each person is responsible to insure his own property.

c) In this case, it was foreseeable that the malfunction would destroy D's woodshed. The spread of the fire to P's house, however, was not a necessary or usual result. It happened instead because of conditions beyond D's control, such as wind, the temperature of the fire, the materials of which P's house was constructed, and so forth.

4) **Comment.** This appears to be an extreme limitation based on proximate cause. Most fire cases result in greater liability for the negligent party. Even in New York, the courts have more recently permitted recovery by the first adjoining landowner whose property is damaged.

b. **Broad liability.** In *Atchison, Topeka & Santa Fe Railroad Co. v. Stanford*, 15 Am. Rep. 362 (Kan. 1874), the court held the railroad liable for fire damage to a farm almost four miles from the point where the fire was negligently started.

Bartolone v. Jeckovich

5. **Psychological Damage from Motor Vehicle Accident--Bartolone v. Jeckovich,** 481 N.Y.S.2d 545 (1984).

a. **Facts.** Bartolone (P), a carpenter with varied interests including body building, art and music, was in a car accident and suffered whiplash and lower back strain. Later, he suffered an acute psychotic breakdown from which he did not recover. He stopped his former activities and became hostile and delusional. P sued Jeckovich (D), who had caused the accident, claiming that the accident aggravated a preexisting paranoid schizophrenic condition. P's witnesses explained that P's mother and sister had died of cancer, and that P's interest in body building was a way to avoid doctors and to deal with his emotional problems. The physical injury impaired his physical abilities and eliminated his means to cope, causing his psychological deterioration. D's witnesses claimed that P suffered from schizophrenia but not because of the accident. The jury found for P, but the court set aside the verdict, finding that P's total mental breakdown could not be attributed to a minor accident. P appeals.

b. **Issue.** Is the person who caused a minor traffic accident, which in turn causes minimal physical injury but serious psychological damage to another, liable for that psychological damage?

c. **Held.** Yes. Judgment reversed and jury verdict reinstated.

1) There are existing cases in which victims of accidents who suffered only minor physical injuries suffered from serious psychological problems as a result of the accident. A person may be able

to cope with underlying psychotic illness until an accident which brings on a chronic psychosis.

2) A defendant must take a plaintiff as he finds him. D could be held liable for damages for aggravation of P's preexisting illness. It does not matter that P's current condition might have occurred even if the accident had not. P was able to function despite his psychotic illness until the accident, and now is totally and permanently disabled.

d. **Comment.** Unforeseeable consequences of physical injury are normally actionable. This rule differs from property damage cases due to the greater values assigned to personal injuries.

6. **Manner in Which Injury Occurs--*In Re* Arbitration Between Polemis and Furness, Withy & Co., Ltd.,** 3 K.B. 560 (1921).

In Re Arbitration Between Polemis and Furness, Withy, & Co. Ltd.

a. **Facts.** Ps, owners of a vessel, chartered it to Ds. While unloading cargo, Ds' servants dropped a plank into the hold of the vessel. Apparently it caused a spark that, in turn, ignited benzine vapors. The resulting fire destroyed the vessel. Arbitrators hearing the case found that Ds' servants were negligent. They also found that, although the spark could not have been anticipated, some damage from the falling plank was foreseeable. The court affirmed the arbitrator's award of damages to Ps. Ds appeal on the ground that the particular damage was not foreseeable.

b. **Issue.** Is a defendant liable for unforeseeable consequences of his acts if some damage is foreseeable, but not the damage that actually occurred?

c. **Held.** Yes. Judgment affirmed.

1) The foreseeability of damages may be important in determining the existence of negligence. But once negligence is established, the negligent party is liable for all damages, regardless of foreseeability.

2) The arbitrators found that the falling plank was due to the negligence of Ds' servants. They also found that some damage was reasonably foreseeable, even if not the creation of the spark and the resulting fire. Ds are liable for the damage actually caused, even though the manner in which it occurred was not foreseeable.

d. **Comment.** The rule that the unforeseeability of the manner in which a particular result is brought about is not a defense has been widely accepted. This is a different concept from the unforeseeability of the result itself.

Overseas Tankship (U.K.) Ltd. v. Morts Dock & Engineering Co. (Wagon Mound I)

7. **Actual Results Must Be Foreseeable--Overseas Tankship (U.K.) Ltd. v. Morts Dock & Engineering Co. (Wagon Mound I),** [1961] App. Cas. 338 (P.C. 1961).

   a. **Facts.** D's freighter, Wagon Mound, was moored approximately 600 feet away from P's wharf. D's ship negligently discharged oil, which spread across the harbor and under P's wharf. P's workers were welding on the wharf. Molten metal dripped from the welding job, set fire to cotton which was floating on the surface of the water, and this in turn ignited the oil. The ensuing fire damaged the wharf and two ships docked alongside. From a judgment for P, D appeals.

   b. **Issue.** Must the actual damage or results be foreseeable?

   c. **Held.** Yes. Judgment reversed.

      1) The actual type of damage or results must be foreseeable. It is not enough that just any damage or results are foreseeable or follow in an unbroken sequence.

      2) Some limitation must be imposed upon the consequences for which a negligent actor is to be held responsible. The better view is reasonable foreseeability, *i.e.*, liability limited to what the reasonable person ought to foresee.

   d. **Comment.** This case represented a repudiation of the direct causation rule of *Polemis*.

8. **Balancing Test.** *Overseas Tankship (U.K.) Ltd. v. Miller Steamship Co. (Wagon Mound II)*, App. Cas. 617 (P.C. 1967), involved the same facts as in Wagon Mound I immediately above. Here, the suit was brought by the owners of the ships damaged in the fire, and the court held for the owners on reasoning similar to that in *Carroll Towing*; *i.e.*, the burden of eliminating a risk must be balanced against the probability of its materializing times the potential gravity of the harm. The court stated that the defendant should have known that there was a serious risk of the oil on the water catching fire in some way and that if it did, serious damage to ships or other property was not only foreseeable, but very likely, thus making it unreasonable to dismiss such a risk.

   a. **Comment.** This case can be viewed as consistent with its sister case involving the wharf by finding that the court in that case erred in determining what a reasonable person would foresee. Here, the result in *Polemis* is approached by charging the reasonable person with the recognition of slight or extremely remote risks.

   b. **Comment.** In cases involving direct results of a defendant's act, proximate cause is nearly synonymous with actual cause.

9. **Foreseeability of the Plaintiff.** The foreseeability criteria have been extended to the question of to whom does the defendant owe a duty.

a. **Duty owed the plaintiff--Palsgraf v. Long Island Railroad Co.,** 162 N.E. 99 (N.Y. 1928). Palsgraf v. Long Island Railroad Co.

1) **Facts.** Palsgraf (P) purchased a railroad ticket and stood on a platform of D's railroad when a would-be passenger carrying a package attempted to leap aboard a moving train. A train guard pulled the passenger aboard while another guard pushed him from behind, causing his package to dislodge and fall upon the tracks. The package, wrapped in newspaper, contained fireworks, which exploded. The shock of the explosion caused some scales at the other end of the platform to fall and strike P. P was awarded damages resulting from her injuries. The Appellate Division affirmed. D appeals.

2) **Issue.** May the defendant's negligence toward a third person be the basis of recovery for injuries to the plaintiff, even though no risk of harm to the plaintiff was foreseeable?

3) **Held.** No. Judgment reversed.

a) The plaintiff must show a wrong to herself; *i.e.*, a violation of her own right, not merely a wrong to someone else or an unsocial act.

b) The reasonably perceivable risk defines the duty to be obeyed. The risk extends to those within the range of reasonable apprehension.

c) The purpose of the guard's act was to make the passenger safe. If there was a wrong at all, it was to the safety of the package. There was nothing in the situation to suggest to the most cautious mind that the parcel would spread wreckage through the station.

d) Negligence itself is not a tort; it must be negligence in relation to the plaintiff.

4) **Dissent** (Andrews, J.). Judgment for P should be affirmed.

a) When an act unreasonably threatens the safety of others, the wrongdoer is liable for all proximate consequences regardless of whether they are unforeseeable or unexpected.

b) The doctrine of proximate cause is a tool that allows the law to arbitrarily decline to trace a series of events beyond a certain point.

c) Due care is a duty imposed on everyone to protect society from unnecessary harm. To say that there is no negligence unless there is a legal duty owed to the plaintiff herself is too narrow a conception. When there is an unreasonable act, there is negligence.

5) **Comment.** This case illustrates the analysis used to determine who is a proper plaintiff in a tort action. To recover, the plaintiff must show that the defendant owed her a duty that was then breached by the defendant.

Yun v. Ford Motor Co.

b. **Unforeseeable extraordinary circumstances--Yun v. Ford Motor Co.,** 647 A.2d 841 (N.J. Super. Ct. App. Div. 1994).

1) **Facts**. Yun (P) owned and operated a van manufactured by Ford Motor Co. Her 65-year-old father, Chang, was a passenger in the van. P heard a "rattling type" noise coming from the rear of the van before the plastic cover, spare tire, and part of the support bracket fell off the van and rolled across the traffic to the center divider. P pulled over and Chang ran across the two lanes of the rain-slicked road in the dark. He retrieved the spare tire and other parts, but in returning to P's van, he was struck and killed by Linderman. P sued Ford as well as Miller, the manufacturer of the spare tire assembly, Universal, which installed the assembly, Castle, the dealer, and Kim, who had changed P's oil and told P that the spare tire assembly was bent. P had asked Kim not to repair it because it had been damaged in another accident and the insurance company had not yet handled it. The trial court granted summary judgment to all defendants except Linderman, who settled. P dropped Ford as a defendant, but appeals regarding the other defendants.

2) **Issue.** May a court grant summary judgment on the issue of causation if it determines that the victim's own conduct was senseless and a supervening cause of the injury?

3) **Held.** Yes. Judgment affirmed.

a) Kim had no duty to repair the bent spare tire assembly, and thus did not breach any duty. The issue of proximate cause does not even apply to Kim, so the summary judgment for Kim is upheld, even if for a different reason than the trial judge gave.

b) P must prove that the alleged defect in the spare tire assembly proximately caused the injuries to Chang. Proximate cause is a standard for limiting liability for the consequences of an act so that a person is not held liable for a highly extraordinary consequence. Proximate cause is a cause that sets off a foreseeable sequence of consequences, unbroken by any superseding cause, and that is a substantial factor in producing the particular injury.

c) The facts in this case demonstrate extraordinary circumstances. Chang's attempt to retrieve the tire and parts under the dark, wet circumstances on a major highway were highly extraordinary and dangerous. Logic and fairness dictate that liability should not be imposed for injuries resulting from the victim's senseless decisions. If Chang had exercised common sense, he would have either waited for assistance or abandoned the tire.

d) The defect in the assembly did not injure Chang. The loss of the spare tire may have created a condition upon which the subsequent intervening force acted; *i.e.*, Chang's decision to cross the road. This does not create a proximate cause between the defect and the injury. Even if the defect was a substantial factor in causing Chang's injuries, his actions in crossing the highway twice are clearly superseding and intervening causes of his own injuries.

4) **Concurrence and dissent.** Questions of proximate cause are normally left to the jury for its factual determination, as are questions of intervening cause. Under these facts, reasonable persons might differ regarding whether Chang's death was proximately caused by the defective tire assembly. A jury might conclude that it would be unusual to abandon a spare tire under the circumstances. Judges generally are more conservative than the general population and should not apply their personal standards of foreseeability and fairness, but leave these questions to a jury.

5) **Comment.** The New Jersey Supreme Court adopted the dissent's rationale and reversed the appellate division. (*See* Yun v. Ford Motor Co., 669 A.2d 1378 (N.J. 1996))

C. INTERVENING CAUSES

1. **Indirect Results of Defendant's Act.** Indirect results occur when there is an intervening force (or forces) between the defendant's act and the harm caused to the plaintiff. Such forces or causes are of external origin, and do not come into operation until after the defendant's negligent act has occurred. Intervening causes generally do not relieve the defendant of liability, unless they are both unforeseeable and bring about unforeseeable results. In such cases, the intervening causes are said to be superseding. However, the test in every case where there is an intervening force or cause is whether the average, reasonable person faced with like or similar circumstances would have foreseen the likelihood that the force or cause would intervene.

Derdiarian v. Felix Contracting Corp.

2. **Intervening Act Within Risk of Negligent Act--Derdiarian v. Felix Contracting Corp.,** 414 N.E.2d 666 (N.Y. 1981).

   a. **Facts.** Derdiarian (P) was employed by a subcontractor and was sealing a gas main in an excavation in a city street. The general contractor, Felix Contracting Corp. (D) had excavated the site and provided one flagman, but did not erect barriers completely around the excavation. A passing driver had an epileptic seizure and lost control of his car, which hit P and caused him to be severely burned by the sealing material. The material had been placed in a kettle on the traffic side of the excavation. The trial court held for P on the question of liability in an interlocutory order. D appeals.

   b. **Issue.** Is an intervening act a superseding cause, when the act is unforeseeable, but the risk of it occurring is the same risk that renders the actor negligent?

   c. **Held.** No. Judgment affirmed.

      1) D claims that the injury resulted solely from the negligence of the driver of the car, and that there was no causal link between D's breach of duty and P's injuries. However, an intervening act does not automatically sever the causal connection. Liability depends on whether the intervening act is a normal or foreseeable consequence of D's negligence.

      2) The prime hazard associated with D's failure to properly protect the work site was that a vehicle might enter and injure a worker. The manner in which the injury actually occurred is irrelevant when it is the same risk that arose from D's negligence. The placement of the kettle does not preclude D's liability either, since the general risk was foreseeable and D's negligence created the situation in which the injury occurred.

3. **Intervening Negligent or Intentional Acts.** A person's negligent conduct may produce a situation that makes possible significant injury through the actions of another person. The original actor's liability may depend on whether the intervenor acted negligently or intentionally.

Watson v. Kentucky & Indiana Bridge & Railroad Co.

   a. **Highly dangerous situation--Watson v. Kentucky & Indiana Bridge & Railroad Co.,** 126 S.W.146 (Ky. 1910).

      1) **Facts.** Gas was spilled from a train when one of the cars was negligently derailed by the railroad company (D). Thousands of gallons flooded through the streets of the town. Three hours later, the gas exploded when ignited by a match thrown on the street by Duerr. There was a factual question as to whether the match was being

used to light a cigar and was then negligently dropped or whether it was intentionally dropped. Watson (P) was injured and sued the owner and operator of the train. The trial court directed a verdict for D, finding Duerr acted intentionally. P appeals.

2) **Issue.** If a person's negligence produces a highly dangerous situation, may that person be held liable for damages caused by an intervenor's foreseeable negligent act which, because of the dangerous situation, actually causes the damages?

3) **Held.** Yes. Judgment reversed.

a) D's negligent act created the dangerous situation of gasoline in the street. It was probable that someone would light a match to light a cigar, and throwing the match away is a common action. If Duerr acted inadvertently or negligently, D's own negligence was the efficient cause of the explosion. In other words, if an intervening negligent act of another brings about the same injury as was threatened by D's negligent act, then the intervening negligent act (foreseeable or not) will not be considered superseding and liability will be incurred by D.

b) However, a malicious act of starting a fire would not be foreseeable. If Duerr acted intentionally, D would not be liable. At the new trial, the jury must determine the nature of Duerr's acts.

4. **Normal Intervening Causes.** There are other intervening causes that may not be foreseeable but are normal incidents of the risk that the defendant has created.

a. **Disease.** Rules similar to those for escape, rescue, etc., apply when the defendant injures the plaintiff and the plaintiff subsequently contracts a disease (*e.g.*, the plaintiff becomes seriously ill from an infection that was a result of her reduced resistance after a miscarriage caused by the injury the defendant negligently inflicted upon her).

b. **Suicide.** In the case of suicide by the decedent after the defendant negligently inflicts injury upon him, the defendant is not liable if the decedent was sane, but if the suicide resulted from insanity caused by the defendant's negligence, the defendant may be liable.

1) **Not superseding as a matter of law--Fuller v. Preis,** 322 N.E.2d 263 (N.Y. 1974). Fuller v. Preis

a) **Facts.** Fuller (P) is the administrator of the estate of Lewis, who committed suicide. Preis (D) drove a vehicle that negligently collided with Lewis's vehicle, causing no immediately apparent injury to Lewis but causing organic brain damage to the portion of the brain controlling emotions and resulting in frequent brain seizures. Lewis was forced to give up his medical practice and, after three particularly severe seizures, shot himself. The trial court rendered judgment for P; the appellate court reversed, holding that suicide was a superseding cause of death and that the judgment was against the weight of the evidence. P appeals.

b) **Issue.** Is suicide a superseding cause of death as a matter of law?

c) **Held.** No. Judgment reversed and remanded.

(1) If the suicide proximately resulted from injuries sustained by the deceased, it would not be a superseding cause. The issue is one for the jury. Since the appellate court held that the verdict was against the weight of the evidence, it is remanded for a new trial.

McCoy v. American Suzuki Motor Corp.

c. **Rescue doctrine--McCoy v. American Suzuki Motor Corp.,** 961 P.2d 952 (Wash. 1998).

1) **Facts.** McCoy (P) was driving down the freeway when the car in front of him, a Suzuki Samarai manufactured by American Suzuki Motor Corp. (D), swerved off the highway and rolled. P stopped to provide assistance to the seriously injured driver. A patrol trooper stopped and asked P to set out flares. He did so, and then walked even further up the road to hold flares in his hand. Once the accident was cleared, P started walking back with a flare in his hand. The patrol trooper left before P reached his car, and P was struck by another car from behind. P sued D for defects in its Samurai that caused the rollover. D moved for summary judgment on the ground that D did not proximately cause the injury. The trial court agreed with D and granted summary judgment of dismissal. The court of appeals reversed, applying the rescue doctrine and holding that the rescuer need not prove proximate causation, but only that D proximately caused the danger and that the rescuer was injured during the rescue. D appeals.

2) **Issues.**

a) Does the rescue doctrine apply in product liability cases?

b) Must a plaintiff show proximate cause in a rescue doctrine case?

3) **Held.** a) Yes. b) Yes. Case remanded.

a) The rescue doctrine allows an injured rescuer to sue the party that caused the danger requiring the rescue in the first place. The doctrine both imposes a duty on tortfeasors regarding rescuers comparable to the duty owed to the person originally imperiled, and also negates a presumption that the rescuer assumes the risk of injury by undertaking the rescue, so long as he does not act recklessly.

b) P satisfied the requirements for a rescuer because (i) D's negligence caused the peril, (ii) the peril was imminent, (iii) a reasonably prudent person would have concluded that the peril existed, and (iv) P acted with reasonable care in performing the rescue.

c) D claims that the rescue doctrine should not apply to product liability actions because it supplants all common law and the rescue doctrine is a common law remedy. However, the rescue doctrine is not a common law remedy, but a reflection of a societal value judgment that rescuers should not be barred from suing for knowingly placing themselves in danger to undertake a rescue. There is no reason to prevent its application to product liability actions.

d) A rescuer-plaintiff must prove that D's wrongdoing proximately caused his injuries. The foreseeability issue in this case is sufficiently close that it should be decided by a jury. If D's Samurai is defective, a jury could find that it is foreseeable that it would roll and that an approaching car would cause injury to either those in the car or to a rescuer.

5. **Summary of Foreseeability.** A defendant need not reasonably foresee the particular event that has occurred, so long as he should have foreseen that some event of the same general nature might occur. If the defendant created the risk, he is liable for foreseeable intervening causes or damages that are normal results of the risks. If the act of the original actor is a substantial factor in the harm, lack of foreseeability will not prevent liability.

D. PUBLIC POLICY

1. **Social Host's Liability for Drunken Guests--Kelly v. Gwinnell,** 476 A.2d 1219 (N.J. 1984). Kelly v. Gwinnell

a. **Facts.** Gwinnell (D) drove Zak home and stayed there for about two hours, drinking several drinks while there. Zak watched D drive off. D then caused a head-on collision, which seriously injured Kelly (P), the other driver. P sued D, who named Zak as a third party defendant. P then added Zak as a defendant. The trial court granted summary judgment for Zak on the ground that a host who provides alcohol to guests was not liable for a drunk adult guest's negligence. The appellate court affirmed. P appeals.

b. **Issue.** May a social host who allows an adult guest to get drunk, knowing the guest will drive home, be held liable for damages caused by the guest's drunken driving?

c. **Held.** Yes. Judgment reversed.

1) If negligent conduct creates a risk of harm or danger to others and in fact is the proximate cause of such injury, the tortfeasor is normally held liable. In this case, Zak did provide alcohol to D even after D was visibly drunk. Zak knew that D would drive home. A reasonably prudent person would foresee the risks presented from this situation. The only issue is whether Zak had a duty to prevent the risk posed by D's intoxication.

2) The common law develops in response to changing circumstances and the demands of fairness and public policy. Drunk driving is an increasingly intolerable activity, as reflected by the significant criminal sanctions attached and the thousands of deaths and significant damage it causes.

3) Although prior decisions limited liability to hosts who provide liquor to minor guests, it is appropriate and fair to extend this approach to hosts who serve alcohol to adult guests, knowing the guest is drunk and will be operating a motor vehicle. Such a host may be held liable for damages suffered by a third party as a result of the guest's drunk driving.

4) Although this decision may impair the relaxed and enjoyable atmosphere of social gatherings, the interest of providing compensation to victims and the deterrent value of the rule outweighs the negative aspects of the expanded scope of liability.

d. **Dissent.** The legislature is more capable of balancing the competing interests involved in this case. Social hosts are not like commercial licensees who serve alcohol as part of their business. Social hosts are not necessarily capable of assessing degrees of intoxication. In addition, guests at a social gathering are not closely supervised. The host frequently drinks along with the guests. It is unclear exactly what measures a host can take to enforce the rule against guests. Finally, unlike a commercial licensee, a host is unable to spread the cost of liability insurance among customers. These factors should be considered through the legislative process before liability is extended to all social hosts.

2. **Public Policy Limitations--Enright v. Eli Lilly & Co.,** 570 N.E.2d 198 (N.Y. 1991). Enright v. Eli Lilly & Co.

a. **Facts.** Karen Enright's (P's) grandmother ingested DES, a miscarriage preventive drug, during pregnancy that allegedly led to abnormalities in the reproductive system of P's mother, causing P's premature birth, to which she attributes her cerebral palsy and other disabilities. The trial court dismissed P's claims against Eli Lilly (D), one of the drug's manufacturers. The appellate division affirmed the dismissal of P's claims for negligence, breach of warranty, and fraud, but reinstated the strict liability count. P appeals.

b. **Issue.** Should the court recognize a cause of action in favor of a child for injuries suffered as a result of a preconception tort committed against her grandmother in the context of a DES case?

c. **Held.** No. Judgment affirmed.

1) We decline to recognize a cause of action on behalf of P because an injury to a mother that results in injuries to a later-conceived child does not establish a cause of action against the original tortfeasor.

2) Although the legislature has modified the statute of limitations and the courts have adopted a market-share theory of liability in the context of DES cases, these actions were in response to unique procedural barriers and problems of proof peculiar to DES litigation and do not establish DES plaintiffs as a favored class for whose benefit all traditional limitations on tort liability must give way.

3) There is no basis for recognizing this cause of action in the context of a strict product liability claim when we have previously refused to recognize this type of action in an ordinary negligence action. The public policy considerations in favor of holding manufacturers of defective products strictly liable (*i.e.*, ability of manufacturer to distribute the burden of product-caused injuries by passing the costs along to customers and encouraging development of safer products) do not outweigh the countervailing considerations that preclude us from recognizing a cause of action here.

4) The rippling effects of DES exposure may extend for generations; it is our duty to confine liability within manageable limits. Limiting liability to those who ingested the drug serves this purpose without unduly impairing the deterrent purposes of tort liability because the manufacturers may be sued by all those injured by exposure to their product.

5) The dangers of overdeterrence, *i.e.*, the possibility that research will be discouraged or beneficial drugs withheld from the market, are

magnified where we are asked to recognize a legal duty toward generations not yet conceived.

E. SHIFTING RESPONSIBILITY

As a general rule, once the defendant has negligently created a risk of harm to the plaintiff, the defendant's liability will not be relieved by the failure of a third person to prevent the harm. Some situations may arise, however, in which the responsibility for the risk, although originated by the defendant, shifts to a third person.

VII. JOINT TORTFEASORS

A. LIABILITY AND JOINDER OF DEFENDANTS

1. **Introduction.** Joint tortfeasors are persons who either act in concert to cause injury to the plaintiff or act entirely independently but cause a single indivisible injury to the plaintiff. Joint tortfeasors are jointly and severally liable for the damage they cause. Thus, the plaintiff may elect to seek the entire amount from any one of the defendants.

2. **Action in Concert--Bierczynski v. Rogers,** 239 A.2d 218 (Del. 1968). Bierczynski v. Rogers

   a. **Facts.** Mr. and Mrs. Rogers (Ps) were injured when their car was struck by one driven by Race. At the time, Race was racing with Bierczynski (D), who stayed in the proper lane while Race was driving in Ps' lane. Ps sued both participants in the race and the trial court found liability against both participants. D appeals.

   b. **Issue.** When two or more parties engage in a common act of negligence, may all parties be held liable even though only one party was immediately involved in causing the injury?

   c. **Held.** Yes. Judgment affirmed.

      1) There was sufficient evidence to allow the jury to find that both D and Race had been engaged in a race. Once the fact of a race was established, both were liable for injuries resulting from their negligent conduct.

   d. **Comment.** Most states have statutes making it negligence per se to be involved in a race on a public highway. This court found negligence from the fact that a reasonable person would not engage in auto racing on a public highway. There was no applicable state statute.

3. **Comparative Negligence and Joint Liability.** Comparative negligence statutes provide for apportionment of damages between negligent parties who cause an injury in proportion to their fault (*e.g.*, $10,000 damages; plaintiff is 30% at fault—plaintiff would be entitled to $7,000). There is a divergence of opinion as to the effect of comparative negligence on the notion of joint and several liability.

4. **Comparative Negligence Does Not Eliminate Joint and Several Liability--Coney v. J.L.G. Industries, Inc.,** 454 N.E.2d 197 (Ill. 1983). Coney v. J.L.G. Industries, Inc.

   a. **Facts.** J.L.G. Industries, Inc. (D) manufactured a hydraulic aerial work platform. Jasper died while operating the platform, and Coney (P), his administrator, brought a wrongful death action against

D and Jasper's employer. The trial court certified questions to the state supreme court regarding joint and several liability in comparative negligence cases.

b. **Issue.** Does the doctrine of comparative negligence eliminate joint and several liability?

c. **Held.** No.

1) Joint and several liability makes all joint tortfeasors responsible for the plaintiff's entire injury. The plaintiff may pursue all, some, or just one of them and recover full damages, leaving the tortfeasors to work out a fair apportionment.

2) Under comparative negligence, damages are apportioned according to each party's fault. D claims that joint and several liability should no longer apply because it would result in one defendant being responsible for more than its share of the damages. However, most states that adopted comparative negligence retained joint and several liability.

3) Even though fault may be apportioned, an indivisible injury is not divisible. Each tortfeasor's negligence remains a proximate cause of the whole injury.

4) If joint and several liability were not retained, the injured party, even if he contributed to the injury and thus could not recover all of his damages, would have to bear a more than proportionate share of the loss if one of the joint tortfeasors was financially unable to contribute to the judgment. It is better that the other tortfeasors, whose negligence endangered another person, bear this loss than the injured party.

Bartlett v. New Mexico Welding Supply, Inc.

5. **Comparative Negligence Does Eliminate Joint and Several Liability--Bartlett v. New Mexico Welding Supply, Inc.,** 646 P.2d 579 (N.M. Ct. App.), *cert. denied*, 648 P.2d 794 (N.M. 1982).

a. **Facts.** In order to avoid colliding with a car that pulled out quickly in front of her, Bartlett (P) slammed on her brakes. The driver of the truck behind P, who was an employee of New Mexico Welding Supply, Inc. (D), hit his brakes but still collided with P's car, injuring P. The driver of the first car was never found. The jury found that P suffered damages of $100,000 and that D's negligence contributed to the accident and P's damages to the extent of 30% while the unknown driver contributed 70%. P moved that judgment for the full $100,000 be entered against D. The trial court instead ordered a new trial and both parties appeal.

b. **Issue.** Does the doctrine of comparative negligence eliminate joint and several liability?

c. **Held.** Yes. Judgment reversed and judgment against D for 30% of the damages is ordered.

1) The doctrine of joint and several liability, under which any one of a group of joint tortfeasors may be held liable for the entire amount of damages, existed in New Mexico before pure comparative negligence was adopted. If the rule still applies, then D or the unknown driver could be held liable for the damage caused by their combined negligence.

2) Other states have retained joint and several liability when comparative negligence is adopted. One rationale is that the injury is not divisible. However, the concept of one indivisible wrong is based on the common law concept of unity of the cause of action whereby the jury could not apportion damages because there was only one wrong. This common law technicality is obsolete and is not a justification for retaining joint and several liability in the comparative negligence context.

3) The other rationale is that as between one defendant and the injured plaintiff, the defendant should bear the loss caused by a joint tortfeasor's absence or inability to pay. However, when there is only one defendant, the plaintiff bears the risk that the tortfeasor is insolvent. There is no reasonable basis for shifting the risk when there are two or more defendants and one is insolvent. Joint and several liability should not be retained simply to favor the plaintiff.

4) Accordingly, under comparative negligence a joint tortfeasor is liable only for that portion of the total damages attributable to its own negligence. A defendant is not required to pay the full damages when the other joint tortfeasors cannot pay their share.

B. SATISFACTION AND RELEASE

1. **Introduction.** An unsatisfied judgment against one of several joint tortfeasors does not bar the plaintiff's action against the others. However, the ***satisfaction*** of a judgment against one joint tortfeasor extinguishes the cause of action and bars any subsequent suit for a greater or additional amount against any of the others. Many courts formerly reached the same result where the plaintiff had merely released one of several joint tortfeasors, regardless of the sufficiency of compensation paid for the release. Most states now reject the latter rule, requiring that the re-

lease specifically waive the right to sue the other joint tortfeasors for them to be released.

a. **Compare.** The covenant not to sue is distinguished from the release in that the latter results in surrender of a cause of action whereas the former obligates the plaintiff by contract to refrain from enforcing the right. Also, both may be negotiated by a plaintiff and defendant for full, partial or no compensation to the plaintiff. They are thus distinguished from "satisfaction," which is deemed an acceptance of full compensation for the plaintiff's injury.

b. **Present Law.**

1) **Majority:** Neither a release nor a covenant not to sue releases other tortfeasors.

2) **Minority:** Release of one tortfeasor releases all; covenant not to sue does not operate as a release of other tortfeasors.

3) **Sub-Minority:** Release with reservation of rights against others is treated as covenant not to sue.

Bundt v. Embro

2. **Judgment and Satisfaction--Bundt v. Embro,** 265 N.Y.S.2d 872 (1965).

a. **Facts.** Bundt and several others (Ps) were passengers in autos involved in a collision resulting from the obstruction of a stop sign by a construction company making repairs to a road. Ps had previously sued and recovered from the state and now sue the owners and drivers of the autos and the construction company. Ds moved to amend their answers to interpose the defense of discharge and satisfaction.

b. **Issue.** May a suit for the recovery of damages be maintained against a joint tortfeasor after full satisfaction of the claim is received from another joint tortfeasor?

c. **Held.** No. Leave to amend is granted.

1) The policy of allowing only one satisfaction is to prevent unjust enrichment. Once the plaintiff has been compensated, he cannot obtain further compensation.

2) The state waived its sovereign immunity and put itself in the same position as any other tortfeasor. It was a joint tortfeasor with Ds in this case. Consequently, Ps' recovery from the state discharged Ds.

d. **Comment.** Partial recovery from one tortfeasor will allow recovery from others to the extent of the unsatisfied claim. Recovery from others, not tortfeasors, will not prevent recovery from tortfeasors. However, an unsatisfied judgment against one of several tortfeasors will not preclude an action by the plaintiff against the others.

3. **Release--Cox v. Pearl Investment Co.,** 450 P.2d 60 (Colo. 1969). Cox v. Pearl Investment Co.

a. **Facts.** Cox (P) sued Pearl Investment Co. (D) for injuries suffered when she fell on property owned by D. P settled with the lessor of the property and the agreement expressly reserved her rights against joint tortfeasors. The trial court ruled the reservation clause ineffective and applied the common law rule that release of one tortfeasor is a release of all and granted summary judgment to D. P appeals.

b. **Issue.** Will a clause in a contract not to sue reserving the right to sue other joint tortfeasors be given effect to the extent of uncompensated injuries?

c. **Held.** Yes. Judgment reversed.

1) The policy of preventing excess recovery is best handled by having the court credit the amount of the settlement against the amount of the verdict. The policy of preventing favoritism among joint tortfeasors by a plaintiff is best executed by examining the sufficiency of the consideration for the release.

4. **"Mary Carter" Agreements--Elbaor v. Smith,** 845 S.W.2d 240 (Tex. 1992). Elbaor v. Smith

a. **Facts.** Smith (P) suffered serious injuries, including a compound ankle fracture, in an automobile accident and received treatment at two hospitals from several physicians, including Elbaor (D), an orthopedic surgeon. After release from the second hospital she received follow-up treatment from other specialists at other facilities over the next few years, resulting in her ankle joint being fused. She then filed medical malpractice actions against both hospitals, D, and the other doctors who treated her. Prior to trial she settled with one hospital and entered into "Mary Carter" agreements with two of the doctors (other than D) and the remaining hospital. Pursuant to the Mary Carter agreements, these defendants agreed to pay P $425,010, remain as defendants, participate in the trial, and be paid back all or part of the settlement money they paid P out of P's recovery from D. D sought to have the Mary Carter agreements declared void as against public policy or, in the alternative, to have the settling defendants dismissed from the trial. The trial court denied D's request, and, after trial and a jury award in favor of P, entered judgment against D for $1,872,848. The court of appeals affirmed and D appeals.

b. **Issue.** Should the Mary Carter agreements between P and some of the defendants be invalidated by the court as against public policy?

c. **Held.** Yes. Judgment reversed and remanded.

1) Mary Carter agreements inflict procedural and substantive damage on the adversarial system and are therefore void as violative of sound public policy. Under such agreements there is a tremendous incentive for settling defendants to ensure that the plaintiff succeeds in obtaining a sizable recovery; this motivates them to greatly assist in presentation of the plaintiff's case, thereby frustrating the adversarial system.

2) Here the trial court made adjustments in the procedure to mitigate the harmful effects of the agreements (reapportioning the peremptory challenges, changing the order of proceedings, etc.); however, these measures do not balance the harmful skewing of the trial process. While as a matter of public policy this court favors settlement, we do not favor partial settlements that promote rather than discourage further litigation.

d. **Dissent.** Most jurisdictions allow Mary Carter agreements when trial courts implement similar procedural safeguards to those adopted here. The opinion in this case represents a minority view accepted in only a few states.

C. CONTRIBUTION AND INDEMNITY

1. **Introduction.** At common law, contribution was not allowed between joint tortfeasors—if one satisfied a judgment, she could not recover from the others their pro rata share. Today under most contribution statutes, each joint tortfeasor is responsible for a pro rata share of the judgment. However, in comparative negligence states, contribution is not pro rata, but is based on relative fault.

Knell v. Feltman

2. **Contribution from Joint Tortfeasor Not Sued by Plaintiff--Knell v. Feltman,** 174 F.2d 662 (D.C. Cir. 1949).

a. **Facts.** Langland was a passenger in a car driven by Knell (D). The car collided with a taxi owned by Feltman (P) and driven by P's employee. When Langland sued P, P filed a third-party complaint against D. The jury found P and D equally at fault and ordered P to pay Langland and D to indemnify P for his share. D appeals, claiming that because Langland did not have a judgment against D, D should not have to pay contribution.

b. **Issue.** In a negligence case, may the joint tortfeasor sued by the plaintiff obtain contribution from another joint tortfeasor not sued by the plaintiff?

c. **Held.** Yes. Judgment affirmed.

1) The right to contribution belongs to the tortfeasor who pays the judgment. It does not depend on the plaintiff's choice of defendants.

2) There is no contribution between intentional tortfeasors, but this rule should not be extended to negligent tortfeasors. Denying contribution in this case would allow plaintiffs to select which parties to sue even though no party committed an intentional tort.

d. **Comment.** The indirect/direct distinction is abandoned in favor of the intentional/unintentional tort standard because the degree of personal involvement by the defendant is immaterial to his entitlement to contribution. This is the prevailing rule.

3. **Contribution Based on Existence of Cause of Action--Yellow Cab Co. of D.C., Inc. v. Dreslin,** 181 F.2d 626 (D.C. Cir. 1950).

Yellow Cab Co. of D.C., Inc. v. Dreslin

a. **Facts.** Dreslin (P) was the owner and operator of a car involved in a collision with a taxi owned by Yellow Cab (D). P's wife and other passengers in P's car were injured and sued D for damages. P joined with them, claiming loss of consortium, medical expenses for his wife, and damage to his car. D counterclaimed for contribution and damages to its taxi. The jury found both parties negligent and allowed D's contribution claim against P for all parties except P's wife. D appeals.

b. **Issue.** Must an injured party plaintiff have a cause of action against the party from whom contribution is sought?

c. **Held.** Yes. Judgment affirmed.

1) A spouse is not liable for tortious acts committed one against the other (in this jurisdiction). The policy of preserving domestic peace and felicity outweighs the policy of requiring contribution in this case.

4. **Indemnity.** Indemnity is an equitable remedy to prevent unjust enrichment. Whereas contribution involves wrongdoers who are jointly and severally liable and requires each to pay a proportionate share of the judgment, indemnity involves wrongdoers who have unequal degrees of responsibility and requires the one primarily liable to bear the entire burden and compensate the one secondarily liable who was initially compelled to compensate the plaintiff.

contribution v. indemnity

5. **Contribution After Other Party Has Settled--Slocum v. Donahue,** 693 N.E.2d 179 (Mass. App. Ct. 1998).

Slocum v. Donahue

a. **Facts.** As Donahue (D) backed out of his driveway, his car's engine began to race and the car accelerated across the street, hit a fence, and killed the 18-month-old son of the Slocums (Ps). D claimed that he inadvertently pushed the floor mat under the throttle, which allowed it to interfere with the power brakes so that they would not work even when D pressed the brake pedal repeatedly during the incident. D also admitted that, prior to the accident, he had been drinking from a bottle of vodka he kept in the car. D pleaded guilty to motor vehicle homicide. Ps sued D for civil damages. D filed a third-party complaint against Ford Motor Company, the car's manufacturer, denying negligence and seeking contribution and indemnity for negligence and breach of warranty. During settlement negotiations, Ford's lawyer proposed a settlement of $300,000, including $150,000 from Ford, the $125,000 maximum under D's insurance policy, and $25,000 from D personally. D's lawyer related that D could not contribute that amount. Ford settled independently for $150,000. Ford moved for summary judgment as to D's claims on the ground that the settlement extinguished D's claims for contribution and that D had no basis for indemnity. The court granted summary judgment. D appeals.

b. **Issue.** When one defendant settles with the plaintiff, is the other defendant entitled to contribution from the settling defendant?

c. **Held.** No. Judgment affirmed.

1) The applicable state statute provides that when a release is given in good faith to one of two or more persons liable in tort for the same injury, it discharges the tortfeasor to whom it is given from all liability for contribution to any other tortfeasor. D claims that the settlement was not made in good faith and was collusive because of the amount and because Ford agreed to let Ps use its experts to prevent D from showing at trial that Ford was at fault.

2) The facts in this case support the judge's finding that the settlement was fair and reasonable. It was reasonable that D would be found liable due to his criminal conviction and his admission about drinking. A jury may not have found any liability on the part of Ford. The settlement was the amount discussed by the parties prior to trial as part of a total settlement package.

3) A settlement may be deemed collusive when it is used to remove a deep-pocket defendant as a tactical advantage because of the experts the defendant could produce. In this case, D merely speculated that Ps settled with Ford because they believed Ford was not responsible for the death. This speculation does not raise a sufficient issue to require a more in-depth hearing on the good faith issue.

4) D also sought indemnity, but contribution and indemnity are mutually exclusive remedies. The right to contribution is based on the shared fault of joint tortfeasors, but indemnity is for someone without fault to recover from the actual wrongdoer when the faultless person is held vicariously

liable for the wrongdoer's act. If the case had gone to trial and Ford had been found liable, it would have been as a result of its own negligence or breach of warranty, not for anything D did. Ford's liability would not have been vicarious. Once Ford settled, the only issue was whether D was negligent. D could claim he was not negligent and that Ford was, but D could not have been held liable for Ford's negligence. Therefore, indemnity would not have been applicable to this case.

D. APPORTIONMENT OF DAMAGES

1. **Introduction.** When two or more defendants acted to cause injury to the plaintiff, or to aggravate a preexisting injury, and the injuries are divisible, liability may be apportioned among the defendants. In such cases, the defendants are not jointly and severally liable.

2. **Burden of Proof--Bruckman v. Pena,** 487 P.2d 566 (Colo. Ct. App. 1971).

Bruckman v. Pena

   a. **Facts.** Pena (P), a passenger in a car, was injured when the car collided with Bruckman's (D's) truck. P was involved in another later accident, which aggravated the injuries received in the first collision. P sued D for damages. The trial court awarded P damages and D appeals.

   b. **Issue.** When injuries are caused by two or more separate acts of negligence and the plaintiff is unable to prove which injuries resulted from the defendant's negligence, does the defendant become liable for the entire injury?

   c. **Held.** No. Judgment reversed.

      1) P has the burden of establishing that his injuries proximately resulted from D's negligence as well as the burden of proving the injuries sustained. Tortfeasors should be liable only for injuries that result from their negligence.

3. **Indivisible Injury Shifts Burden of Proof--Michie v. Great Lakes Steel Division, National Steel Corp.,** 495 F.2d 213 (6th Cir. 1974).

Michie v. Great Lakes Steel Division, National Steel Corp.

   a. **Facts.** Michie and 36 other people (Ps) were residents of Canada. Great Lakes and several other industrial corporations (Ds) in the United States emitted pollutants into the air, which were blown onto Ps' premises. The separate effects of each pollutant could not be identified, but as a whole, the pollutants created a nuisance. Ds moved for dismissal of the complaint and the trial court denied the motion. Ds appeal.

b. **Issue.** When it is impractical to prove the damage resulting from each of several tortfeasors when each tort contributed to the injury, may the burden be shifted to the tortfeasors by holding them jointly and severally liable?

c. **Held.** Yes. Judgment affirmed as modified (modification was of punitive damage issue).

1) If some reasonable means of apportioning damages is available, joint and several liability will not be imposed. If the harm is not theoretically divisible, most jurisdictions will impose joint and several liability. If the harm is not practically divisible, Michigan law will impose joint and several liability to prevent a tortfeasor from escaping liability at the expense of an innocent plaintiff.

Dillon v. Twin State Gas & Electric Co.

4. **Damages Reduced by Other Contingency--Dillon v. Twin State Gas & Electric Co.,** 163 A. 111 (N.H. 1932).

a. **Facts.** Dillon (P) was the parent of a 14-year-old boy who, with his friends, had habitually played on a bridge over which Twin States (D) had strung electric wires. While seated on a girder, P's son lost his balance and was electrocuted when he grabbed the electric wire to keep from falling and suffering death or serious injury. P sued to recover damages for wrongful death. D appeals the denial of a motion for a directed verdict.

b. **Issue.** If, but for a negligent injury, the injured person would still have suffered other injury, may the court in awarding damages consider the other injury and its potential effects on the injured person?

c. **Held.** Yes. Denial of the motion for directed verdict affirmed.

1) To constitute actionable negligence there must be damage.

2) If, but for the wires, the boy would have fallen, then D did not deprive him of a life expectancy long enough to be given pecuniary allowance and D would only be liable for conscious suffering sustained by the shock.

3) Likewise, evidence that P's son would have been crippled by the fall should be taken into account in determining damages to earning capacity as though P had already been crippled.

4) The above issues of fact may lead to different conclusions and therefore must be tried.

VIII. DUTY OF CARE

A. PRIVITY OF CONTRACT

1. **Old English Case--Winterbottom v. Wright,** 152 Eng. Rep. 402 (1842). Winterbottom v. Wright

   a. **Facts.** Winterbottom (P), a coach driver, was injured when a coach collapsed. Wright (D) had contracted with the owner of the coach to keep the coach in repair, but failed to do so. P brings suit against D.

   b. **Issue.** May a plaintiff who is not in privity of contract sue a defendant in contract?

   c. **Held.** No. Judgment for D.

      1) There is no privity of contract between P and D. The most absurd and outrageous consequences would result if those not in privity of contract were allowed to sue in contract. There would be no limit. If a party is responsible to the public, the real ground of liability is public duty or public nuisance.

   d. **Concurrence.** If we allowed this case, there would be no point to stop. We must confine the right to recover to those who enter into the contract.

   e. **Concurrence.** D's duty to keep the coach safe arises solely from the contract. There was no duty to P.

   f. **Comment.** The privity of contract theory developed in the English courts as a shield to manufacturers and suppliers against injured users and parties other than the buyer. Unless the injured plaintiff was the buyer, no recovery could be had, either in tort or contract, no matter how negligent the seller's conduct. Modern developments distinguish between nonfeasance and misfeasance—where breach of contract constitutes misfeasance such breach may also constitute a tort. The privity limitation was abolished as to sellers of negligently made goods in *McPherson v. Buick Motor Co.,* below.

2. **Landmark Case--MacPherson v. Buick Motor Co.,** 111 N.E. 1050 (N.Y. 1916). MacPherson v. Buick Motor Co.

   a. **Facts.** MacPherson (P) purchased a Buick from a dealer, who had purchased the car from Buick Motor Company (D), the manufacturer. While P was driving the car, a wheel with defective wooden spokes collapsed and P was thrown out and injured. The wheel was not made by D, but was purchased from a subcontractor. Evidence indicated that D could have discovered the defect by reasonable inspection, which was not done. On a judgment for P, D appeals.

b. **Issue.** Is privity between the manufacturer and the plaintiff necessary for the plaintiff to be able to recover against the defendant?

c. **Held.** No. Judgment affirmed.

1) If the nature of a product is such that it is reasonably certain to place life and limb in peril when negligently made, then it is a thing of danger. If the manufacturer knows or can reasonably foresee that it will be used by persons other than the immediate purchaser (supplier) without new tests, then, irrespective of contract, the manufacturer is under a duty to make it carefully.

2) This holding can be drawn from prior cases involving poisons, explosives, and deadly weapons, which had placed a duty on the manufacturer thereof based on the fact that such products were "implements of destruction" in their normal operation.

3) The negligence of the wheel manufacturer, such as to constitute an actionable wrong with respect to users of the finished product incorporating the wheel, was a question of proximate cause and remoteness. However, in order for the wheel manufacturer's original negligence to become a cause of the danger, it was necessary for an independent cause to intervene, *i.e.,* the omission of the car manufacturer to fulfill its duty of inspection.

d. **Comment.** The rule as originally propounded by the court (Judge Cardozo) in *MacPherson* was as follows: If a reasonable person would have foreseen that the product would create a risk of harm to human life or limb if not carefully made or supplied, the manufacturer and supplier are under a duty to all foreseeable users to exercise reasonable care in the manufacture and supply of the product.

H.R. Moch Co. v. Rensselaer Water Co.

3. **Application of the *MacPherson* Rule--H.R. Moch Co. v. Rensselaer Water Co.,** 159 N.E. 896 (N.Y. 1928).

a. **Facts.** Rensselaer Water Co. (D) contracted with the city of Rensselaer to provide water for, among other purposes, service at fire hydrants. It specifically agreed to provide certain quantities of water and at a certain pressure to the fire hydrants. A fire broke out near Moch Company's (P's) warehouse. Although D was notified of the fire in a timely manner, it failed to provide either the quantity or pressure of water that it contracted to provide. The fire spread and destroyed P's warehouse. P sued for damages arguing alternative theories of breach of contract, common law tort under *MacPherson v. Buick Motor Company* or breach of a statutory duty. The trial court denied a demurrer. The appellate division reversed. P appeals.

b. **Issue.** Is a third party beneficiary able to recover for damages caused by a promisor's failure to perform its contractual obligations?

c. **Held.** No. Judgment of the appellate division affirmed.

1) Contractual liability does not exist because the parties did not originally intend that the water company should be liable to individual members of the public. Also, the water company is not an insurer and did not anticipate becoming one.

2) If D's conduct was such that inaction would normally result in working an injury, it might have owed a duty to P. But D's conduct was not such and if it were deemed to be so, it would subject such supply companies to an infinite circle of tort claimants.

3) Finally, there is no statutory basis for imposing liability.

4) Thus, D is not liable to P for failing to maintain adequate water quantity or pressure.

d. **Comment.** Possibly the real reason Cardozo decided *Rensselaer Water* as he did was out of a belief that fire insurance companies were the proper social institution for bearing the loss in such circumstances.

4. **Attorney's Liability to Nonclient--Clagett v. Dacy,** 420 A.2d 1285 (Md. Ct. Spec. App. 1980). Clagett v. Dacy

a. **Facts.** Clagett (P) was the high bidder at a foreclosure sale on two occasions but on both occasions the sale was set aside because the attorneys conducting the sale failed to follow the necessary procedures. The debtor satisfied the debt and P lost any further opportunity to buy the property. P sued the attorneys for lost profits, but the trial court dismissed the claim. P appeals.

b. **Issue.** Does a successful bidder at an auction have a cause of action against the attorneys conducting the auction when the sale is invalid because improper procedures were followed?

c. **Held.** No. Judgment affirmed.

1) In some situations, a third party beneficiary may sue an attorney just as he could sue any other tortious party. This does not allow third parties to sue attorneys on a pure negligence theory, however, unless the third party was a person intended to be benefited by the attorney's performance.

2) In determining an attorney's liability, the special limitations that attorneys work under must be considered. An attorney may not rep-

resent two parties if a conflict of interest is involved. Thus, an attorney's duty will not be presumed to flow to a third party if the effect would be tantamount to a prohibited employment.

3) Here, the attorneys were representing the debtor at the auction. It would be a conflict of interest if they were also representing P. The fees paid were to come out of the debtor's pocket, not P's. Therefore, no relationship to P may be inferred.

B. FAILURE TO ACT

1. **General Rule.** Under the general common law rule, the defendant owes no duty to go to the aid of a stranger in an emergency, at least when the defendant was in no way responsible for that person's injury or predicament. The rationale is that tort law is not concerned with purely moral obligations.

Hegel v. Langsam

2. **University's Duty to Students--Hegel v. Langsam,** 29 Ohio Misc. 147 (1971).

a. **Facts.** Hegel (P) alleged that Langsam (D) permitted P's minor child, a student at the university, to become associated with criminals, to be seduced, to become a drug user, and to absent herself from the dormitory. P sought damages for D's alleged negligence, and D moved the court for a judgment on the pleadings.

b. **Issue.** Does a university have the legal duty to regulate the private lives of its students in order to protect them from getting into difficulties?

c. **Held.** No. D's motion granted.

1) There is no requirement of the law placing on the university, or its employees, any duty to regulate the private lives of the students, to control their comings, and to supervise their associations. A university is an institution for the advancement of knowledge and learning, not a boarding school or prison. The Ohio statutes cited do not apply to the fact situation here.

3. **Moral vs. Legal Responsibility.** In *Yania v. Bigan*, 155 A.2d 343 (Pa. 1959), the defendant taunted and dared the plaintiff's husband to jump into a deep pool of water. When he did, the defendant watched him drown. The court found no legal duty to rescue or attempt the rescue of the plaintiff's husband.

a. Some authorities believe this decision is bad. The court could have found several theories under which the defendant had a duty. This case illustrates the reluctance of courts to recognize nonfeasance as a basis for liability.

b. Unless there is some legal relation imposing a duty to rescue, the law does not enforce a mere moral obligation that should be observed out of common decency or common humanity.

4. **Instrumentality Under the Control of Defendant.** When the plaintiff is injured by an instrumentality under the control of the defendant, whether through the plaintiff's own negligence or that of a third party, the defendant is obligated to take affirmative steps to effectuate rescue but is liable only for the aggravation of the plaintiff's injury when such duty is not exercised.

a. **Escalator injury--L.S. Ayers & Co. v. Hicks,** 40 N.E.2d 334 (Ind. 1942).

L.S. Ayers & Co. v. Hicks

1) **Facts.** Hicks (P), a six-year-old child, caught his fingers in L.S. Ayers & Co.'s (D's) escalator and D negligently delayed shutting down the escalator, which aggravated P's injury and caused him to lose his hand. P won at trial and D appeals.

2) **Issue.** Does a defendant have a duty to rescue when the injury is caused by an instrumentality under its own control?

3) **Held.** Yes. Judgment reversed due to improper jury instructions.

a) Although D's conduct was in the first instance innocent (*i.e.*, there is nothing negligent about operating the escalator), its failure to exercise proper care to effectuate rescue when P suffered injury by reason of the instrumentality under D's control subjected D to liability.

b) At the new trial, the jury must be instructed that D may be held liable only for injuries caused by D's negligence (the aggravation of P's injury).

b. **Comment.** Liability in this case could also have been predicated on the obligation of a shopkeeper to its invitees (*see infra*).

5. **Misfeasance and Nonfeasance.** There is a difference between acting negligently and failing to act. One who has no duty to take affirmative action, but does so anyway, may become liable if she acts negligently. To encourage people with no duty to come to the assistance of those in need, many states have Good Samaritan statutes that protect a doctor who acts reasonably in an emergency. Typically, liability turns on determining at what point the defendant began to render assistance. For example, an employer who has no obligation to give employees a physical exam may still incur liability if it provides the exam but then negligently fails to inform the employee about dangerous or

diseased conditions revealed in the exam. [Coffee v. McDonald-Douglas Corp., 503 P.2d 1366 (Cal. 1972)]

6. **Protecting Plaintiff from Acts of Third Persons.** There are three basic circumstances that may impose a duty to protect a plaintiff from acts of third parties: voluntary undertaking, control, and relationship. The care that the defendant must exercise is reasonable care under the circumstances.

   a. **Voluntary undertaking.** When a person voluntarily undertakes to protect another and the plaintiff relies upon that, the undertaking may raise a duty of care. Often this voluntary undertaking involves special knowledge. In *Crowley v. Spivey*, 329 S.E.2d 774 (S.C. 1985), the grandparents assured the father that they would supervise the children on a visit to their mother, who the grandparents knew had a history of mental disease. The mother killed the children, and the grandparents were held liable for not properly supervising them in light of their special knowledge.

   b. **Control.** Any person who stands in a position of control over the conduct of an individual has a duty to control that person's conduct so as to protect third parties, even strangers. For example, parents have a duty to control their children.

   c. **Relationship.** A defendant may have a particular relation to the plaintiff that may require that the defendant exercise care for the protection of the plaintiff. Examples of these relationships include innkeeper-guest, shopkeeper-invitee, carrier-passenger, employer-employee, teacher-pupil, etc.

J.S. and M.S. v. R.T.H.

      1) **Wife's duty to protect children from husband--J.S. and M.S. v. R.T.H.,** 714 A.2d 924 (N.J. 1998).

         a) **Facts.** R.T.H. or "John" (D), a 64-year-old man, and his wife R.G.H. or "Mary" moved next door to J.S. and M.S. (Ps). Ps had two daughters, ages 12 and 15, who spent a lot of time with D at his horse barn, riding and caring for D's horses. D began sexually abusing the girls and continued to do so for over a year. He eventually pleaded guilty to endangering the welfare of minors and was sentenced to 18 months in prison. Ps sued D for damages and added Mary as a defendant, alleging that she was negligent because she knew and/or should have known of D's propensities. Mary responded that she did not owe a duty to Ps, that any alleged negligence on her part did not proximately cause any of Ps' damages, and that Ps' damages were caused by a third party over whom she exercised no control. Mary also crossclaimed against D for contribution and indemnification. The trial court granted Mary summary judgment, but the court of appeals reversed. The New Jersey Supreme Court granted certiorari.

b) **Issue.** Does a wife who suspects or should suspect her husband of actual or prospective sexual abuse of children have a duty of care to prevent such abuse?

c) **Held.** Yes. Judgment affirmed.

(1) A variety of factors must be considered in determining whether to impose a duty of care, including: (i) the foreseeability and severity of the underlying risk of harm; (ii) the opportunity and ability to exercise care to prevent the harm; (iii) the comparative interests of and relationships between the parties; and (iv) the societal interest in recognizing the duty.

(2) Foreseeability is based on the defendant's knowledge of the risk of injury. It may be actual or constructive, where the defendant is in a position to discover the risk of harm. When the risk of harm is posed by third persons, the plaintiff may be required to prove that the defendant knew or had reason to know from past experience that there was a likelihood of conduct on the part of the third person to endanger the safety of another.

(3) A duty in tort law is imposed where the plaintiff's interests are entitled to legal protection against the defendant's conduct. Imposition of a duty thus requires a relationship between the parties that would give the defendant sufficient control, opportunity, and ability to avoid the risk of harm. Ultimately, it is a question of public policy based on fairness, common sense, and morality. The notion of duty may change over time to adjust to changing social relations.

(4) The scope of a duty is determined by the totality of the circumstances. If the defendant's actions are relatively easy to correct and the harm at stake is serious, it is fair to impose a duty.

(5) In this case, D criminally sexually assaulted neighboring adolescent children. The abuse occurred on his property, which he shared with Mary. This type of conduct is normally difficult to identify, anticipate, and predict. Yet it may be foreseeable to a wife that her husband would sexually abuse a child. Relevant factors are whether the husband had previously committed sexual offenses and the circumstances of any such abuse, whether the wife facilitated unsupervised contact between her husband and the child victims, the presence of pornographic materials in the marital home, and the extent to which the victims may have made inappropriate sexual comments in the wife's presence.

(6) Statistically, most abusers are male, most child victims are female acquaintances or relatives, and most of these sexual assaults occur in the offender's or victim's home. Thus, a wife of a sexual abuser of children is in a unique position to observe signs of sexual abuse, and she may be

the only person with the knowledge or opportunity to know that a particular person is being sexually abused by her husband.

(7) These circumstances support a standard of foreseeability based on "particular knowledge" or "special reason to know" that a particular class of plaintiffs would suffer a particular type of injury. This type of test protects a wife against a broad duty that may expose her to liability for any child whom her husband may threaten and harm.

(8) The nature of the parties' interests obviously supports a duty of care because of the strong public policy against child sexual abuse. Every citizen has a statutory duty to report abuse if they have a reasonable cause to believe it is occurring.

(9) The societal interest in enhancing marital relationships, represented by interspousal immunity, does not outweigh the societal interest in protecting children from sexual abuse. There is a compelling basis for imposing a duty on a wife whose husband poses a threat of sexually abusing young children.

(10) Accordingly, when a spouse has actual knowledge or special reason to know of the likelihood of her spouse engaging in sexually abusive behavior against a particular person or persons, the spouse has a duty of care to take reasonable steps to prevent or warn of the harm.

(11) Proximate cause can arise from a wife's failure to prevent or warn of her husband's sexual abuse or propensity for sexual abuse, when it results in the occurrence or continuation of such abuse. If in fact Mary was negligent in this case, that negligence could be found to be a proximate cause of Ps' injuries.

Tarasoff v. Regents of University of California

2) Duty to warn--Tarasoff v. Regents of University of California, 551 P.2d 334 (Cal. 1976).

a) Facts. The Tarasoffs (Ps) are the parents of a girl who was murdered by a psychiatric patient of a psychologist employed by the University of California (D). Ps alleged that the murderer confided his intent to kill their daughter to the psychologist two months before the killing and that, although the killer was briefly detained, no further action was taken to restrain him or to warn Ps. D demurred to the complaint. The trial court and lower appellate court upheld the demurrer and Ps appeal.

b) Issue. Does a therapist who determines that a patient poses a serious danger of violence to others have a duty to exercise reasonable care to protect the foreseeable victim of that danger?

c) Held. Yes. Judgment reversed.

(1) When prevention of a foreseeable harm requires the defendant to control the conduct of another person, or to warn of such conduct, the common law imposes liability only if the defendant bears some special relationship to the dangerous person or to the potential victim. D's therapist has such a relationship with the murderer.

(2) D claims that therapists cannot accurately predict violent behavior and in fact are more often wrong than right. We do not require perfection, but once the existence of a serious danger of violence is determined, or should have been determined, the therapist has a duty to exercise reasonable care to protect the foreseeable victim. If such care includes warning the victim, the therapist is liable for his failure to do so.

(3) D claims that such a warning could damage the professional relationship and the patient. Weighing this uncertain damage against the peril to the victim's life compels the conclusion that inaccuracy in predicting violence cannot negate the therapist's duty to protect the threatened victim. The containment of such risk lies in the public interest.

C. PURE ECONOMIC LOSS

1. **Physical Damage Rule--State of Louisiana *ex rel.* Guste v. M/V Testbank,** 752 F.2d 1019 (5th Cir. 1985), *cert. denied*, 477 U.S. 903 (1986).

State of Louisiana *ex rel.* Guste v. M/V Testbank

a. **Facts.** The M/V Testbank (D) collided with another ship in the Mississippi River Gulf outlet. Containers of PCP aboard D were damaged and spilled overboard. The Coast Guard closed the outlet to all maritime activity for almost three weeks. Numerous parties sued D, including the State of Louisiana (P). D moved for summary judgment on all claims for economic loss not accompanied by physical damage to property. The district court granted D's motion except as to claims by fishermen, shrimpers, and others who commercially harvested food from the waters. A panel of the Fifth Circuit affirmed, and the court granted reexamination en banc.

b. **Issue.** May the defendant in an unintentional maritime tort be held liable for economic loss not accompanied by physical damage to a proprietary interest?

c. **Held.** No. Judgment affirmed.

Rule: physical damage with economic loss -

1) In *Robins Dry Dock v. Flint*, 275 U.S. 303 (1927), the Court held that a plaintiff may not recover for economic loss if the loss resulted from physical damage to property in which the plaintiff had no proprietary interest. The fact that the plaintiff was under contract to the person whose property was damaged did not make any difference. No recovery for negligent interference with contractual rights was permitted.

2) This rule has been followed since that decision. The *Robins* case was not limited to interference with contract, but provides a pragmatic limitation on the tort doctrine of foreseeability. Because under *Robins* a plaintiff connected to the damaged property through contract cannot recover, others more remotely connected may certainly not recover.

3) The physical damage rule provides a clear limit to liability. If the rule were not followed, the various plaintiffs would each bring suit and each claim would be evaluated based on remoteness from the negligent acts. While in some sense the physical damage rule may be unfair, any limitation of liability has some unfairness. The importance of having a rule of law that can be consistently applied outweighs the fairness problems.

4) P also asserts particular damages attributed to a public nuisance. Such damages may be recovered if they are sufficiently distinct from the damages suffered by the public in general, but this presents a problem as difficult as that of determining which foreseeable damages are too remote to justify recovery in negligence. Consequently, the physical damage rule applies to public nuisance cases as well.

d. **Concurrence.** Courts have limited abilities in managing disasters, and should limit adjudication to nonspeculative damages such as those involved in physical damage cases.

e. **Dissent.** The normal tort principles of proximate cause, foreseeability, and particular damage sufficiently limit liability and are manageable by the courts. The *Robins* case, contrary to the majority's characterization, actually held that those who were neither proximately nor foreseeably injured by a tortious act could not recover merely because they had a contract with the injured party. However, that rule should not bar application of traditional tort principles to cases in which they should apply.

D. MENTAL DISTURBANCE

1. **Introduction.** Mental disturbance is the negligent infliction of severe mental suffering on the plaintiff. Under the older view, some physical

impact or contact was required before the courts would allow recovery by the plaintiff. The rationale was that this gives the defendant reasonable grounds for declaring a defense and acts as a deterrent to fraudulent claims. Today, as with the tort of intentional infliction of mental distress, a majority of states have moved away from the requirement that there must be physical impact before the tort will be recognized, but most still require a threat of physical injury; *i.e.*, that the plaintiff was in the "zone of danger" from the defendant's conduct. In addition, physical injury manifestations from the emotional disturbance caused by the defendant's negligent act are still generally required for the plaintiff to be entitled to any damages.

Negligent infliction of emotional distress

2. **Physical Impact Rule Rejected--Daley v. La Croix,** 179 N.W. 2d 390 (Mich. 1970). Daley v. La Croix

   a. **Facts.** La Croix (D) negligently crashed his car into Daley's (P's) home. Although no physical impact with P resulted, P suffered substantial emotional and nervous injury as a consequence of the accident. P sued D for negligent infliction of emotional distress, an action that traditionally required proof of physical impact. Absent such proof, the court directed the verdict for D. P appeals.

   b. **Issue.** May a plaintiff recover damages for negligent infliction of emotional distress absent a showing of direct physical impact?

   c. **Held.** Yes. Judgment reversed and remanded.

      1) Recovery in such cases has generally been denied, except in extreme circumstances, such as negligent handling of corpses. However, the traditional rule is being repudiated, even in the English courts that initiated it.

      2) In view of the changed circumstances relating to the factual and scientific information now available to prove emotional injury, the rule requiring physical impact is no longer needed.

   d. **Dissent.** No-physical-impact cases should be restricted to those situations in which definite and objective physical injury occurs.

3. **Contemporaneous Observance of Event--Thing v. La Chusa,** 771 P.2d 814 (Cal. 1989). Thing v. La Chusa

   a. **Facts.** A child was injured when he was struck by an automobile driven by La Chusa (D). The child's mother (P) was nearby but neither saw nor heard the accident. P became aware of the accident when her daughter told P that her son had been struck by a car. When P arrived at the scene, she saw her bloody and unconscious child, whom she believed was dead, lying in the roadway. P sued D for negligent infliction of emotional distress that she suffered as a result of these events. The trial court granted D's motion for summary judgment. The court of appeals reversed. P appeals.

b. **Issue.** May a mother, who did not witness the accident in which an automobile struck and injured her child, recover damages from the driver for emotional distress she suffered when she arrived at the accident scene?

c. **Held.** No. Judgment reversed.

1) A plaintiff may receive damages for emotional distress caused by observing a negligently inflicted injury to a third person only if the plaintiff: (i) is closely related to the injured victim; (ii) is present at the scene of the injury-producing event at the time it occurs and is then aware that it is causing injury to the victim; and (iii) as a result suffers serious emotional distress.

2) Here, P was not present at the scene of the accident in which her son was injured, did not observe D's conduct, and was not aware that her son was being injured. Thus, she may not recover for the emotional distress she suffered when she subsequently learned of the accident and observed its consequences.

E. PRENATAL INJURIES

Today, seemingly all jurisdictions allow recovery for prenatal injuries. Medical science has advanced to the point where causation of injury to a fetus in the early stage of development can be ascertained.

1. **Stillborn Children.** The courts disagree as to whether or not the child must be born alive. Actions for wrongful death are purely statutory—there is great variance among the statutes and interpretations of the statutes.

Endresz v. Freidberg

2. **Wrongful Death--Endresz v. Freidberg,** 284 N.E.2d 901 (N.Y. 1969).

a. **Facts.** Endresz (P) delivered stillborn twins after being injured in an automobile accident that allegedly occurred as a result of Freidberg's (D's) negligence. P brought an action against D for wrongful death, which was dismissed on D's motion. P appeals.

b. **Issue.** May an action be maintained for the wrongful death of an unborn child?

c. **Held.** No. Dismissal sustained.

1) Except insofar as it is necessary to protect the unborn child's own rights, the law has never considered the fetus as having a

separate judicial existence. Since any limitation on liability would be arbitrary in nature, a tangible and concrete event such as birth would be the most acceptable and workable boundary. The damages recoverable by the parents in their own right afford ample redress for the wrong done. To allow more would punish D and result in an unmerited bounty to P.

d. **Dissent.** If no right of action is allowed, there is a wrong without a remedy. Moreover, to adopt such a rule would produce the absurd result that an unborn child who was badly injured by the tortious acts of another, but who was born alive, could recover damages, while an unborn child who was more severely injured and died as a result of the tortious act of another could recover nothing.

3. **Birth Defects.** Parents have sued when their children have been born with birth defects. The claim is usually that the child would have been better off not to have been born. The alternative to the birth is, of course, abortion. Courts have generally denied recovery by the child (wrongful life), but have permitted recovery by the parents (wrongful birth). Courts disagree on the proper measure of damages.

4. **Action for Wrongful Life--Procanik by Procanik v. Cillo,** 478 A.2d 755 (N.J. 1984). Procanik by Procanik v. Cillo

a. **Facts.** Procanik (P) was born with congenital rubella syndrome after Cillo (D), his mother's doctor, failed to diagnose that his mother had contracted German measles in the first trimester of her pregnancy. D had failed to order further tests despite indications that P's mother had contracted German measles. As a result of D's assurances that she had nothing to worry about, P's mother was deprived of the choice of terminating the pregnancy. P sought damages for his pain and suffering, for his parents' impaired capacity to cope with P's problems, and for the expenses of his health care. The lower courts dismissed the case and the New Jersey Supreme Court granted certification.

b. **Issue.** May a person obtain damages for wrongful life based on his mother's doctor's negligent failure to diagnose birth defects?

c. **Held.** Yes. Judgment affirmed in part and reversed in part.

1) In *Gleitman v. Cosgrove*, 227 A.2d 689 (N.J. 1967), the court held that a child and his parents had no cause of action against a doctor who negligently diagnosed or treated a pregnant woman for conditions that could cause birth defects. The rationale was that the doctor did not cause the birth defects, so it was impossible to compare the child's actual condition with what that condition would have been if the doctor had not been negligent. This would have required

comparison between a life with impairments and the nonexistence of life. The parents had no cause of action because of the impossibility of weighing the intangible benefits of parenthood against the injuries alleged.

2) Since 1967, the rights of pregnant women and their children have been re-evaluated. Women now have a constitutional right to an abortion. In *Berman v. Allan*, 404 A.2d 8 (N.J. 1979), the court held that parents could recover damages for the deprivation of a woman's right to choose whether to have an abortion. Still, no cause of action by the infant was permitted, nor could the parents recover the expenses of raising the child, including medical expenses.

3) The term "wrongful life" means a cause of action brought by the child afflicted with birth defects who would not have been born had the doctor properly advised or treated his mother. "Wrongful birth" is the parents' cause of action for the deprivation of the right to choose an abortion.

4) D owed a duty to P before he was born. Assuming D was negligent in treating P's mother and thereby deprived her of the choice of aborting P, it is still impossible to compare the value of even a burdened life to the value of nonexistence. P never had a choice between a healthy life and a burdened life; his only options were a handicapped life or nonexistence. Nor is it possible to accurately and fairly determine the damages claimed for diminished childhood. Thus P may not recover for pain and suffering or for a diminished childhood.

5) P's claim for special damages for medical treatment is reasonably certain. These extraordinary medical expenses are attributable to D's negligence. Parents have been permitted to recover medical expenses for birth-defective children in other cases. The fact that P's parents are barred by the statute of limitations from directly suing should not prevent P from personally recovering those expenses. Thus, P may recover special damages.

IX. OWNERS AND OCCUPIERS OF LAND

In this area, duties are divided into fairly rigid and arbitrary categories, depending on the type of landowner or occupier and the plaintiff involved. These duties are generally the result of historical precedent and often would be considered inconsistent with what reasonable persons under the same or similar circumstances would do.

A. PERSONS OUTSIDE OF THE PREMISES

The person in possession of land is required to exercise reasonable care with regard to her activities for the protection of those outside the premises.

1. **Natural Conditions.** A landowner/occupier is not liable for damages resulting from conditions on the premises arising in a state of nature.

   a. **Rural/urban distinction.** The natural conditions rule has been applied rather strictly; however, a number of cases have held that the urban landowner/occupier with trees on her premises is under a duty to inspect since the burden imposed is relatively small. And, if a rural owner knows of a dangerous tree, she is under a duty to remove it or take such other steps as may be necessary to eliminate the danger to those outside the premises.

   b. **Consideration of circumstances--Taylor v. Olsen,** 578 P.2d 779 (Or. 1978). Taylor v. Olsen

      1) **Facts.** Taylor (P) was injured when her car ran into a tree that had fallen from Olsen's (D's) property onto the road. The trial court directed a verdict for D and P appeals. There was evidence that the road was used fairly heavily and that D had been logging in the area before the accident occurred.

      2) **Issue.** Does a landowner have a duty to go beyond common methods of examining conditions on his property when the conditions could result in danger to persons outside the premises?

      3) **Held.** No. Judgment affirmed.

         a) A fact question arises when a suit depends on a landowner's attention to the condition of his roadside trees. The duty depends on the circumstances of each case, and simple distinctions such as "urban" and "rural" are not sufficient.

         b) If there had been evidence that an inspection would have disclosed the hazardous condition of the tree, it would be a jury question whether D did use reasonable care. However, there was no evidence that the condition could have been discovered by observing the tree. Nor was there evidence that cutting through the bark, which was the only way the defect could have been discovered, was a common and ordinary way to examine trees generally.

2. **Public Highways.** The public right of passage on a highway carries with it an obligation on the part of the abutting landowners to use reasonable care for the protection of those on the highway.

Salevan v. Wilmington Park, Inc.

a. **Activities--Salevan v. Wilmington Park, Inc.,** 72 A.2d 239 (Del. 1950).

1) **Facts.** Salevan (P) brought an action in damages for the personal injuries he received when struck by a baseball while walking on a street adjacent to the ballpark owned by Wilmington Park (D). D appeals from a judgment for P.

2) **Issue.** Do landowners have a duty to exercise due care in the use of their land so as not to injure passersby on public highways adjacent to their land?

3) **Held.** Yes. Judgment affirmed.

a) The nature of the game of baseball is such as to require the landowner to take reasonable precautions for the protection of the traveling public. D knew or should have known that the precautions taken initially were insufficient to protect the public using the highway. The evidence shows that two or three times in each game, baseballs went out of the park into the area in which P was passing at the time of the accident.

b. **Artificial conditions.** If the landowner/occupier creates artificial conditions on the land, he is obligated to inspect them and protect against danger to others. In *Tremblay v. Harmony Mills*, 171 N.Y. 598 (1902), the court indicated that a landowner/occupier is not liable for damage resulting from the natural flow of water from his premises. However, since the defendant had altered that flow, he was then under a duty to insure that flowage from his land would not harm his neighbor.

c. **Extent of duty.** The rule is that a person is under a legal duty to take reasonable precautions against foreseeable and unreasonable risks of harm to persons entering his land where the entry is for purposes incident to travel upon a highway abutting his property (*e.g.*, detour because road blocked) and where the risk is created by an artificial condition existing on the land. The landowner/occupier need not have notice of the hazard to be liable for public nuisance; nor need he be requested to abate the nuisance before liability will attach. The general public cannot impliedly consent to such a hazard.

B. ON THE PREMISES

1. **Trespassers.** Trespassing adults enter the land of another with no right or privilege, must take the premises as found, and are presumed to assume the risk of looking out for themselves. Thus, the general rule is that a landowner/occupier is not liable for injuries to adult trespassers caused by her failure to exercise due care, to put her land in a safe condition for them, or to carry on her activities in such a manner as not to endanger them. In most jurisdictions, the foreseeability of a trespass is deemed to create no duty on the part of the landowner/occupier. However, when the trespassers are known generally (*i.e.*, the identity or presence of the particular trespasser is not known), occur on a particular part of the property (walking path, etc.) and are tolerated, there is a tendency on the part of the courts to treat the trespasser as a licensee, requiring the landowner/occupier to warn the trespasser of, or make safe, known natural or artificial conditions or activities involving any risk of harm that he is unlikely to discover, though some courts limit the obligation of the landowner/occupier to a duty to discover and warn the trespasser of, or make safe, known artificial conditions and activities that could cause death or serious bodily injury to the trespasser. (Under this position, there is no duty with respect to natural conditions or artificial conditions presenting a risk less than death or serious bodily injury.)

   a. **General rule--Sheehan v. St. Paul & Duluth Railway Co.,** 76 F. 201 (7th Cir. 1896).

   Sheehan v. St. Paul & Duluth Railway Co.

      1) **Facts.** Sheehan (P) was walking along St. Paul & Duluth's (D's) tracks (not at a crossing) and his foot slipped between the rail and a cattle guard. P was unable to extricate his foot and a train ran over it. From a directed judgment for D, P appeals.

      2) **Issue.** Does a landowner owe a positive protective duty to unknown trespassers in unexpected locations?

      3) **Held.** No. Judgment affirmed.

         a) A railroad, or for that matter, any landowner, owes no positive duty to a trespasser to anticipate his presence. A trespasser assumes the risk of all conditions existing on the premises.

         b) Once the landowner/occupier discovers the trespasser, it must exercise reasonable care in its activities for the trespasser's safety. If the landowner has reasonable cause to believe that a trespasser is present (*e.g.*, if told by a witness), it must exercise due care—it is not essential that the landowner actually perceive the trespasser for there to be discovery.

b. **Easement holder.** Only the actual possessor of land has immunity with respect to injuries suffered by a trespasser.

c. **Adjoining landowners.** Nor does the immunity extend to adjoining landowners.

d. **Independent contractors.** There is a great division among the cases relating to independent contractors upon the land. The Restatement suggests granting independent contractors immunity only when they come on the land on behalf of the landowner.

2. **Licensees.** A licensee is one who goes on the land of another with the consent of the owner/occupier, through authority of law, or through necessity and is deemed to take the land as the occupier uses it. However, the landowner-occupier must warn the licensee of, or make safe, known natural or artificial conditions or activities involving any risk of harm which he is unlikely to discover, whether existing at the time of entry or arising thereafter. The licensee has the occupier's consent and nothing more.

Barmore v. Elmore

a. **Duty owed--Barmore v. Elmore,** 403 N.E.2d 1355 (Ill. App. Ct. 1980).

1) **Facts.** Barmore (P) and Elmore (D) were officers of a Masonic Lodge. P visited D at D's home to discuss lodge business. During the visit, D's son attacked P and stabbed him several times, despite D's attempt to restrain him. P sued D for negligently failing to protect him from the dangerous condition on D's premises, since D knew his son had a history of mental illness. The trial court directed a verdict in favor of D and P appeals.

2) **Issue.** Is a licensee entitled to less protection by the landowner than an invitee?

3) **Held.** Yes. Judgment affirmed.

a) A social guest is considered a licensee as opposed to a person who enters the owner's premises in furtherance of the owner's business. The latter is an invitee, and the owner must make his premises reasonably safe for the use of an invitee. A licensee, however, generally must take the premises as he finds them, although the owner has a duty to warn of any hidden dangers.

b) Although the transaction of business of a fraternal organization may make a person on the premises of the organization an invitee, here P entered D's house, which was not the premises of the organization. P was a social guest and therefore a licensee, not an invitee.

c) The evidence is conclusive that D did not know or have reason to know that his son would attack P. The son's history of violence was 10 years old and the son had previously had contact with P without incident. Therefore, the judgment is affirmed.

b. **Social guest.** "Invitee" is a word of art (*see infra*); it does not include all persons invited onto the premises. A social guest, though invited, is only a licensee. The fact that a guest renders some incidental service or that he was invited out of economic motives does not remove him from the status of licensee.

c. **Known danger.** The owner of premises is under a duty to warn a known licensee of known dangerous conditions that the owner cannot reasonably assume that the licensee knows or can detect through a reasonable use of his faculties, or to make such conditions safe. In *Laube v. Stevenson*, 78 A.2d 693 (Conn. 1951), the landowners were held liable for injuries sustained by the plaintiff in a fall when they did nothing to warn the plaintiff, a social guest, of a defective dark stairway that the plaintiff was going to use.

d. **Duty to inspect.** The duty of a landowner/occupier extends only to known dangerous conditions; there is no duty to inspect to discover dangerous conditions.

e. **Guest statutes.** In the absence of a "Guest Statute," most states treat a gratuitous guest in an automobile as a licensee.

3. **Invitees.** An invitee is one who goes upon the land of another with the consent of the owner/occupier for some purpose connected with the use of the premises; *e.g.*, a business or public invitee. The duty owed is coextensive with the invitation. The basis of liability is an implied promise that the premises are, or will be, safe or reasonably so. This means that the invitor is under a duty to make a reasonable inspection of the premises and discover any dangers that may exist. Thereafter, the duty owed the invitee is one of ordinary care. The limitations of responsibility of the invitor in the case of the business invitee are generally determined by specific time, length of stay, part of premises visited, etc. Until 1960, those entering under public authority were deemed mere licensees.

a. **Business invitee--Campbell v. Weathers,** 111 P.2d 72 (Kan. 1941). Campbell v. Weathers

1) **Facts.** Campbell (P) entered Weathers' (D's) lunch counter where he was a regular customer and loitered for several minutes without making any purchases. P went towards the toilet in the back part of the store and fell through an open trap door in the dark. P sued for negligence but the trial court sustained D's demurrer. P appeals.

2) **Issue.** Is a visitor to a restaurant's toilet facilities a business invitee?

3) **Held.** Yes. Judgment reversed.

a) P was a regular customer who had used the toilet previously. There was no indication that the toilet was not intended for public use.

b) The fact that P had not bought anything on this occasion is irrelevant, because he was a regular customer.

c) If P had had no intention to become a customer that day or anytime in the future, he would not be an invitee.

b. **Public invitees.** In most jurisdictions, the government owes a duty to use reasonable care to keep public premises safe for all persons who come on the property. It does not matter whether the person comes on the premises as an invitee for the intended purpose or as a licensee for an unintended purpose.

c. **Limitations on invitation.** A person remains an invitee only while in those areas or parts of the premises held open to him for the purposes for which he came.

1) **Beyond scope of invitation.** If an invitee goes outside the area of invitation, but under the consent of the owner, he becomes a licensee. If the owner does not consent, the person may become a trespasser. Of course, the owner could not endanger a customer through an intentional act or allow him to encounter a known peril.

Whelan v. Van Natta

2) **With owner's permission--Whelan v. Van Natta,** 382 S.W.2d 205 (Ky. 1964).

a) **Facts.** Whelan (P) entered Van Natta's (D's) store and bought cigarettes. He asked for a box and D told him to go in back where P could find some. While looking around the unlit storage room, P fell down a stairwell. P sued. At trial, D claimed the light in the storage room had been on earlier that day but he did not know whether it was on when P fell. The trial court found for D. P appeals.

b) **Issue.** Does an invitee become a licensee if he goes beyond the premises to which he was invited but has the owner's permission to do so?

c) **Held.** Yes. Judgment affirmed.

(1) An invitee may exceed the scope of the invitation either by the expiration of a reasonable time within which to accomplish the purpose of the invitation, or by going outside that part of the land to which the invitation extends. The area included

within the invitation depends on the purpose of the invitation.

(2) Once an invitee exceeds the invitation, he becomes a trespasser or a licensee, depending on whether the possessor consents to his activity.

(3) In this case, P clearly exceeded the scope of the invitation when he went into the storage area. He was an invitee for purposes of shopping in the store, but he went to the storage area for a different purpose. As he did so with D's permission, P became a licensee. Thus D owed him no duty to provide a safe place, other than to abstain from intentional acts endangering P or knowingly letting P encounter a hidden peril. D satisfied his duty.

d. **Invitee's knowledge of the danger--Wilk v. Georges,** 514 P.2d 877 (Or. 1973). Wilk v. Georges

1) **Facts.** Wilk (P) was injured from falling down while searching for a Christmas tree at a nursery operated by Georges (D). P brought an action for damages against D, claiming that D was negligent in failing to cover the walkway with a nonskid surface and otherwise maintain it in a safe condition. D claimed that the warning signs he erected were sufficient to satisfy his duty toward P. P appeals from a verdict for D.

2) **Issue.** If a possessor of land should anticipate that a dangerous condition will cause harm to the invitee despite the latter's knowledge, must he warn of or correct the condition, if necessary?

3) **Held.** Yes. Judgment reversed and remanded.

a) If the possessor should anticipate an unreasonable risk of harm to the invitee, notwithstanding his knowledge or warning, something more in the way of precautions may be required. The evidence shows that notwithstanding the posted signs, D should have anticipated an unreasonable risk of harm to the invitee.

4. **Persons Outside the Established Categories.**

a. **Children.** Except with respect to extrahazardous activities, such as maintaining a turntable, recognized in 1873 in *Sioux City & Pacific Railroad Co. v. Stout*, 84 U.S. 657 (1873), children were treated the same as adults until about the 1920s, when trespassing children began to be recognized as a special class. The rationale for the special classification lies in the facts that: (i) children are often incapable of protecting themselves because of their inability to perceive the risk; (ii) out of necessity the parent cannot be expected to follow the child around all day; (iii) maintaining an "attractive nuisance" is deemed undesirable; and (iv) the cost to alleviate the risk of harm is usually slight in comparison with the damages that might be suffered.

1) **Turntable doctrine.** In *Keffe v. Milwaukee & St. Paul Railway Co.*, 21 Minn. 207 (1875), a child was injured while playing on a railroad turntable. The defendant railroad company was held liable even though the child was trespassing because the turntable had attracted the child onto the land and the railroad should have had reason to believe that such a temptation would lead children into danger.

2) **Restatement rule.** Restatement (Second) of Torts, section 339, sets out the duty of a property owner with respect to artificial conditions when infant trespassers are involved. A property owner will be liable for injuries to infant trespassers from dangerous artificial conditions on his land under the following circumstances:

    a) If he knows or should know that they are likely to trespass upon the places where the dangerous condition is maintained; and

    b) If he knows or should know that the condition involves an unreasonable risk of injury to them; and

    c) If the children, because of their immaturity, do not realize the danger involved; and

    d) If the utility of maintaining the condition is slight in relation to the risk of injury to the children; and

    e) If he fails to exercise reasonable care to eliminate the danger or otherwise protect the children.

3) **Water hazard.** In *King v. Lennen*, 348 P.2d 98 (Cal. 1959), all of the above criteria were met when the plaintiff's one and one-half year old son drowned in the defendant's pool near which children often played. The case illustrates that California has purged itself of some of the rigid categories formerly applied to infant trespassers. One can no longer posit any fixed rules in this area—courts generally apply the principles of the Restatement to the facts.

4) **Comment.** Contributory negligence on the part of the parent has not been held a bar to recovery.

b. **Privilege to enter without consent.**

1) **"Public entrants" defined.** This refers to any public employee entering the land under a privilege recognized by law, and irrespective of any ex-

press or implied consent from the land occupier; *i.e.*, someone whose entry the land occupier has no right to prevent. This includes firefighters, police officers, sanitation inspectors, mail carriers, meter readers, tax assessors, etc.—as long as they are acting in the scope of their official duties.

2) **Duty owed depends on reason for entry.**

a) If they enter for some purpose involving business dealings with the land occupier (entrants such as mail carriers, garbage collectors, meter readers, sanitation inspectors, tax assessors, etc.), they are owed the same duties as invitees.

b) However, if the entry is not for a business visit with the land occupier, but under some other privilege afforded by law, such as entry by police to chase a burglar, most courts hold that the public entrant is entitled only to the status of a licensee. [Restatement (Second) of Torts, §345] A few consider the entrant an invitee.

5. **Rejection of Common Law Categories--Rowland v. Christian,** 443 P.2d 561 (Cal. 1968). Rowland v. Christian

a. **Facts.** Rowland (P), a social guest in Christian's (D's) apartment, was injured when a cracked water faucet handle in D's bathroom broke in P's hand, causing severe injuries. D knew the handle was cracked and had asked the landlord to repair it, but she did not warn P of the condition of the handle. P sued to recover for the injury and appealed the trial judge's granting of D's motion for summary judgment.

b. **Issue.** If the occupier of land is aware of a concealed condition that presents an unreasonable risk of harm to others, is the land occupier's failure to warn or to repair the condition negligence?

c. **Held.** Yes. Judgment for D reversed.

1) In the past, the common law divided a landowner's visitors into three categories: (i) invitees-business guests; (ii) licensees-social guests; and (iii) trespassers.

2) While the landowner owed a duty of ordinary care to invitees, licensees and trespassers were obliged to take the premises as they found them. This exception to the rule of liability for negligence grew out of the high place that land has held in English and American law and is no longer justifiable.

3) Applying negligence liability equally regardless of the visitor's status will eliminate complexity and confusion in the law.

4) A person's life or limb is not less worthy of protection because he has come upon the land of another without a business purpose or without permission.

5) The basic policy set forth by the legislature is that everyone is responsible for an injury caused to another by his want of ordinary care. We adhere to it.

d. Dissent. The judgment should be sustained.

1) The majority opinion allows for decisions on a case-by-case basis bereft of the guiding principles and precedent of tort law.

2) This sweeping modification falls within the domain of the legislature.

3) Social guests ought to take the premises as they find them.

e. Comment. This case has met with complete acceptance in some states, partial acceptance in others, and rejection in most states. Under *Rowland*, the same duty is owed to trespassers as to invitees. This aspect of the case is the most troublesome.

C. LANDLORD AND TENANT

1. Duty Owed by Landlord to Persons Outside the Land.

a. The landlord has a duty to repair or warn the tenant of known dangerous artificial conditions or of conditions that may become dangerous.

b. This duty continues only until the tenant has a reasonable opportunity to discover the condition and remedy it. But if the landlord actively concealed the danger, the duty continues until the tenant actually discovers and has time to remedy it.

c. No duty is owed with respect to dangers arising after the property is leased unless the landlord covenants to repair or voluntarily undertakes to do so.

2. Duty Owed by Landlord to the Lessee.

a. The landlord has a duty to repair or warn of known latent dangerous conditions. If the condition is reasonably apparent, no duty is owed.

b. No duty is owed with respect to conditions arising after the property is leased except that the landlord is liable for his negligent repairs, and modern cases hold the landlord liable in tort for failure to make repairs covenanted in the lease.

3. **Landlord's Knowledge of Defective Condition--Borders v. Roseberry,** 532 P.2d 1366 (Kan. 1975).

Borders v. Roseberry

a. **Facts.** As a result of a condition known to Roseberry (D), the landlord, water dripped from the roof of a house leased from D, and froze on the steps below, causing Borders (P), a social guest of the tenant, to slip and fall. P sought damages from D, but the trial court concluded as a matter of law that D had no duty to any social guest to make such repairs. P appeals.

b. **Issue.** Is a lessor liable to social guests for injuries resulting from a defective condition on the leased premises where the lessee has had sufficient opportunity to discover and remedy the dangerous condition?

c. **Held.** No. Judgment sustained.

1) As a general rule there is no liability upon the landlord, either to the tenant or to others entering the land, for defective conditions existing at the time of the lease. The pertinent exceptions to this rule do not apply in the instant case because D did not contract to keep the premises in repair, and the lessee was fully aware that D had made the repair negligently.

d. **Comment.** The Restatement (Second) of Torts, section 358, indicates that for a landlord to be held liable for a dangerous condition existing at the time the tenant takes possession, the landlord must have knowledge of a danger and reason to expect that the tenant will not discover it, and the tenant must have no knowledge of the danger. However, the landlord's knowledge need not be actual. It is sufficient that he has reason to know of the danger and that it presents an unreasonable risk of physical harm to persons on the premises.

4. **Rejection of Contract Theory and Privity Requirement.** Because the lease is deemed a contract, breach of a repair covenant was the traditional theory that supported landlord liability. This theory excluded from the category of potential plaintiffs any persons who could not show that they were in privity with the landlord. Modern courts have adopted tort theories of liability and have abandoned the privity requirements.

a. **Duty to tenant's invitees--Pagelsdorf v. Safeco Insurance Co. of America,** 284 N.W.2d 55 (Wis. 1979).

Pagelsdorf v. Safeco Insurance Co. of America

1) **Facts.** Pagelsdorf (P) was helping an apartment dweller move her furniture. P leaned against a railing on a second story balcony and fell when the railing collapsed. The railing was rotted. P sued the landlord. The trial court instructed the jury that P was a licensee of the landlord and the jury found that the landlord had no knowledge

of the dangerous condition. The complaint was dismissed and P appeals.

2) **Issue.** Does a landlord have a duty to exercise ordinary care toward his tenant's invitees?

3) **Held.** Yes. Judgment reversed.

a) The distinction between the different duties owed by an occupier of land to licensees and to invitees has been previously abolished. Traditionally, however, a landlord has not been liable for injuries to his tenants and their guests because a lease was considered a conveyance of property and, therefore, control and possession passed to the tenant.

b) The modern lease is treated as a contract rather than a conveyance. Since the distinction between licensees and invitees has been abolished, and landlords have a contractual duty to keep the premises in good repair, it follows that landlords have a duty to exercise ordinary care toward their tenants or anyone on the premises with the tenants' consent.

c) At trial, the jury will consider whether the landlord exercised ordinary care in maintaining the premises under the circumstances.

5. **Common Passageways.** A landlord may be liable to a tenant or third persons other than trespassers for failure to maintain those portions of the premises over which he retains control. This is known as the "common passageways" doctrine. Anything that is not rented out to anyone in particular and is used in common by all tenants is considered within the landlord's control.

Kline v. 1500 Massachusetts Ave. Apartment Corp.

a. **An apartment stairway--Kline v. 1500 Massachusetts Ave. Apartment Corp.,** 439 F.2d 477 (D.C. Cir. 1970).

1) **Facts.** Kline (P), a lessee of the Apartment Corp. (D), sustained serious injuries when she was criminally assaulted and robbed while in the common hallway of a large, unguarded office-apartment owned by D. P brought an action against D for personal injuries and the court dismissed her complaint. P appeals.

2) **Issue.** Should a duty be placed on a landlord to take steps to protect tenants from foreseeable criminal acts committed by third parties?

3) **Held.** Yes. Judgment reversed and remanded.

a) The general rule that exonerates a third party from protecting another from criminal attack has no applicability to the landlord-tenant relationship in multiple dwelling houses. Since the landlord is the only one in the position to take the necessary acts of protection required, while not an insurer, he is obligated to minimize the risks to his tenants.

b) In view of the applicable standard of care, it is clear that D is liable to P. Here the risk of criminal assault and robbery on any tenant was clearly predictable, a risk of which D has specific notice, which became a reality with increasing frequency, and which materialized on the very premises under D's control.

c) Although this duty must be applied regardless of the expense to the landlord, he is justified in passing on the cost of increased protective measures to his tenants.

X. DAMAGES

Damages is the sum of money that may be recovered in the courts by a plaintiff who has suffered damage (*i.e.*, loss, detriment, or injury), whether to person, property, or rights through the conduct of the defendant.

A. THREE KINDS OF DAMAGES

1. **Nominal Damages.** Nominal damages are a small sum of money awarded to the plaintiff for a technical invasion of his rights (*i.e.*, no substantial loss or injury), in order to make the judgment a matter of record so that prescriptive rights can be avoided and to cover at least part of the costs of bringing the action.

2. **Compensatory Damages.** Compensatory damages are the sum of money deemed the equivalent of the full loss or harm suffered by the plaintiff (*i.e.*, to compensate him for the wrong suffered).

3. **Punitive (Exemplary) Damages.** Punitive damages are the sum of money over and above what will compensate the plaintiff fully for the loss suffered. The purpose of punitive damages is to punish the defendant and to make an example of her to others in instances when her conduct is of an aggravated nature (*e.g.*, intent to injure, willful and wanton conduct, or gross disregard of the consequences).

B. PERSONAL INJURIES

1. **Introduction.** If the plaintiff suffers personal injuries, he is entitled to recover a sum that will fairly and adequately compensate him for all injuries that are the direct and proximate result of the defendant's conduct. This can include, among other things, the following: physical and mental pain and future suffering; loss of earnings and future loss of earnings; and reasonable expenses incurred in treatment of the injury, including doctor, hospital, and nursing care expenses. Of course, the damages that the plaintiff is expected to suffer in the future must be proved with reasonable certainty.

   a. **Future pain and suffering.** It is up to the jury to estimate future pain and suffering, and the amount that will compensate the plaintiff. Often, counsel for the plaintiff will use a "per diem" argument such as "the plaintiff's pain and suffering should be compensated at the rate of one penny per second" because small amounts seem rather trivial to the jury. However, arguing damages on a unit of time basis has been prohibited by a minority of courts because it tends to deceive the unwary. (In the example, one penny per second equals $315,536 per year.)

b. **Mortality and annuity tables.** Mortality and annuity tables are admissible in a case involving permanent injuries that affect future earning capacity.

c. **Collateral benefits rule.** If hospital and medical services are furnished gratuitously to the plaintiff, he may still recover the value of those services from the defendant. Furthermore, compensation received from an accident insurance policy does not reduce the damages recoverable from the defendant.

d. **Court review of jury awards.** The trial court has the power to set aside a verdict on the ground that it is either excessive or inadequate because it is not sustained by the evidence. To avoid the expense of a new trial, when the jury brings in an excessive verdict, the court may grant the defendant's motion for a new trial only if the plaintiff refuses to accept a lesser amount.

e. **Income tax.** A plaintiff's award for personal injuries is not taxable, including punitive damages (except in libel and slander suits).

f. **Interest.** The courts normally do not require payment of interest on a judgment for monetary damages for personal injury until the judgment is actually entered. This has the effect of discouraging early settlements by defendants. Several states have prejudgment interest statutes that require calculation of interest on the award from a specified date (*e.g.*, when the suit was filed).

2. **Remittitur Denied--Anderson v. Sears, Roebuck & Co.,** 377 F. Supp. 136 (E.D. La. 1974). Anderson v. Sears, Roebuck & Co.

a. **Facts.** Anderson (P), her husband, and her daughter were all injured when their house burned down. The fire started when a heater that Sears (D) had negligently manufactured malfunctioned. The jury awarded P $250,000, her husband $23,000 and her daughter $2 million in damages and D moved for a remittitur.

b. **Issue.** If a damage award is tremendously large, but does not exceed the maximum that the jury could reasonably find, should a motion for remittitur be granted?

c. **Held.** No. Motion for remittitur denied.

1) The court's task is to scrutinize all of the evidence in order to ascertain what amount would be the maximum the jury could have reasonably awarded. In this case there are five cardinal elements of damages: (i) past physical and mental pain; (ii) future physical and mental pain; (iii) future medical expenses; (iv) loss of earning capacity; and (v) permanent disability and disfigurement.

2) Considering the gravity of P's daughter's injuries, the tremendous amount of suffering that she has undergone and that she will yet undergo, and the complete loss of earning capacity that has resulted, the jury's award is well within the periphery established by the maximum award test. The infant girl was burned over 40% of her body; her scarring required multiple surgeries and hinders the movement of her arms, hands, and legs.

Richardson v. Chapman

3. **Remittitur in Interest of Fairness--Richardson v. Chapman,** 676 N.E.2d 621 (Ill. 1997).

a. **Facts.** Richardson (P), a 23-year-old flight attendant, was driving a car with McGregor, another flight attendant who was 22 years old, as a passenger. Chapman (D) drove a semi-trailer and hit P's car from behind as P was stopped at a traffic light. The collision fractured P's spine and made her quadriplegic, retaining only limited functions in her arms. She also had several facial scars that could not be repaired. She would require extensive living assistance for the rest of her life. McGregor suffered minor injuries. P and McGregor sued for damages. At trial, the judge directed a verdict in favor of the plaintiffs on the question of liability. The jury granted P over $22 million and McGregor over $100,000, of which $100,000 was for pain and suffering. P's damages included $258,814 for past medical care; $11 million for future medical care; $900,000 for past and future lost earnings; $3.5 million for disability; $2.1 million for disfigurement; and $4.6 million for pain and suffering. P's expert testified that her future medical expenses would fall between $7.4 and $9.6 million. The court of appeals upheld the amount of damages. D appeals, claiming the award was excessive.

b. **Issue.** May a court modify a damage award for unspecified future expenses in the interests of fairness?

c. **Held.** Yes. Judgment reversed in part and remanded for a new trial unless the plaintiffs consent to a partial remittitur.

1) P's expert gave an upper and lower range for his damage estimates, based on two different assumptions regarding inflation. This was a reasonable approach.

2) D claims that the jury could not properly award P more damages for future medical treatment than her own expert testified to. P notes that there were several items listed in the future medical expenses that did not have assigned values attached, so the jury could add these to the award. However, the additions totaled $1.5 million. While there may be higher increases in some medical costs, most of P's care involves personal services that are expected to increase at nor-

mal rates. Hence, it is appropriate to reduce by $1 million the $1.5 million awarded in excess of the highest estimate in the record.

3) D also claims that some of the remainder of the award damages is duplicative or excessive or lacks support in the record. Reviewing courts must defer to jury determinations about the facts, including damage awards. These awards do not shock the conscience of the court, nor do they lack support in the evidence.

4) D claims that awarding McGregor $100,000 for pain and suffering was excessive. The record shows that she was not seriously injured in the accident and incurred only a laceration on her forehead that was treated the same day. She did miss two weeks of work and testified that she continues to suffer from nightmares. A more appropriate figure for pain and suffering would be $50,000.

d. **Concurrence and dissent.** The court should not order remittitur in this case. There is no medical treatment that can repair the damage to P's spine. She needs daily assistance, including for emptying her bladder and bowel. She has lost the use of her legs, fingers, and the fine muscles of her hand, and her chest and abdomen are paralyzed. She is subject to risk of serous infections and may expect to be hospitalized on a regular basis for the balance of her life. P's expert testified that using a different calculation, P's future care could cost $12.1 million. The upper estimate did not include hospital admissions for emergencies and complications. The majority has applied an arbitrary limit on the jury's ability to assess the evidence. The jury's award for lost future wages was $1.265 million less than the highest estimate. The majority also should not reduce McGregor's damage award because her injury took six months to heal and she has ongoing trauma. There is no good reason to arbitrarily reduce that award.

4. **Collateral Source Rule--Montgomery Ward & Co., Inc. v. Anderson,** 976 S.W.2d 382 (Ark. 1998).

Montgomery Ward & Co. v. Anderson

a. **Facts.** Anderson (P) was badly injured in a fall while she was shopping at Montgomery Ward & Co., Inc. (D). D's personnel sent P to a hospital for treatment. P had surgery and other care that cost over $24,000. P sued for damages. D filed a motion in limine to limit P's proof of the amount of damages to the actual amount for which she would be responsible to pay. The hospital had agreed to reduce P's bill by 50%, but P asserted that the collateral source rule prohibited D from introducing evidence of the discount. The trial court agreed with P. D appeals.

b. **Issue.** Is the forgiveness of a debt for medical services a collateral source that is covered by the collateral source rule?

c. **Held.** Yes. Judgment affirmed.

1) The collateral source rule applies unless the evidence of the benefits from the collateral source is relevant for a purpose other than the mitigation of damages. Recoveries from collateral sources such as private insurance or government benefits do not intend to benefit the tortfeasor, even though the injured party may end up with a double recovery for the same damage.

2) The collateral source doctrine has been criticized by commentators as being inconsistent with the modern compensatory goal of tort law. However, public policy still favors having the claimant benefit from the collateral source rather than the tortfeasor, for whom it would be a total windfall. Here, for example, D had nothing to do with P getting the discount from the hospital.

3) As exceptions to the rule, evidence of a collateral source may be used (i) to rebut a plaintiff's testimony that financial necessity required an early return to work or incomplete medical care; (ii) to show that the plaintiff had attributed her condition to another cause such as sickness; (iii) to impeach the plaintiff's testimony that she had paid her own medical expenses; and (iv) to show that the plaintiff had actually continued to work instead of being out of work as claimed. It may also apply when the plaintiff opens the door to her financial condition. This case does not fit any of these exceptions.

4) A tortfeasor is responsible for compensating for all the harm that it causes, not merely the net loss suffered by the injured party. The Restatement uses the example of a doctor who does not charge for medical services. Other jurisdictions have held that gratuitous medical services may not be an item for recovery, but this is not the better approach.

Zimmerman v. Ausland

5. **Avoidable Consequences--Zimmerman v. Ausland,** 513 P.2d 1167 (Or. 1973).

a. **Facts.** Ausland (D) negligently caused an automobile accident in which Zimmerman's (P's) knee suffered a torn cartilage. P's damage award of $7,500 was partially based on the jury's conclusion that P has suffered permanent injury. Medical testimony submitted by D asserted that P's condition could be corrected by surgery. D appeals.

b. **Issue.** May an injured party recover damages for permanent injury even though surgery could correct the condition?

c. **Held.** Yes. Judgment affirmed.

1) It is well established that a plaintiff cannot claim damages for permanent injury if the permanency of the injury could have been avoided by submitting to medical treatment, when a reasonable person would do so under the circumstances. However, if a reasonable person might decline to proceed with a particular surgery, the plaintiff's failure to submit to the surgery does not prevent recovery of full damages. Relevant factors include the risks of the procedure, the probability of success, the money and effort involved, and even the accompanying pain.

2) If the facts involved in deciding such an issue are not so clear and convincing as to be ruled on by the court as a matter of law, they must be submitted to the jury for a finding of fact. The verdict of the jury was supported by substantial evidence and should not be disturbed.

C. PHYSICAL HARM TO PROPERTY

Damages for physical harm to property are measured by the property's fair market value at the time and place of its destruction or conversion. If the property is not wholly lost, the difference in value before and after the tort is the measure of damages. Temporary deprivation of use allows the possessor to recover the fair rental value. In some situations, consequential damages are allowed.

D. PUNITIVE DAMAGES

1. **Introduction.** Because punitive damages are intended to punish the defendant and make an example of him, they may be allowed in a suit for battery, where the defendant intends to injure the plaintiff. They may be allowed in certain cases for defamation, malicious prosecution, misrepresentation, and products liability cases. Punitive damages are not allowed for negligent conduct, although some states permit such damages when the defendant has engaged in reckless conduct, such as drunk driving.

2. **Purpose of Punitive Damages--Gryc v. Dayton-Hudson Corp.,** 297 N.W.2d 727 (Minn. 1980).

Gryc v. Dayton-Hudson Corp.

   a. **Facts.** Dayton-Hudson Corp. (D) had at one time manufactured children's pajamas made of "flannelette," a material that met the minimum federal standards of product flammability but was still highly flammable and could have easily been made less dangerous. Gryc (P), a four-year-old, was wearing flannelette pajamas made by D when she reached across a stove to stop a timer and the pajamas burst into flames and badly burned P. P sued for damages. The jury awarded $750,000 compensatory and $1million punitive damages. D appeals.

b. **Issue.** May a corporation be held liable for punitive damages for injuries caused by a product it no longer produces?

c. **Held.** Yes. Judgment affirmed.

1) The jury was given several factors to consider in determining whether D had acted in willful or reckless disregard of P's rights, including the magnitude of the danger, the cost of reducing the danger, D's awareness of the danger, and the time that had elapsed since manufacture of the product. The evidence supports the jury's verdict.

2) D claims that since there is a potential for future suits, it may be subject to severe economic hardship if punitive damages are awarded. However, D is protected because its wealth is a factor considered by the jury.

3) D also argues that since it no longer makes the product, no deterrent is needed, and that compensatory damages and adverse publicity are sufficient deterrents. However, the deterrent effect is prospective, and the alternative deterrents D points out did not deter it in the past.

4) Another reason why punitive damages are awarded is to punish past misconduct. For this reason, the fact that D no longer makes the product does not require that punitive damages be disallowed.

BMW of North America, Inc. v. Gore

3. **Constitutional Limitations on Punitive Damages--BMW of North America, Inc. v. Gore,** 517 U.S. 559 (1996).

a. **Facts.** Gore (P) purchased a BMW sports sedan from a dealer in Alabama for over $40,000. He drove the car for nine months before taking it to an independent dealer to have it customized. This dealer found evidence that P's car had been repainted. P sued BMW of North America, Inc. (D), seeking $500,000 in compensatory and punitive damages. At trial D, admitted that it had a nationwide policy of repairing cars damaged during manufacturing or transportation and not disclosing the repair if the damage was less than three percent of the car's suggested retail price. If the damage was more than that, the car would be put into company service for a time before being sold as used. The cost of repainting P's car was $601, which was less than the three percent threshold, so D did not notify the dealer or P that the car had been repaired. P claimed that his actual damages were $4,000, representing the decrease in value for a car that had been damaged and repaired. On the issue of punitive damages, P showed that D had sold 983 refinished cars as new, including 14 in Alabama. P claimed punitive damages of $4 million, representing the $4,000 times the nearly 1,000 cars sold. D responded that it had no obligation to disclose repairs of minor damage and that the repair did not affect the value of P's car. D also claimed that transactions outside Alabama were irrelevant. The jury found for P and awarded $4 million in punitive damages on the ground that the nondisclosure policy constituted "gross, oppressive or malicious" fraud. The trial court refused to set aside the punitive damages award. The Alabama Supreme Court held that the award did not exceed the constitutionally permissible amount. It did hold that the jury should not have considered the sales in other jurisdictions. That court ordered a remittitur to $2 million. D appeals.

b. **Issue.** Is a $2 million punitive damages award unconstitutionally excessive where the plaintiff's actual damages are only $4,000?

c. **Held.** Yes. Judgment reversed.

1) Punitive damages are appropriate for furthering a state's legitimate interests in punishing unlawful conduct and deterring its repetition. Most states give the jury flexibility in determining the level of punitive damages in a particular case, requiring that the damages awarded be reasonably necessary to vindicate the state's legitimate interests in punishment and deterrence. However, an award that is grossly excessive is arbitrary and in violation of the Due Process Clause of the Fourteenth Amendment.

2) Federal courts that review punitive damages awards must first identify the state interests that the award is designed to serve. States clearly may protect their citizens by prohibiting deceptive trade practices. They may require vehicle distributors to disclose presale repairs that affect the value of a new car. In fact, most states have done so, although the rules vary considerably from state to state.

3) The sovereignty of each state prevents one state from imposing economic sanctions on violators of its own laws with the intent of changing the tortfeasors' lawful conduct in other states. In this case, the Alabama courts may require D to comply with Alabama law, but they cannot punish D for conduct that was lawful where it occurred. Therefore, the Alabama Supreme Court properly limited the punitive damages award to conduct that occurred within Alabama.

4) However, a person is entitled to fair notice not only of the conduct that will subject him to punishment, but also of the severity of the penalty that a state may impose. Three guideposts should be followed in assessing whether a particular award is grossly excessive.

5) The degree of reprehensibility of the defendant's conduct is the first guidepost. In this case, none of the aggravating factors associated with par-

ticularly reprehensible conduct was present. The harm P suffered was purely economic; the repairs had no effect on the car's performance or safety features. D had no indifference to or reckless disregard for the health and safety of others. Other states required disclosure of repairs only if they cost in excess of three percent of the suggested retail price, which could reasonably have been interpreted by D to be a safe harbor. There was no evidence that D persisted in the course of conduct once it had been found unlawful. For these reasons, D's conduct was not sufficiently reprehensible to warrant imposition of the $2 million exemplary damages award.

6) The second guidepost is the ratio between the punitive damages award and the actual harm inflicted on the plaintiff. In *TXO Production Corp. v. Aliance Resources Corp.*, 509 U.S. 443 (1993), the Court upheld a $10 million punitive damages award where the actual harm likely to result form the defendant's conduct was over $1 million. In this case, the punitive damages were 500 times the amount of the actual harm, which again is clearly excessive.

7) The third guidepost is a comparison to civil or criminal penalties that could be imposed for comparable misconduct. Alabama authorizes a civil penalty of $2,000 for violation of its Deceptive Trade Practices Act, although other states allow as much as $10,000 in fines. Thus, D had no notice that a violation such as this would subject it to a multimillion dollar penalty.

8) There is no bright line rule for defining the constitutional limits for a punitive damages award, but in this case, it is clear that the award of $2 million in punitive damages was grossly excessive.

d. **Comment.** On remand, P accepted punitive damages of $50,000 as ordered by the Alabama Supreme Court. Some state legislatures have limited punitive damages. For example, Virginia limits total punitive damages to $350,000. New Hampshire only allows punitive damages if specifically provided for by statute.

Price v. Hartford Accident and Indemnity Co.

4. **Insurance--Price v. Hartford Accident and Indemnity Co.,** 502 P.2d 522 (Ariz. 1972).

a. **Facts.** Price (P) purchased an insurance policy from Hartford (D), which promised to pay for all sums that P might become liable to pay as damages arising out of the ownership, maintenance, and use of his automobile. When P was successfully sued for compensatory and punitive damages as the result of an auto accident, D refused to indemnify P for punitive damages. P seeks a declaratory judgment that the policy includes coverage for punitive damages.

b. **Issue.** Does public policy make P's insurance contract illegal insofar as it relates to punitive damages?

c. **Held.** No. Judgment reversed and remanded.

   1) Even though a driver is insured for punitive damages, he cannot engage in wanton conduct with impunity. He would be subjected to criminal penalties, and his insurance rates would soar. The possibility that punitive damages will exceed a driver's policy limits will provide a deterrent effect.

   2) An insurance company that accepts a premium for covering all liability should honor its obligations. Since P's policy was actuarily adjusted for the possible payment of punitive damages, holding for P should not raise insurance rates generally.

XI. WRONGFUL DEATH AND SURVIVAL

A. WRONGFUL DEATH

1. **Common Law.** The common law rule was that one could not maintain an action for the wrongful death of a person. However, all jurisdictions today grant some remedy for wrongful death. Some statutes only allow for the survival of any causes of action that the deceased might have just before his death, although most statutes create a new cause of action for the benefit of the particular surviving relatives.

Moragne v. States Marine Lines, Inc.

2. **Rejection of Common Law Rule--Moragne v. States Marine Lines, Inc.,** 398 U.S. 375 (1970).

   a. **Facts.** Moragne (P) is the widow of a man who was killed while working aboard a vessel for States Marine Lines, Inc. (D). P brought a suit for wrongful death. A prior United States Supreme Court case (*The Harrisburg*) had held that maritime law does not afford a cause of action for wrongful death. On this basis, the lower courts denied P's claim. The Supreme Court granted certiorari to consider the question.

   b. **Issue.** May a cause of action for wrongful death be recognized under general maritime law?

   c. **Held.** Yes. Judgment reversed and remanded.

      1) Under English common law, no action for wrongful death was recognized. The reason was the felony-merger doctrine, under which no civil recovery was allowed for an act that was both a tort and a felony. The penalty for a felony was death and forfeiture of the felon's property to the Crown, so that there was nothing left to satisfy a civil recovery. All intentional or negligent homicide was felonious.

      2) The British rule was followed in this country, although the felony punishment here did not include forfeiture of property. As a result, damages could be obtained for injuries short of death, but not for injuries that resulted in death.

      3) Since the *Harrisburg* case, state legislatures have enacted wrongful death statutes. Congress has also done so in particular situations. The courts should recognize the public policy expressed by the legislatures, and since there are no valid judicial reasons against recovery, suits for wrongful death should be recognized under the common law.

4) The difficulty in defining the class of beneficiaries should be addressed by the lower courts. The fact that the cause of action accrues in the survivors rather than in the decedent does not make the action unmanageable.

3. **Damages.** Generally, the surviving beneficiaries can recover for loss of support, services, contribution, and other damages of a pecuniary nature; for loss of consortium (if applicable); but not for decedent's pain and suffering or the beneficiary's mental anguish. Under this rule it would seem that parents could recover nothing for the wrongful death of their child, since under the traditional "pecuniary loss" standard, they would be entitled only to the difference between the expected earnings of the child until majority less the expected expenses of raising the child. However, courts have developed different rules for the wrongful death of a child. (*See* below.)

4. **Damages for Wrongful Death of a Child--Selders v. Armentrout,** 207 N.W.2d 686 (Neb. 1973). Selders v. Armentrout

a. **Facts.** The Selders (Ps) brought an action against Armentrout (D) to recover damages for the wrongful deaths of their three minor children. Ps were awarded damages in the exact amount of medical and funeral expenses, and now appeal claiming that the amount awarded was insufficient.

b. **Issue.** In assessing damages for the wrongful death of a minor child, should the measure of damages include the loss of society, comfort, and companionship?

c. **Held.** Yes. Judgment reversed and remanded with directions.

1) To disallow the damages sought by Ps would be to stamp almost all modern children as worthless in the eyes of the law. Recovery for the loss of society, comfort, and companionship has been allowed for the wrongful death of a spouse, and there is no logical reason for treating the wrongful death of a child more restrictively. It is no more difficult for juries and courts to measure damages for the life of a child than many other abstract concepts with which they are required to deal.

d. **Dissent.** Such a verdict is a mistake because it does not reflect the policy of the legislature, makes the job of reducing excessive verdicts much more difficult, and permits a jury to translate subjective, emotional, conjectural, and sentimental values into an award of money.

B. SURVIVAL OF ACTIONS

1. **Common Law.** The common law rule was that tort actions did not survive the death of either the person injured or the tortfeasor. The

only exception to this rule recognized in the American cases was in actions for injury to personal property—here the executor or administrator could prosecute an action.

2. **Modern Survival Statutes.** Today, the common law rule has been changed extensively by survival statutes in almost all jurisdictions. Generally, death of the tortfeasor does not affect survival of the action, but under modern statutes there is usually some restriction on the actions that can be maintained upon the injured party's death. All jurisdictions allow causes of action for injury to real property and tangible personal property to survive the injured party's death; most allow causes of action for personal injury to survive; but only a small minority permit survival of actions for injury to intangible personal interests (defamation, privacy, etc.).

3. **Damages.** All damages that the decedent could have recovered had he lived are recoverable, except that punitive damages against the estate of the tortfeasor are not recoverable under the general rule, and many jurisdictions do not permit recovery for pain and suffering of the decedent.

Murphy v. Martin Oil Co.

4. **Contemporaneous Actions--Murphy v. Martin Oil Co.,** 308 N.E.2d 583 (Ill. 1974).

   a. **Facts.** Murphy (P) brought a claim against Martin Oil Co. (D), both under the state Wrongful Death Statute and the state Survival Statute, after P's husband was injured on D's premises, and died nine days later from his injuries. The second part of P's claim was dismissed in part, and both P and D appeal.

   b. **Issue.** In addition to seeking damages for wrongful death, may P also bring an action under the state Survival Statute for damages occurring in the interval between injury and death?

   c. **Held.** Yes. Judgment affirmed, insofar as it is held that an action may be maintained.

      1) The majority of jurisdictions that have considered the question now allow both actions to be brought contemporaneously. To say that there can be recovery only for the decedent's wrongful death is to provide an obviously inadequate justice, which holds the wrongdoer to answer only for a portion of the damages he has caused.

XII. DEFENSES TO NEGLIGENCE

A. PLAINTIFF'S CONDUCT

1. **Contributory Negligence.** Contributory negligence is conduct on the part of the plaintiff that contributes, as a legal cause, to the harm she has suffered, which conduct falls below the standard to which she must conform. Contributory negligence is much like negligence itself—the criteria are the same—but it involves a person's duty to exercise reasonable care for her own safety rather than the safety of others. While the formula for determining negligence and contributory negligence is the same (Learned Hand's formula), the results are not necessarily the same. The same act may be negligent when done by the defendant yet not so when done by the plaintiff. The standard of care, as in negligence, is determined by what the reasonable person would have done under the same or similar circumstances.

    a. **General Rule.** Under traditional contributory negligence rules, a plaintiff's action for negligence is barred by her own negligent conduct if such conduct was a substantial factor in bringing about her injury. Thus, its effect is to give the defendant a complete defense—*i.e.*, no liability to the defendant.

        1) **Ordinary care--Butterfield v. Forrester,** 103 Eng. Rep. 926 (1809). Butterfield v. Forrester

            a) **Facts.** Butterfield (P) was injured when he failed to use ordinary care to guide his horse around an obstruction that Forrester (D) had placed in the road. P's action for damages was dismissed, and P appeals.

            b) **Issue.** Since P failed to use ordinary care in avoiding the accident, may he still recover damages from D?

            c) **Held.** No. Judgment sustained.

                (1) Two things must concur to support this action: (i) an obstruction in the road by the fault of the defendant, and (ii) no want of ordinary care to avoid it on the part of the plaintiff. One person being at fault (here D) will not dispense with another's duty to use ordinary care.

    b. **Compare—avoidable consequence.** Contributory negligence should be distinguished from "avoidable consequence." If the plaintiff fails to act as a reasonable person to mitigate her damages, she will be barred from recovering the damages that could have been avoided. Note that this doctrine is a rule as to damages and not as to liability.

c. **Limitation to the particular risk.** The defense of contributory negligence is not available to the plaintiff if her injury did not result from a hazard with respect to which she failed to exercise reasonable care. In *Smithwick v. Hall & Upson Co.*, 21 A. 924 (Conn. 1890), the plaintiff negligently failed to heed a warning about an icy platform but was injured when a wall fell on him. Since his actions were reasonable in regard to the danger that actually caused his injury (the falling wall), the defendant was held liable.

d. **Injuries intentionally or recklessly caused.** Contributory negligence is not a defense to intentional torts, willful and wanton conduct, or reckless misconduct.

1) In *Kasanovich v. George*, 34 A.2d 523 (Pa. 1943), the plaintiff's decedent was negligently walking along streetcar tracks, yet the driver saw him a long distance away and did not slow down to avoid him, instead hitting the decedent at a speed of 30-35 mph. The court did not accept the defense of contributory negligence because the defendant's conduct exhibited a deliberate and conscious disregard of a known serious risk.

2) If the plaintiff's conduct is also reckless, courts will balance the recklessness of the plaintiff against the recklessness of the defendant to determine whether recovery should be denied.

e. **Last clear chance.** This doctrine was promulgated to ameliorate the harsh effects of contributory negligence as a complete defense. It applies when the defendant was negligent and the plaintiff, through her contributory negligence, placed herself in a position of either "helpless" or "inattentive" peril; the defendant must be aware of the plaintiff's presence or peril or, in helpless peril situations, under a duty to discover the plaintiff; and the defendant, by the exercise of due care, should have been able to recognize the plaintiff's peril and avoid injury to the plaintiff.

Davies v. Mann

1) **Origin of the doctrine--Davies v. Mann,** 152 Eng. Rep. 588 (1842).

a) **Facts.** P fettered his donkey and turned it onto a public highway. D drove his wagon into the animal and killed it. The jury found for P. D appeals.

b) **Issue.** If D could have avoided the animal, can P recover, notwithstanding any contributory negligence on his part?

c) **Held.** Yes.

(1) (Abinger) D has not denied that the animal was lawfully in the highway, but if it were otherwise, D could have avoided injuring the animal with proper care.

(2) (Parke) D was obligated to drive at a pace that would be likely to prevent mischief.

d) **Comment.** This case is the origin of the doctrine of last clear chance and reflects the reluctance courts have for denying recovery on the basis of contributory negligence. Until the adoption of comparative negligence by almost all states, the doctrine was applied everywhere in one form or another.

2. **Comparative Negligence.**

a. **Introduction.** Comparative negligence is a civil law doctrine. Those countries that have adopted the 1909 Brussels agreement follow admiralty law and therefore accept comparative negligence. However, until 1975, United States admiralty law rejected comparative law in favor of the common law practice of dividing damages equally. Today in most states there are statutes or judicial decisions providing for apportionment of damages between negligent parties who injure one another in proportion to their fault (*e.g.*, \$10,000 damages; plaintiff 30% at fault—plaintiff would be entitled to \$7,000).

b. **Adoption of comparative negligence doctrine--McIntyre v. Balentine,** 833 S.W.2d 52 (Tenn. 1992).

McIntyre v. Balentine

1) **Facts.** McIntyre (P) pulled his pickup truck onto a highway and was struck by a Peterbilt tractor-truck driven by Balentine (D). Both P and D had consumed alcohol the night of the accident and P's blood alcohol level was at .17% after the accident. Testimony at trial indicated that D was speeding before he hit P's truck. In response to P's allegation of negligence, D answered that P was contributorily negligent, partly because he was operating his truck while intoxicated. The jury found P and D equally at fault and, under Tennessee's contributory negligence rule, judgment was entered for D. P then appealed, alleging error by the trial court for refusing to instruct the jury regarding the doctrine of comparative negligence and for instructing the jury that a blood alcohol level greater than .10% creates an inference of intoxication, since this inference arises under a criminal and not a civil statute. The court of appeals affirmed, holding that comparative negligence is not the law of Tennessee and that the presumption of intoxication set forth in the criminal statute is admissible in a civil case. P appeals to the Tennessee Supreme Court, requesting that it adopt a system of comparative fault in Tennessee to replace the contributory negligence

standard and that it declare the criminal presumption of intoxication inadmissible in a civil case.

2) **Issues.**

a) Should the common law defense of contributory negligence be replaced with a system of comparative fault?

b) Is the criminal presumption of intoxication admissible in a civil case?

3) **Held.** a) Yes. b) Yes. Judgment reversed in part, affirmed in part, and remanded.

a) We hold that the common law defense of contributory negligence should be replaced with a system of comparative fault wherein a plaintiff will be allowed to recover so long as the plaintiff's negligence remains less than the defendant's negligence. In tracing the history of contributory negligence, we note that 11 states (plus Tennessee with this decision) have judicially adopted comparative fault while an additional 34 states have legislatively adopted it.

b) Making this change to a comparative fault system affects other legal principles; henceforth, the following rules will apply in Tennessee: (i) the doctrines of remote contributory negligence and last clear chance are obsolete, though circumstances formerly taken into account by those two doctrines will be addressed when assessing relative degrees of fault; (ii) in cases of multiple tortfeasors, a plaintiff may recover so long as the plaintiff's fault is less than the combined fault of all tortfeasors; (iii) the doctrine of joint and several liability is obsolete; and (iv) where a defendant alleges negligence on the part of a nonparty, the trial court must instruct the jury to assign such nonparty the percentage of the total negligence for which she is responsible.

c) We find no error in the instruction that a criminal presumption of intoxication is admissible in a civil case.

4) **Comment.** With this decision, Tennessee became part of only a small minority of states that have eliminated joint and several liability after adopting comparative negligence. The jurisdictions have split over the doctrine of last clear chance, with some retaining it after adoption of a comparative negligence system and others, like Tennessee, determining that it is no longer necessary.

c. **"Pure" vs. "partial" comparative negligence.** There are two basic types of comparative negligence formulas for assessing liability:

1) **"Pure."** A number of jurisdictions have "pure" comparative negligence, which allows the plaintiff to recover a percentage of her damages even if her own negligence exceeds that of the defendant (*e.g.*, if the jury determines that the plaintiff was 90% at fault, she can still recover 10% of her damages).

2) **"Partial."** Other states, however, recognize only "partial" comparative negligence in that they ***deny any recovery*** to a plaintiff whose own negligence ***equals or exceeds*** that of the defendant. This is the so-called "less than" or "49% limit" plan.

a) **"50% limit" plans.** Some jurisdictions turn this around and allow the plaintiff to recover if the defendant's negligence equals or exceeds the plaintiff's (the so-called "equal to or less than" or "50% limit" plans). Under this approach, if the jury finds that the plaintiff was 50% at fault, she can still recover half of her damages.

b) **Multiple defendants.** When several defendants are negligent, but are ***not jointly*** liable, some states hold that the plaintiff's negligence must be less than that of any defendant. For example, if the jury determines that two defendants acting independently were each one-third at fault, and the plaintiff was one-third at fault, no recovery would be possible. Others consider the negligence of multiple defendants in the ***aggregate***, permitting the plaintiff to recover something if her fault is less than the combined negligence of the defendants.

3. Assumption of Risk.

a. **Introduction.** The defense of assumption of risk arises when the plaintiff voluntarily encounters a known danger and by her conduct expressly or impliedly consents to take the risk of the danger. In such a case, the defendant will be relieved of responsibility for his negligence.

b. **Not negligence.** The plaintiff's voluntary assumption of risk need not be a negligent act on her part—*e.g.*, a spectator at a baseball game assumes risks of flying balls.

c. **Agreement--Winterstein v. Wilcom,** 293 A.2d 821 (Md. Ct. Spec. App. 1972). Winterstein v. Wilcom

1) **Facts.** Due to Wilcom's (D's) negligence in maintaining his racetrack, Winterstein (P) was injured when he struck debris left on the track while driving in an auto race. Prior to the race, P had signed an agreement releasing D from liability for negligence. P brought an

action for damages against D, arguing that under public policy the agreement should be invalidated. P appeals from a dismissal of his claim.

2) **Issue.** Is there any public policy justification for invalidating the agreement between P and D?

3) **Held.** No. Judgment affirmed.

a) Generally, there is no public policy in opposition to assumption of risk agreements. The facts of this case satisfy the several provisos to the general rule. The bargaining (i) was free and open; (ii) did not involve a business affected with the public interest; and (iii) did not seek a release from liability for willful, wanton, reckless, or gross actions.

b) An exculpatory provision involves the public interest if it (i) concerns a business that is commonly regulated; (ii) involves a service of some necessity to the public, such as a common carrier; (iii) is a service available to the public; and/or (iv) results in the plaintiff submitting to the tortfeasor's control. D's business of running a racetrack does not fall within the public interest category.

4) **Comment.** In addition to this list of exculpatory agreements that are not enforceable, an agreement that excludes liability for intentional torts would violate public policy. Also, any exculpatory clause must have been known to the party whose cause of action is forfeited.

d. **Knowledge required.** The plaintiff may be contributorily negligent for failing to discover danger that a reasonable person should be aware of. Yet there can be no assumption of risk if the plaintiff had no knowledge or awareness of the particular danger involved.

Rush v. Commercial Realty Co.

e. **Must be voluntary--Rush v. Commercial Realty Co.,** 145 A. 476 (N.J. 1929).

1) **Facts.** Rush (P) rented a home from Commercial Realty Co. (D). P went into the detached privy and fell through a trapdoor in the floor, which P knew to be defective. P had to be rescued by use of a ladder. The trial court refused a nonsuit and refused to direct a verdict for D. D appeals.

2) **Issue.** Did P assume the risk?

3) **Held.** No. Judgment affirmed.

a) P had no real choice in the matter—nature had called.

4) **Comment.** The plaintiff's assumption of risk must be voluntary, and if the defendant's acts leave the plaintiff with no reasonable alternatives to encountering the danger, then there is no assumption of risk.

f. **Unreasonable assumption.** On the other hand, the plaintiff's action may constitute contributory negligence if the plaintiff is unreasonable in assuming the risk of the defendant's conduct. In *Hunn v. Windsor Hotel Co.*, 193 S.E. 57 (W. Va. 1937), a lodger was injured in a passageway of the defendant's hotel, which he knew to be dangerous. Since other safe entrances were available, there was a possible issue of contributory negligence. However, what was decisive on the issue of assumption of risk was the fact that the plaintiff, by his conduct, impliedly agreed that the defendant be relieved from his responsibility to exercise due care with respect to the plaintiff.

g. **Relation between assumption of risk and comparative negligence--Blackburn v. Dorta,** 348 So. 2d 287 (Fla. 1977).

Blackburn v. Dorta

1) **Facts.** The state supreme court consolidated three cases involving the doctrine of assumption of risk.

2) **Issue.** Does the doctrine of assumption of risk act as an absolute bar to recovery after the state has adopted the rule of comparative negligence?

3) **Held.** No.

a) Assumption of risk is not a favored defense and it has been abrogated in a number of comparative negligence jurisdictions.

b) There are various categories of assumption of risk. One, express assumption of risk, is a contractual concept that is not reached in this opinion. The various types of implied assumption of risk are discussed.

(1) *Primary assumption of risk*. This is a term used to refer to situations where the defendant was not negligent either because he owed no duty or because he did not breach the duty owed. The same concept is expressed by the notion of standard of care. The latter term is preferable and consistent with state law; therefore, the term "primary assumption of risk" is meaningless.

(2) *Secondary assumption of risk*. This term has two branches. The first, labeled "pure" or "strict," bars recovery whenever the plaintiff exposes himself to a known risk, including saving a child from a burning building when the fire was negligently caused by the defendant. This principle of law has no credence in Florida. The second branch, "qualified" assumption of risk, is no different from contributory negligence.

c) Therefore, the defense of implied assumption of risk is merged into the defense of contributory negligence and the principles of comparative negligence.

B. STATUTE OF LIMITATIONS

As stated *supra*, damages is an essential element of a cause of action for negligence. Therefore, the statute of limitations does not begin to run against a negligent act until there has been some damage.

1. **Actual Damage Required.** The possibility of future damage is insufficient to state a cause of action. There is an actionable breach only when injury happens.

2. **Medical Malpractice.** This has caused problems in medical malpractice cases where the statute runs before the plaintiff discovers the injury; *e.g.*, finding a sponge or forceps in the body. Several legal fictions such as "continuing negligence" have been used to skirt this problem. Another approach is to find that the statute begins to run only after the damage is manifest and the plaintiff has or should have discovered the damage.

Teeters v. Currey

3. **Discovery Doctrine--Teeters v. Currey,** 518 S.W.2d 512 (Tenn. 1974).

   a. **Facts.** As a result of Currey's (D's) negligence in performing surgery to sterilize Teeters (P), P gave birth to a premature child, with severe complications. P brought an action for malpractice and D pleaded the statute of limitations. The court held for D and P appeals.

   b. **Issue.** Does the statute of limitations for a medical malpractice claim begin to run from the date of the injury?

   c. **Held.** No. Judgment reversed and remanded.

      1) In recognition of the harshness of the traditional rule, under which the statute begins to run from the date of the injury, the court adopts the so-called "discovery doctrine," under which the statute does not begin to run until the injury is, or should have been, discovered.

C. IMMUNITIES

An immunity is an exemption from all tort liability because of the defendant's status or relation to the plaintiff or injured party. The defendant's conduct may still be tortious but it cannot result in his liability.

1. **Inter-Family Immunities.**

   a. **Husband and wife.**

      1) **Common law.** At common law, husband and wife were considered a single legal entity; therefore, one spouse could not sue the other in tort.

2) **Modern rule.** Today, in most states, either spouse may sue the other for both torts to property and personal injury torts, rejecting the doctrine of interspousal immunity entirely. The rationale for abolition of the doctrine is two-fold:

a) The common law fiction of single identity is abolished.

b) Losses are probably covered by insurance so that allowing suit should not threaten the marriage institution.

3) **Abolition of rule--Freehe v. Freehe,** 500 P.2d 771 (Wash. 1972).

Freehe v. Freehe

a) **Facts.** P brought an action against D, his wife, after sustaining injuries due to D's negligence in maintaining a tractor, and failing to warn P of the unsafe condition thereof. The court granted D's motion for summary judgment, on the basis of interspousal tort immunity and P appeals.

b) **Issue.** Does the defense of interspousal tort immunity preclude recovery in a tort action brought by one spouse against another?

c) **Held.** No. Judgment reversed and remanded.

(1) The traditional "supposed unity" of husband and wife is no longer a valid premise for the rule. If peace and tranquility really exists between spouses, it is illogical to think that the abolition of the rule would destroy it. In other jurisdictions, where the rule has been abrogated, there has not been a problem with increased litigation. Although there is a possibility of fraud, absent express statutory provision or compelling public policy, the court should not immunize tortfeasors or deny remedy to their victims. Clearly spouses do not have an adequate alternative remedy through the criminal and divorce laws.

b. **Parent and child.**

1) **Common law.** At common law, an action could not be maintained between parent and child for personal torts. There was no immunity with regard to torts to property.

2) **Minority rule.** In a growing minority of the states, a child may recover for the willful misconduct of his parents and for parental negligence in automobile accident cases. As with the interspousal immunity doctrine, several jurisdictions have abolished the doctrine of parent-child immunity entirely.

Renko v. McLean

3) **Parent-child immunity after emancipation--Renko v. McLean,** 697 A.2d 468 (Md. 1997).

a) **Facts.** Renko (P), a 17-year-old girl, suffered serious injuries when she was riding with her mother, McLean (D), and D negligently drove into the back of another vehicle. After P turned 18, she sued D for negligence. D moved to dismiss based on parent-child immunity. P unsuccessfully asked the court to recognize an exception to the parent-child immunity doctrine where the child has been emancipated. The court granted D's motion. P appeals.

b) **Issue.** Should the parent-child tort immunity doctrine remain in effect once the injured child becomes emancipated?

c) **Held.** Yes. Judgment affirmed.

(1) The parent-child tort immunity doctrine has been followed for nearly 70 years, with the only exceptions being cruel or unusually malicious conduct by the parent and a child's action against a parent's business partner for negligence. It is a common law rule, first recognized in the United States, that serves to protect the integrity of the family unit and parental authority in the parent-child relationship.

(2) P claims that immunity should not apply once the injured child becomes an adult. A state statute does specifically give minors a right to sue for injuries sustained in minority within three years after reaching the age of majority. If this law outweighed the parent-child immunity doctrine, the threat of imminent litigation would be just as sentimental to family peace and harmony and parental authority as would be an actual suit itself.

(3) P also claims that compulsory motor vehicle liability insurance eliminates the source of potential problems that the immunity was designed to prevent. Apparently only eight states, including Maryland, have retained parent-child immunity without exception for motor torts. One rationale for eliminating the immunity is that any harm to the familial relationship was caused by the negligence itself, not potential litigation, and that access to liability insurance may help family reconciliation.

(4) The problem with relying on insurance is that the parent's insurer is faced with defending a suit that its insured has great incentives to lose. In addition, if a child recovered for pain and suffering and other noneconomic damages, the family might be unable to pay to the extent the award exceeds available insurance. These factors suggest that abrogating immunity would result in additional family discord and interference with parental discretion in raising children.

2. **Charities.** At common law, tort immunity was granted on behalf of all charitable organizations under the theory that the charity is working for the public good. This immunity has now been rejected entirely in almost all states and, where it does remain, it appears that exceptions have arisen that, practically speaking, "swallow up" the rule.

   a. **Immunity abolished--Abernathy v. Sisters of St. Mary's,** 446 S.W.2d 599 (Mo. 1969). Abernathy v. Sisters of St. Mary's

      1) **Facts.** While a patient in a hospital operated by the Sisters of St. Mary's (D), Abernathy (P) suffered injuries as a result of D's negligence. P's action for damages was dismissed on D's motion for summary judgment. P appeals.

      2) **Issue.** Should charitable institutions continue to be protected from liability for their tortious conduct by the doctrine of charitable immunity?

      3) **Held.** No. Judgment reversed and remanded.

         a) Today, charity is a large-scale operation, and should properly include the expense of liability insurance in its costs of doing business. Immunity encourages neglect and irresponsibility, while liability promotes care and caution. The defense of "implied waiver" by patients in charitable hospitals is a mere fiction that cannot be applied alike to all persons. The "trust fund" defense (that money given to charitable institutions is not for the purpose of paying liability claims) is illogical because it does not go to the real issue of whether the plaintiff has a right to maintain an action for damages against the defendant.

3. **Governmental Immunity.** The government has historically enjoyed tort immunity under the common law doctrine that "the King can do no wrong." The rationale in the United States was that whatever the State did must be lawful. Following this doctrine, it was held that not only are state and federal governments immune from tort liability, but so also are various state and federal agencies such as hospitals and schools.

   a. **State governments.** State government immunity has the same common law basis as federal immunity. The Eleventh Amendment to the United States Constitution provides that the several states cannot be sued in the federal courts by a private citizen without the states' permission. State constitutions have similar provisions with regard to such actions in state courts.

   b. **Municipal corporations.** Traditionally, municipal corporations were extended immunity as arms of the state. In response to considerable criticism, municipal corporation immunity has given way to many recognized exceptions. Some jurisdictions have abrogated this immunity entirely.

1) **Dual nature.** Municipal corporations have a dual nature. They are subdivisions of the state and act as its agent in exercising certain functions and responsibilities. They are also corporate bodies capable of the same acts as private corporations and may have local interests not shared by the state.

2) **Functions.** For those jurisdictions that retain immunity, the law distinguishes between governmental or public functions, which are immune, and proprietary or private functions, which are not immune from tort suits.

Ayala v. Philadelphia Board of Public Education

3) **Immunity abolished--Ayala v. Philadelphia Board of Public Education,** 305 A.2d 877 (Pa. 1973).

a) **Facts.** Ayala (P) was severely injured when machinery malfunctioned in D's upholstery classroom. P brought an action for damages against D, alleging that D negligently failed to maintain the machinery in proper condition and warn of its dangerous condition. D moved for a dismissal on the ground of governmental immunity and the dismissal was granted, and affirmed on appeal. P appeals.

b) **Issue.** Should the defense of governmental immunity continue to protect D from tort liability?

c) **Held.** No. Judgment reversed and remanded.

(1) The medieval maxim "the King can do no wrong" should not be applied in the modern era to exempt government entities from tort liability. The evidence does not support the assertion that the rejection of this doctrine will cause increased litigation and curtailment of government functions. The abandonment of this doctrine also includes the rejection of the confusing distinction between governmental and proprietary functions. It is better that losses due to tortious conduct should fall on the municipality rather than the injured individual.

Riss v. New York

4) **Failure to provide police protection--Riss v. New York,** 240 N.E.2d 860 (N.Y. 1968).

a) **Facts.** Riss (P) repeatedly asked the city of New York (D) to protect her from the terrorizing tactics of her rejected suitor. Finally, after several refusals by D, P was severely injured through the actions of the suitor. P brought an action for damages, which was dismissed. P appeals from an affirmance of the dismissal.

b) **Issue.** Should the doctrine of governmental immunity bar recovery for the negligent failure of a municipality to provide its citizens with adequate police protection?

c) **Held.** Yes. Dismissal affirmed.

(1) The imposition of such tort liability would be warranted only by specific legislative action. In view of the continuing increase in crime, such a rule would severely tax the resources of state and local government.

d) **Dissent.** The essence of the majority's argument, "because we owe a duty to everybody we owe it to nobody," would be dismissed as preposterous were it not hallowed by tradition. The evidence refutes the argument that financial disaster would result from the adoption of this rule. The argument of judicial interference ignores the fact that in almost every case against the state or municipality the court reviews administrative practices. To visit liability on the city would no doubt encourage the adoption of better and more considered police procedures.

5) **Assumption of rescue duty--DeLong v. Erie County,** 455 N.Y.S.2d 887 (1982).

DeLong v. Erie County

a) **Facts.** Mrs. DeLong dialed 911 on her telephone and asked that the police come to her house, 319 Victoria, right away because she heard a burglar and saw his face. The complaint writer who took the call told her the police would come right away. However, he incorrectly wrote the address as 219 Victoria, which turned out to be a nonexistent address. He also failed to ask the caller's name, determine where she called from, address the caller by name, or repeat the address, all of which are required. The police were unable to find the house, and Mrs. DeLong was savagely attacked, receiving seven knife wounds, one of which was fatal. DeLong (P), the executor of the estate, brought this action against Erie County (D), which managed the 911 number. The jury found that D was at fault and D appeals.

b) **Issue.** If the government establishes a phone number to be called by someone needing assistance, is it liable for negligent operation of the number that prevents assistance from being rendered?

c) **Held.** Yes. Judgment affirmed.

(1) D's procedures require that when an address proves incorrect, the police dispatcher is to notify the complaint writer so the recording of the call can be replayed. This was not done in this case; instead, the call was treated as a fake.

(2) There is no legal liability for a government's failure to provide police protection. However, if a relationship between the police and an individual creates a special duty, the government may incur liability. Such a duty has been recognized with respect to informers, undercover agents, and schoolchildren for whom crossing guards are provided.

(3) In this case, the creation of the 911 number, by itself, did not create a duty, but in this case, Mrs. DeLong acted on D's representation that 911 was the number to call for help. D assumed a duty toward Mrs. DeLong which required that D act with reasonable care. Because D's complaint writer acted negligently in failing to comply with established practices, liability was properly found.

(4) D claims that its conduct did not increase the risk. In fact, Mrs. DeLong was assured that help would be forthcoming, which prevented her from seeking help from another source or from leaving her house. This indicates that she relied on the response to her 911 call. If D had acted properly, the police might have been able to save her life.

4. **The United States.** The federal government and its agencies have a general tort immunity. However, under the Federal Tort Claims Act, 28 U.S.C. sections 1346, 2671 *et seq.*, the federal government, by its consent, is stripped of immunity for specified torts. The statute is strictly construed.

Deuser v. Vecera

a. **Discretionary function exemption--Deuser v. Vecera,** 139 F.3d 1190 (8th Cir. 1998).

1) **Facts.** The city of St. Louis obtained a special use permit from the Secretary of the Interior to hold a fair on the grounds of the Jefferson National Expansion Memorial, a federal park. The National Park Rangers had jurisdiction over the park. During the fair, Vecera and Bridges (Ds), National Park Rangers, arrested Deuser (P), who after grabbing women on the buttocks, urinated in public. When the city was unable to process the arrest, Ds released P in a parking lot somewhere else in the city, alone and without money or transportation. P subsequently walked onto an interstate highway and was struck and killed by a motorist. At the time of his death, P's blood alcohol level was 0.214. P's survivors sued for wrongful death under the Federal Tort Claims Act ("FTCA"). The district court found for Ds on the ground that their conduct fell within the discretionary function exception. P appeals.

2) **Issue.** May the federal government and its employees be held liable under the FTCA for conduct that falls within the discretionary function exemption from liability?

3) **Held.** No. Judgment affirmed.

a) The discretionary function exception applies when actions taken by the federal agents were discretionary and involved the use of judgment of the kind the exception was designed to protect.

b) To be discretionary, an action must involve a matter of choice. The action cannot be specifically controlled by a federal statute, regulation, or policy. The handbook governing operations of the fair in this case included guidelines for making an arrest. These guidelines are general and by their terms are not intended to substitute for the sound judgment and discretion of the officers, but were intended to provide guidance regarding the extent to which certain laws should be enforced.

c) Once Ds arrested P, there were prescribed procedures for processing, which Ds followed, including a search and handcuffing. Normally an arrestee is booked and held, but once Ds released P, the arrest was terminated so there was no reason to follow incarceration procedures. A ranger's decision to terminate an arrest would involve the same judgment and choice as would the initial decision to make the arrest. The release was therefore a discretionary function reserved to Ds' judgment.

d) Ds' conduct in releasing P also fell within the type of judgment the exception is intended to protect. Ds' duty at the fair included the protection of visitors. Removing P served the social goals of protecting the other fairgoers. The decision to release P once he was away from the fair, rather than charge him for a criminal offense, allowed Ds to return to the fair to continue their protection activity, thus furthering their primary mission. Releasing P preserved already scarce law enforcement resources. It also reflected an appropriate deference to the local police department, which declined to process P's arrest.

5. Liability of Governmental Officers.

a. **High-ranking officers.** Judges, legislators, and high-ranking members of the executive branch (*e.g.*, cabinet members and department heads) are totally immune from tort liability for acts carried out within the scope of their duties, even if they involve "malice" or "abuse of discretion."

b. **Lower-level administrative officers.** Lower-level officers or employees are immune from claims of negligence under ***federal*** law, and some states also follow this position.

c. **Common law dichotomy.** Other states retain the common law rule, which grants immunity to lower-level governmental officers or employees only when performing "discretionary"—as opposed to "ministerial"—functions.

   1) **Discretionary functions.** "Discretionary" functions are those in which the officer has some element of personal judgment or decisionmaking, such as evaluating property for assessment purposes, or designing or routing a highway. In carrying out these functions, the officer is granted immunity as long as he was acting ***honestly and in good faith***.

   2) **Ministerial functions.** "Ministerial" functions are those in which the officer is left no choice of his own; he is merely carrying out orders of others or established duties of his office; *e.g.*, repairing roads, driving vehicles. Here, there is no tort immunity. If the officer fails to perform his required duties properly, he can be held personally liable for any damages resulting therefrom, regardless of whether he was acting in good faith.

XIII. VICARIOUS LIABILITY

Under the theory of vicarious liability (*i.e.*, imputed negligence or respondeat superior), if X is negligent and if there exists a special relationship between X and Y, the negligence of X may be "imputed" or charged to Y, even though Y has had nothing to do with X's conduct and may even have tried to prevent it. The effect of "imputed negligence" may be either (i) to make Y liable to Z, who has an action against X for negligence, which negligence may be imputed to Y (*e.g.*, in master (Y)-servant (X) situations), or (ii) to bar recovery by Y against Z where X has been contributorily negligent and such contributory negligence is imputed to Y (*e.g.*, driver (X)-passenger (Y) versus other driver (Z) where both drivers are negligent and Y seeks recovery from Z, who defends on the basis of imputed contributory negligence).

A. RESPONDEAT SUPERIOR

The master will be liable for the torts of his servant that occur in the scope of the servant's employment. What type of conduct is considered within the scope of employment is a subject in itself, but as a general rule, it may be considered to be any acts done to further the purposes of the master plus reasonably expected deviations therefrom, but not including acts done while the servant is on a frolic of her own. As is apparent, "scope" is a question of fact and precedent. If the servant can be shown to be acting within the scope of her employment, the master may be held liable for both the negligent and intentional torts of the servant within such scope.

1. **Travel to Work--Lundberg v. State,** 255 N.E.2d 177 (N.Y. 1969). Lundberg v. State

   a. **Facts.** Lundberg, P's decedent, was killed in a car accident as a result of the negligent driving of a state of New York (D) employee. At the time, the employee was driving to a work project and was being paid travel expenses. P was awarded damages, and her award was affirmed on appeal. D appeals.

   b. **Issue.** Should D be held liable under respondeat superior for the injury to P's decedent?

   c. **Held.** No. Judgment reversed and suit dismissed.

      1) Under the doctrine of respondeat superior, an employer will be held liable for the negligence of his employee only if it is committed while the latter is acting within the scope of his employment.

      2) It has been established as a matter of law that D's employee was not acting within the scope of his employment, but that he was merely satisfying a desire to get to work.

3) To hold that merely by paying travel expenses, D opened itself up to liability for any tortious act committed by its employee while driving, would be to unfairly enlarge the scope of respondeat superior.

d. **Dissent.** The test for liability should be whether the travel engaged in was required in the work of the employee. The facts of the instant case show that this test has been met. The fact that D paid travel expenses indicates that it recognized that the work of its employee necessitated such travel.

Fruit v. Schreiner

2. **Enterprise Theory--Fruit v. Schreiner,** 502 P.2d 133 (Alaska 1972).

a. **Facts.** While attending an insurance convention, Fruit (D) had an auto collision, which resulted in injuries to Schreiner (P). P sued both D and his employer, Equitable Life, and was awarded a judgment in damages. This appeal, by Equitable, follows.

b. **Issue.** Since Equitable had no control over D's actions, can it be held liable under respondeat superior?

c. **Held.** Yes. Judgment affirmed.

1) Since D's negligent acts were not committed with the implied authority, acquiescence, or subsequent ratification of his employer, Equitable would not be liable under the "control" theory of respondeat superior. However, since in the context of D's actions, Equitable would have benefited, liability may be found under the "enterprise" theory of respondeat superior. Employees' acts sufficiently connected with the enterprise are in effect considered deeds of the enterprise itself. Where, through negligence, such acts cause injury to others, it is appropriate that the enterprise bear the loss incurred. A determination of whether the acts are sufficiently connected with the employer will depend on the findings of fact in each case.

B. INDEPENDENT CONTRACTOR

Subject to numerous exceptions, the prevailing view is that the employer of an independent contractor is not liable for the independent contractor's torts. The most important exceptions arise when the employer is negligent and this negligence is connected with the improper selection, control, directions, etc., from the employer to the contractor; when the employer has attempted to delegate nondelegable duties; and when the work being performed by the contractor is of a dangerous nature requiring her to take special precautions.

1. **Newspaper Carrier--Murrell v. Goertz,** 597 P.2d 1223 (Okla. 1979). Murrell v. Goertz

a. **Facts.** Murrell (P) questioned Goertz (D), her newspaper carrier, about damage caused by a newspaper thrown against her screen door. The parties argued and D struck P, causing injuries. P sued D and the newspaper, claiming that D was an agent of the newspaper. The trial court granted summary judgment for the newspaper on grounds that D was an independent contractor. P appeals.

b. **Issue.** Does the performance of services for a party under broad guidelines, by itself, make the party a principle and liable for the acts of the one performing the services?

c. **Held.** No. Judgment affirmed.

1) P argues that D's services were an important part of the newspaper's business. The newspaper controls D's boundaries and time of delivery. The paper also handles complaints from D's customers.

2) The newspaper argues that D was hired by an independent contractor to whom D is responsible. The newspaper had no control over D's hiring, nor the manner in which he performed his job. D received his pay from the independent contractor.

3) On this evidence, the only inference is that D was an independent contractor, who really had no contact with the newspaper. The standards imposed by the newspaper do not rise to the level of supervision and control necessary to make D the agent of the newspaper.

2. **Mechanic--Maloney v. Rath,** 445 P.2d 513 (Cal. 1968). Maloney v. Rath

a. **Facts.** As a result of brake failure, Rath's (D's) car collided with Maloney's (P's) auto, causing injuries to P. P brought an action for damages, and the court held for D, on the basis that the brakes failed due to a mechanic's negligence. P appeals.

b. **Issue.** Can D avoid liability by delegating the responsibility to maintain her car to an independent contractor?

c. **Held.** No. Judgment reversed.

1) Under state law, the responsibility for minimizing the risk of an improperly maintained automobile or compensating for the failure to do so properly rests with the person who owns and operates the vehicle, and cannot be delegated to an independent contractor. Thus, the fact that D's brake failure resulted from the negligence of her mechanic is no defense.

C. JOINT ENTERPRISES

In a joint enterprise, each member is considered the agent or servant of the other and the negligence of one is imputed to the others engaged in the same enterprise. Generally, there must be a sharing of expense and control and a common purpose for a joint enterprise to be found. Imputed negligence has been applied to bar one member of a joint enterprise from recovering from the defendant because another member of the joint enterprise was negligent, and probably has had more use as a defendant's doctrine than as a tool for the plaintiff.

Popejoy v. Steinle

1. **Business or Pecuniary Purpose--Popejoy v. Steinle,** 820 P.2d 545 (Wyo. 1991).

   a. **Facts.** While on a trip to purchase a calf for her daughter to raise on the family ranch, Connie Steinle's vehicle collided with a vehicle driven by Popejoy (P). Connie died as a result of the accident; P sustained injuries that were initially diagnosed as muscle strain. A year and a half after the accident, P underwent two neurosurgeries when he experienced severe pain in his neck and back. After unsuccessfully attempting to reopen Connie's closed estate, P filed a complaint against the representatives (Ds) of the estate of William Steinle, Connie's husband, who had died in the interim following Connie's death. The complaint sought to impute Connie's negligence to her husband by claiming that the Steinles were engaged in a joint enterprise at the time of the accident because they were securing an appreciable business asset for their family business. The trial court granted Ds' motion for summary judgment. P appeals.

   b. **Issue.** Did a joint venture relationship exist between a husband and wife when the wife was on a trip to purchase a calf for their daughter to raise on the family ranch?

   c. **Held.** No. Judgment affirmed.

      1) The four elements of a joint enterprise are: (i) an agreement, express or implied, among members of a group; (ii) a common purpose to be carried out by the group; (iii) a pecuniary interest in that purpose among the members; and (iv) an equal right to a voice in the direction of the enterprise that gives an equal right of control.

      2) The doctrine of joint enterprise is limited to a venture having a distinct business or pecuniary purpose. The evidence shows that the proceeds of the sale of the calf would have gone solely to the daughter and not to William. Thus, since William did not have a pecuniary or financial interest in the profits of the

sale of the calf, William and Connie were not engaged in a joint enterprise when Connie went to purchase a calf for their daughter.

D. BAILMENTS

Most courts do not impute the negligence of a bailee in suits brought by the bailor against a third party for negligence.

1. **Special Statutory Rule--Shuck v. Means,** 226 N.W.2d 285 (Minn. 1974). Shuck v. Means

   a. **Facts.** An auto leased by Hertz to Codling and driven by Means (D), who was uninsured, collided with a car in which Shuck (P) was a passenger. P brought an action for damages against Hertz under the Minnesota owner-consent statute, and was awarded damages. This appeal follows.

   b. **Issue.** May the owner of a rental car be liable for injuries caused by a collision involving one of its cars leased by one person but operated by another in violation of the rental agreement?

   c. **Held.** Yes. Judgment affirmed.

      1) The Minnesota owner-consent statute provides that "whenever any motor vehicle shall be operated . . . by any person other than the owner, with the consent of the owner, express or implied, the operator thereof shall, in case of accident, be deemed the agent of the owner of such motor vehicle in the operation thereof."

      2) The essential consent mentioned in that statute relates to the vehicle being driven, and not the driver thereof. The presence of the permittee as a passenger in an auto being driven by a subpermittee is not a necessary condition to liability of the owner. The trial court's finding that implied consent existed is justified under the aforementioned principles.

E. IMPUTED CONTRIBUTORY NEGLIGENCE

1. **Introduction.** A difficult legal situation arises when the owner of a vehicle is traveling in the vehicle as a passenger. If the driver negligently causes a collision, the injured party has an obvious cause of action against the driver. In addition, the injured party may sue the owner-passenger on the theory that the driver's negligence is imputed to the owner-passenger, who presumably has control over the driver. This theory was extended to situations in which the driver was contributorily negligent. If the third party causes the collision and injures the owner-passenger, the third party's defense that the driver's negligence contributed to the acci-

dent may be imputed to the owner-passenger. This rule had the effect of making the injured party bear all the costs of the injury. The same notion has been applied to master-servant relationships. This concept has been referred to as the "both ways" test.

Smalich v. Westfall

2. **Repudiation of Doctrine--Smalich v. Westfall,** 269 A.2d 476 (Pa. 1970).

   a. **Facts.** While riding as a passenger in her own car, which Westfall (D) was driving, Smalich was killed in a collision with another auto. Smalich's estate (P) sued D and the driver of the other car for damages. The jury found that D's negligence was a proximate cause of the accident, but the court ruled that D's contributory negligence had to be imputed to Smalich as the owner. P appeals.

   b. **Issue.** Should an injured owner-passenger be precluded from recovery because of the driver's contributory negligence?

   c. **Held.** No. Judgment reversed and remanded.

      1) A driver's negligence will not be imputed to a passenger unless the relationship between them is such that the passenger would be vicariously liable, as a defendant, for the driver's negligent acts. Only a master-servant relationship or a finding of joint enterprise will justify the imputation of contributory negligence.

      2) It is very doubtful that the driver agrees to submit to the backseat driving of the owner-passenger, except with regard to such things as destination. Such would constitute an agency relationship, not one of master-servant, and so there would be no liability.

   d. **Concurrence.** In adopting a limited "both ways" test, the majority falls short of accomplishing the needed reform in this area. The only attractiveness of the "both ways" test is logical symmetry. In the real world, a passenger can in no safe way exercise control over the vehicle in which she is traveling, even if she is the owner. Moreover, the test fails to distinguish between the application of the fiction of "control" to situations where the passenger-owner is the defendant, and those where she is the plaintiff.

XIV. STRICT LIABILITY

Strict liability is liability without fault. It is based on a policy of the law that the particular injured plaintiff must be given a right of recovery notwithstanding that there is no fault in the conduct of the defendant. However, strict liability does not mean absolute liability. There still remain problems of causation, and there are some defenses.

A. ANIMALS

1. **Trespassing.** The general rule is that the owner of animals that are likely to stray and that do stray onto the land of another is strictly liable for any damage caused by such animals. An exception to this rule was made for domestic pets.

2. **Wild Animals.** The possessor of wild animals is strictly liable for harm done by the animals if such harm results from their normally dangerous propensities. However, where animals are kept under a public duty, strict liability does not apply. Negligence must be shown, although a high degree of care will be required. In *Filburn v. People's Palace & Aquarium Co., Ltd.*, 25 Q.B.D. 258 (C.A. 1890), the plaintiff was injured in an attack by the defendant's elephant. The court held that unless an animal is within a class recognized as harmless, either by nature or as so classified by rule of law (horses, sheep, dogs, etc.), the defendant keeps such animal at his peril and is responsible for any damages caused by it.

3. **Known Dangerous Domestic Animals.** If the defendant has knowledge of the dangerous propensities of his animal (*i.e.*, that the animal threatens serious bodily harm or property damage to others), he will be strictly liable for all injuries resulting from that dangerous propensity.

4. **"Dog Bite" Statutes.** "Dog bite" statutes have been enacted in several jurisdictions. Basically, these statutes reversed the common law rule that every dog was entitled to one bite before it became known to be an animal with dangerous propensities. The statutes make an animal's keeper liable for all damage or harm caused by the animal, unless the plaintiff was a trespasser or was committing a tort.

B. ABNORMALLY DANGEROUS ACTIVITIES

1. **Introduction.** Certain activities are so dangerous that they involve serious risk of harm to others despite the use of utmost care to prevent harm. Strict liability is imposed upon those who engage in such activities. Ultrahazardous activities are those abnormal to the area, which necessarily involve a risk to persons, land, or chattels and which cannot be eliminated by the use of utmost care. [Restatement (Second) of Torts, §520]

2. Unnatural Conditions on Land.

Fletcher v. Rylands

a. **Construction of reservoir--Fletcher v. Rylands,** L.R. 1 Exch. 265 (1866).

1) **Facts.** Rylands (D) constructed a reservoir on his land, which, when filled with water, burst, causing water to flow into coal mines on Fletcher's (P's) adjoining property. Unknown to D, there were old coal mine shafts under his property, which were discovered by his employees during construction of the reservoir and which weakened the reservoir and permitted the flow of water onto P's property. P sued for damages, and the trial court awarded a verdict in his favor. The Exchequer reversed, and P appeals to the Exchequer Chamber.

2) **Issue.** Does a person who brings on his land something that will cause harm to another if it escapes have an absolute duty to prevent its escape?

3) **Held.** Yes. Judgment affirmed.

a) One who brings onto his land anything likely to do mischief if it escapes keeps it at his peril and is prima facie answerable for all damage that is the natural consequence of its escape.

b) He can only excuse himself by showing that the escape was the plaintiff's fault.

c) But for D's act, no mischief could have accrued.

d) This case is distinguishable from traffic and other cases, which require proof of a defendant's negligence for recovery. They involve situations where people have subjected themselves to some inevitable risk. Here, there is no ground for saying that P took upon himself any risk arising from the use to which D chose to put his land.

Rylands v. Fletcher

b. **On appeal--Rylands v. Fletcher,** L.R. 3 H.L. 330 (1868).

1) **Facts.** Same facts as above. D appeals the affirmance of the trial court by the Exchequer Chamber.

2) **Issue.** Is a person who makes a nonnatural use of his land strictly liable for any damages that result to another's property?

3) **Held.** Yes. Judgment affirmed.

a) An owner of land may use it for any purpose for which it might, in the ordinary course of enjoyment, be used. Thus, if the water had accumulated naturally and run off onto adjoining land, there could be no complaint.

b) Nevertheless, a landowner who introduces onto the land that which in its natural condition was not present does so at the peril of absolute liability for consequences arising therefrom.

c. **The *Rylands* rule.** The rule of *Rylands* is that one is liable to adjacent landowners when he brings an artificial and unnatural device onto the land, and the unnatural device causes something to escape from the land and harm another's land or property.

d. **Reason for the case.** England had suffered a series of dam failures and the *Rylands* decision appears to have been a response to claims for relief for victims of those failures. The case, however, was not used extensively even in England.

3. **Intervening Tortfeasor--Bridges v. The Kentucky Stone Co.,** 425 N.E.2d 125 (Ind. 1981). Bridges v. The Kentucky Stone Co.

a. **Facts.** The Kentucky Stone Co. (D) stored dynamite and other hazardous explosives at one of its plants. D discovered that some of its dynamite had disappeared, and it reported this loss within 24 hours as required by federal regulations. Three weeks later, the home of Bridges (P) was dynamited with the explosives taken from D's plant. One of P's sons was killed and P and another son were injured. P lived over 100 miles from the plant from which the dynamite was taken. P sued Webb, who allegedly set and ignited the dynamite after stealing it from D. P also sued D, claiming that D had negligently stored the dynamite in a manner permitting Webb to get it. The trial court granted summary judgment for D on the ground that as a matter of law its storage of the dynamite, even if negligent, was not the proximate cause of the explosion. The court of appeals reversed, and D appeals.

b. **Issue.** Is the storage of dynamite an ultrahazardous activity in all cases?

c. **Held.** No. Judgment reversed.

1) Although in some cases storage of dynamite has been held to be, by itself, an ultrahazardous activity, it is not a per se ultrahazardous activity. It depends on the circumstances. Normally such storage will be considered to be an ultrahazardous activity if it results in contemporaneous damages to the inhabitants and property of the area surrounding the storage site.

2) In this case, the damage took place three weeks after the theft and over 100 miles from the storage site. D reported the loss within the required time frame. Webb's theft, transportation, setting up, and

igniting of the dynamite constituted a superseding cause of the explosion, which precludes liability for any negligence on D's part.

Indiana Harbor Belt Railroad Co. v. American Cyanamid Co.

4. **Shipment of Hazardous Chemicals--Indiana Harbor Belt Railroad Co. v. American Cyanamid Co.,** 916 F.2d 1174 (7th Cir. 1990).

a. **Facts.** American Cyanamid Co. (D) manufactured and loaded a hazardous chemical, acrylonitrile (highly toxic and flammable at and above 30 degrees Fahrenheit), into a leased 20,000 gallon railroad tanker car at its plant in Louisiana. The car was then turned over to the Missouri Pacific Railroad Corp. for transport to one of D's plants in New Jersey, which is served by Conrail. Indiana Harbor Belt Railroad Co. (P) is a small switching line in metropolitan Chicago and has a contract with Conrail to switch cars from other lines to Conrail. Several hours after the car arrived at P's yard, P's employees noticed fluid gushing from the bottom outlet of the car and after two hours, finally succeeded in stopping the leak. Approximately 4,000 gallons had leaked from the car, and decontamination measures that P was required to take cost P $981,022.75. P sued to recover these damages from D, alleging that D negligently maintained the leased tank car and that the transportation of acrylonitrile in bulk through the Chicago metropolitan area is an abnormally dangerous activity for which the shipper (here D) should be held strictly liable. The trial court held for P on the strict liability count and D appeals.

b. **Issue.** Is the shipper of a hazardous chemical by rail strictly liable for the consequences of a spill or other accident to the shipment?

c. **Held.** No. Judgment reversed and remanded.

1) This is not a case for strict liability. No reason has been given to suggest that an action for negligence is not perfectly adequate to remedy and deter, at reasonable cost, the accidental spillage of acrylonitrile from the rail cars. The leak in this case was not caused by the inherent properties of acrylonitrile but by carelessness. Accidents that are due to a lack of care can be prevented by taking care, and when a lack of care can be shown, such accidents are adequately deterred by threat of liability for negligence.

2) We note the six factors considered relevant to strict liability as set forth in *Restatement (Second) of Torts*, section 520, and the policy rationale behind them. There is a distinction between the shipper and the storer of a hazardous chemical because there is more control on the part of a storer than a shipper, thus justifying strict liability in the case of a storer. The difference between a shipper and a carrier points to a deep flaw in P's case—*i.e.*, here it is not the actors or transporters of the hazardous chemicals but the shipper whom P seeks to hold strictly liable. In emphasizing the flammability and

toxicity of acrylonitrile rather than the hazards of transporting it, P overlooks the fact that ultrahazardousness or abnormal dangerousness is viewed by the law as not a property of substances, but of activities—the transportation by rail through populated areas.

5. **Other Activities.**

a. **Airplanes.** Ordinary flying is so common today that it is no longer considered an ultrahazardous activity. Properly handled and cared for mechanically, a plane is not considered inherently dangerous. However, experimental planes may be considered dangerous such that the defendant may be held strictly liable for damage.

b. **Earthmoving.** Likewise, earthmoving has been held to be too commonplace to allow imposition of strict liability (as a basis for recovery other than on a theory of negligence) on the part of the defendant.

c. **Blasting.** In some jurisdictions, whether or not blasting is an activity subject to strict liability depends on the location of the activity. If it is done in the city or in populated areas, it is considered an ultrahazardous activity, for which the defendant actor is subject to strict liability. [*See* Spano v. Perini Corp., *supra*] If it is done in rural or unpopulated areas, the defendant's conduct is judged on traditional negligence standards.

C. LIMITATIONS ON STRICT LIABILITY

For strict liability to be imposed, the injury must have been within the group of risks that made the activity ultrahazardous.

1. **Remoteness of Risk of Harm--Foster v. Preston Mill Co.,** 268 P.2d 645 (Wash. 1954). Foster v. Preston Mill Co.

a. **Facts.** Preston Mill Co. (D) used blasting to clear a road necessary to its logging operation. The vibrations from the blasting frightened mother mink at Foster's (P's) mink ranch over two miles away, causing them to kill their young. D was informed of the effect of the blasting on the mink but continued blasting, using smaller charges. P sued and the trial court awarded damages based on D's absolute liability for the loss of mink after notice was given to him of the effect of his blasting. D appeals.

b. **Issue.** Where injuries that result from ultrahazardous activity are not the consequence of the extraordinary risk, may strict liability be used as a basis of recovery?

c. **Held.** No. Judgment for P reversed.

1) One who carries on an ultrahazardous activity is liable to another, who the actor should recognize will suffer damage by the unpreventable miscarriage of the activity, for harm resulting from that which makes the activity ultrahazardous.

2) Blasting is ultrahazardous because of the risk that property or persons may be damaged by flying debris or concussions of the air.

3) The risk that an unusual vibration may cause a wild animal to kill its young is not the risk that made D's activity ultrahazardous.

4) The nervous disposition of the mink, not the hazard of blasting, is responsible for the loss.

d. **Comment.** This is the majority position.

2. **Unforeseeable Intervening Cause.** Even where the damage is within the foreseeable risk, the majority of courts hold that there is no strict liability if it was brought about by an unforeseeable intervening cause.

Golden v. Amory

3. **Act of God--Golden v. Amory,** 109 N.E.2d 131 (Mass. 1952).

a. **Facts.** Amory (D) operated a hydroelectric plant. D had not obtained a permit for the operation of a particular dike, and allegedly maintained it negligently. A hurricane caused the river to overflow and damaged the Goldens' (Ps') real estate. Ps sued, but the trial court entered judgment for D. Ps appeal.

b. **Issue.** Does strict liability apply when the damage was caused by an unforeseen act of God, which the owner could not have anticipated?

c. **Held.** No. Judgment affirmed.

1) The rule of *Rylands v. Fletcher* is the rule in this state, but the rule does not apply where the injury results from an act of God, which the owner had no reason to anticipate. The flood here fits the exception.

4. **Contributory Negligence.** Generally, contributory negligence is not a defense to strict liability, unless the plaintiff's negligence and not the ultrahazardous activity was the cause of the injury.

Sandy v. Bushey

5. **Contributory Negligence Short of Assumption of Risk No Defense--Sandy v. Bushey,** 128 A. 513 (Me. 1925).

a. **Facts.** Sandy (P) kept his horse in a pasture also used by Bushey's (D's) horses. P went out to give his horse some grain and was kicked by D's horse and seriously injured. P did not know that D's horse was dangerous. P sued and recovered; D appeals.

b. **Issue.** Is contributory negligence a defense to a suit based on strict liability?

c. **Held.** No. Judgment affirmed.

1) The owner of an animal is strictly liable for injuries the animal inflicts if he keeps the animal and knows that it has vicious propensities. The jury found that these facts were present and its verdict is supported by substantial evidence.

2) Strict liability is not grounded in negligence, so the defense of contributory negligence does not apply.

3) D would escape liability if he could prove that P's injury was attributable to P's unnecessarily and voluntarily putting himself in a situation where P knew he would probably be hurt, rather than attributable to D's keeping the animal. However, the facts do not support such a conclusion.

XV. PRODUCTS LIABILITY

A. THEORIES OF RECOVERY

1. **Development of Products Liability.** At early English common law, liability for defective products was grounded in either tort or contract. Legal doctrines were added and modified to deal with changing conditions in society.

   a. **Tort actions.** Originally, the action in tort was in the nature of deceit—an action on the case by the purchaser for breach of an assumed duty.

   b. **Contract actions.** By the beginning of the nineteenth century, the plaintiff's action gained substantial recognition in contract, but only those injured plaintiffs in "privity of contract" with the manufacturer or supplier of the defective product were permitted a cause of action against them. This cause of action sounding in contract was in assumpsit, either express, implied-in-fact, or implied-in-law, and the recoverable damages were determined by application of the *Hadley v. Baxendale* rules. Recall that in *Winterbottom v. Wright*, *supra*, Lord Abinger rejected the claim against a coach repairman by a passenger injured when the coach collapsed (the repairman had agreed with the owner to keep it in repair), stating that the most absurd and outrageous consequences would result if those not in privity of contract were allowed to sue in contract. Thus, early cases sounding in contract developed the privity of contract theory as a shield to the manufacturer and supplier of a defective product not in privity with the injured plaintiff.

   c. **Privity requirement.** Unless the injured plaintiff was the buyer, no recovery could be had, either in tort or in contract, no matter how negligent the seller's conduct. On the tort side, the early cases generally involved defects known to the seller but undisclosed to the buyer.

   d. **The foreseeable plaintiff.** Gradually the courts began to make cracks in the privity wall, moving from contracts to torts, and accepting a theory that manufacturers and suppliers of products owe a duty of due care with respect to the condition of the product. Breach of this duty (*i.e.*, supplying the plaintiff with a defective product), was held to be negligence. As the crack opened wider, the courts began to extend this duty to nonpurchasers. At first, special relationships were required between the purchaser and the injured nonpurchaser (*e.g.*, husband-wife, family members, employer-employee). Later the rule was relaxed and, in some instances, unrelated bystanders could be recognized as plaintiffs. Thus, the concept of the foreseeable plaintiff came into play.

e. **Strict liability.** The next step in the development of products liability law, which proceeded to some extent in parallel with the development of negligence theory, was a move away from negligence and into the area of strict liability, and in some jurisdictions toward absolute liability (*i.e.*, manufacturers and suppliers are absolutely liable for injuries sustained through use of defective products). The strict liability theory, which at first was applied in cases involving inherently dangerous products (such as firearms, poisons, and explosives) was extended into the area of products foreseeably dangerous by reason of the defendant's failure to exercise due care. Today, both the strict liability and negligence theories have become alternative theories upon which injured plaintiffs often rely in stating their cause of action in tort.

f. **Warranty.** While this dual theory approach is common, there is also an increased emphasis being placed on the contract theory of warranty, both express and implied, especially with respect to commercial loss. Part of this trend toward use of warranty as a basis for recovery lies in the fact that the Uniform Commercial Code (U.C.C.) has now been adopted in the District of Columbia and 49 of the 50 states, and specifically places substantial burdens in the warranty area on manufacturers and suppliers of goods. (*See* U.C.C. §§2-312, 2-314, and 2-315.)

2. **Intentional Acts as a Basis of Liability.** If a manufacturer or supplier of a chattel sells it with knowledge, or with reason to know, that it is dangerous or defective, and fails to warn of the danger or defect, the party may be liable for a battery to ***any*** person injured through use or consumption of the product. The requisite intent is established by showing that the injuries suffered were substantially certain to result from use of the chattel in the condition as sold by the manufacturer or supplier.

3. **Negligence as a Basis of Liability.**

a. **Foreseeable risk of harm.** The real breakthrough in providing the plaintiff recourse against manufacturers and suppliers of defective products on a negligence theory came in the *MacPherson* case, below.

b. **Landmark case--MacPherson v. Buick Motor Co.,** 111 N.E. 1050 (N.Y. 1916).

MacPherson v. Buick Motor Co.

1) **Facts.** MacPherson (P) purchased a Buick from a dealer, who had purchased the car from Buick Motor Company (D), the manufacturer. While P was driving the car, a wheel with defective wooden spokes collapsed and P was thrown out and injured. The wheel was not made by D, but was purchased from a subcontractor. Evidence indicated that D could have discovered the defect by reasonable inspection, which was not done. On a judgment for P, D appealed.

2) **Issue.** Is privity between the manufacturer and the plaintiff necessary for the plaintiff to be allowed to recover against the defendant?

3) **Held.** No. Judgment affirmed.

   a) (Cardozo, J.) If the nature of a product is such that it is reasonably certain to place life and limb in peril when negligently made, then it is a thing of danger. If the manufacturer knows or can reasonably foresee that it will be used by persons other than the immediate purchaser (supplier) without new tests, then, irrespective of contract, the manufacturer is under a duty to make it carefully.

   b) This holding can be drawn from prior cases involving poisons, explosives, and deadly weapons that had placed a duty on the manufacturer thereof, based on the fact that such products were "implements of destruction" in their normal operation.

   c) The negligence of the wheel manufacturer, such as to constitute an actionable wrong with respect to users of the furnished product incorporating the wheel, was a question of proximate cause and remoteness. However, in order for the wheel manufacturer's original negligence to become a cause of the danger, it was necessary for an independent cause to intervene; *i.e.*, the omission of the car manufacturer to fulfill its duty of inspection.

4) **Comment.** The rule as originally propounded by the court in *MacPherson* was as follows: If a reasonable person would have foreseen that the product would create a risk of harm to human life or limb if not carefully made or supplied, then the manufacturer and supplier are under a duty to all foreseeable users to exercise reasonable care in the manufacture and supply of the product.

c. **Extensions of the *MacPherson* rule.** The *MacPherson* rule has been further developed in subsequent cases to cover the following situations:

   (i) Damage to the product sold resulting from its own defects.

   (ii) Damage to reasonably foreseeable nonusers in the vicinity of the expected use of the product.

   (iii) Damage caused by defects in design as opposed to defects in manufacture.

   (iv) Damage to property in the vicinity of expected use, where the product itself is dangerous to life and limb because it is negligently made.

   (v) Liability for products negligently manufactured but posing a foreseeable risk to property only.

(vi) Liability of a processor of a product at an intermediate stage.

(vii) Liability of those who sell another's products.

1) **Dealer's duty to inspect inherently dangerous products.** Restatement (Second) of Torts, section 401, places a duty on dealers and distributors to make a reasonable inspection of their products that are inherently dangerous in normal use and to remedy, or warn buyers against, such defects or dangers. The failure of the dealer to inspect, however, does not relieve the manufacturer of its obligations since the dealer's omissions are considered foreseeable.

2) **Dealer's duty for products not inherently dangerous.** However, section 402 of the Restatement does not place such a duty on the dealer when the products are manufactured by others and are not inherently dangerous in normal use. In such cases, the manufacturer is still liable under the MacPherson rule, and the dealer may be liable under the theory of warranty or the theory of strict liability. But if the dealer discovers the defect, the common law rule will make the dealer liable to any injured plaintiff who was not warned of the defect prior to the sale. This failure to warn of known defects will operate as an unforeseeable intervening force with respect to the manufacturer's negligence and will relieve it of liability under a negligence theory.

d. **Defenses.** The defenses available to a defendant under a typical negligence action (*e.g.*, contributory negligence, assumption of risk) may be raised by a defendant in a products liability action grounded in negligence.

4. **Warranty.** As stated above, a products liability action can be based in contract upon breach of warranty. The "warranty" upon which the plaintiff will rely will generally be a statement or representation, either express or implied, made by the seller (or attributed to him) with respect to the character, quality, function, performance, reliability, or other matter of the item sold.

a. **Cause of action.** If the plaintiff brings his cause of action on a warranty theory, he must show:

1) The existence of the warranty;

2) Breach of the warranty (sale of the product in a condition that does not comply with the warranty); and

3) Injury proximately caused by reason of the warranty defect in the product. With respect to this last element, if, for example, a war-

ranty states that a widget has five coats of waterproof paint and in fact it has only one coat, the fact that this warranty is breached will not give the plaintiff a cause of action for physical injuries suffered as a result of some mechanism unrelated to the warranty (though the plaintiff would have a breach of contract action for contract damages based on the failure of the widget to comply with the express warranty).

b. **Privity.** In the past, courts considered an action for breach of warranty as a contracts action and required privity of contract between the plaintiff and the defendant as a precondition to a finding of liability. However, this notion and the concept of privity have been stretched by the courts and in a few states entirely discarded or modified by statute.

c. **Express warranties.** An express warranty is an affirmation of fact or promise made by the seller about the product sold, which acts as an inducement to the purchaser to buy the product.

1) **U.C.C. section 2-213.** U.C.C. section 2-213 states that an express warranty can be created by such an affirmation of fact or promise, by any description of the product that is made part of the basis of the sales transaction, or by furnishing a sample or model when the product is represented to conform to such sample or model. This U.C.C. section further states that the words "guarantee" or "warranty" need not appear anywhere in the transaction for such a warranty to arise. The affirmation of fact or promise may be expressly included in the contract by written representations or oral statements made by the supplier, or by a salesperson, or through advertising, or otherwise. The courts, however, have made an exception for statements of opinion or "puffing language"; however, the risk that such a statement may be construed by the courts as an express warranty is on the seller, and the tendency has been to find that such statements are warranties where such a construction is reasonable.

Baxter v. Ford Motor Co.

2) **Privity not required--Baxter v. Ford Motor Co.,** 12 P.2d 409 (Wash. 1932).

a) **Facts.** Baxter (P) purchased an automobile from a dealer who had purchased it from Ford Motor Co. (D). The manufacturer had made misrepresentations, through its advertising, that the windshields of its automobiles were constructed of nonshatterable glass. P was injured when a pebble thrown by a passing truck struck the windshield and glass flew into his eyes, resulting in loss of his left eye and damage to his right eye. D claimed no liability and the trial court held for D. P appeals the judgment and the exclusion of advertising matter from evidence by the trial court.

b) **Issue.** Can there be an express (or implied) warranty running to the benefit of a consumer even without privity of contract?

c) **Held.** Yes. Judgment reversed.

(1) D, as the manufacturer, is liable, notwithstanding a lack of privity, because its misrepresentation as to the quality of its product was not readily discovered by the plaintiff by the usual and customary examination.

(2) It would be unjust to permit a manufacturer of goods to create a demand for its products by representing that the goods possess qualities that they in fact do not possess and then escape liability because of a rule such as privity.

d) **Comment.** On the second trial in *Baxter*, a verdict was entered for P and D appealed. The judgment was affirmed for P. The appellate court noted the fact that D's expert testified that there were no better windshields available, but held that even if this were true, it would have no effect because it still would not make the representations of D true.

3) **Effect of action.** The action in *Baxter* was on the breach of an express warranty, but the effect of the breach thereof was to hold the manufacturer strictly liable for its misrepresentation.

d. **Implied warranties.** Implied warranties are creatures of the law and become part of a sales transaction by operation of law rather than by the acts or agreements of the parties.

1) **Privity not required--Henningsen v. Bloomfield Motors, Inc.,** 161 A.2d 69 (N.J. 1960).

Henningsen v. Bloomfield Motors, Inc.

a) **Facts.** Henningsen (P) was seriously injured when the steering gear in her car malfunctioned and the car crashed into a wall. P sued the manufacturer (Chrysler) and the dealer (Bloomfield) from whom her husband purchased the car (Ds). The husband had signed a contract with 8½ inches of fine print on the backside, which he did not read. The fine print contained a disclaimer of warranties, express and implied, except for a warranty to repair or replace, at the factory, any parts that became defective within 90 days or 4,000 miles after delivery of the car to the original purchaser, whichever occurred first. P's claim based on negligence was dismissed and the case went to the jury solely on the basis of an implied warranty of merchantability. On a verdict for P, Ds appeal.

b) **Issues.**

(1) Is privity a requirement for an implied warranty of reasonable suitability (fitness) to run from manufacturer to P?

(2) Is the disclaimer of the warranty and limitation of liability on the reverse side of the contract effective?

(3) Is there an implied warranty of merchantability from the dealer to P?

c) **Held.** (1) No. (2) No. (3) Yes. Judgment affirmed for P.

(1) Traditional concepts of privity would work a social injustice and are therefore overruled. Under modern marketing conditions, when a manufacturer puts a new automobile into the stream of trade and promotes its purchase to the public, an implied warranty that it is reasonably suitable for use accompanies it into the hands of the ultimate purchaser. The absence of an agency relationship between the manufacturer and the dealer who makes the ultimate sale is immaterial to the flow of the warranty.

(2) The general rule is that one who chooses not to read a contract cannot later relieve himself of its burdens. However, this rule takes into consideration the bargaining power or relative economic position of the parties and recognized the adhesion character of automobile industry contracts. Chrysler's attempted disclaimer of the implied warranty of merchantability and its limitation on liability were contrary to public policy and therefore invalid.

(3) For similar reasons, the dealer's attempted disclaimer of the warranty of merchantability and limitation of liability to replacement of defective parts was against public policy.

d) **Comment.** This case disposed of the requirement of privity on the basis that social policy requires that a manufacturer be held liable for defects in its products and that warranty disclaimers and limitations on liability in consumer situations are "unconscionable" because of the relative inequality of bargaining positions.

(1) Thus, even an express disclaimer of liability in a contract will not bar a products liability action. Note also that this decision extended the concept of manufacturer's liability beyond consumer products intended for bodily use.

(2) Difficulties remained, however, because actions based on "warranty" were still subject to limiting commercial rules that were unsuited to protection of consumers.

2) **Statutes.** Until adoption of the U.C.C., the principal statute giving buyers implied warranties was the Uniform Sales Act ("USA"), originally drafted in 1905. The USA provisions, however, were designed to apply only between the seller and his immediate buyer. The U.C.C., while specifically applicable

only to the sale of "goods," followed in general the USA's "privity" format in sections 2-314 and 2-315, but attempted in one version of section 2-318 to create rights in remote purchasers and any "natural person who may reasonably be expected to use, consume, or be affected by the goods and who is injured in person by breach of the warranty." This version has not been widely adopted, though some states have adopted similar, even more encompassing consumer legislation. [*See*, *e.g.*, Cal. Civil Code §§1790 *et. seq.*] Also, in 1972, the federal government adopted the Consumer Products Safety Act (discussed below).

a) **Merchantability: U.C.C. section 2-314.** Where goods are supplied by a merchant who deals in goods of that description, the law implies a warranty in the sales transaction that the goods are of fair average quality and reasonably fit for the general purposes for which they were sold.

b) **Fitness for particular purpose: U.C.C. section 2-315.** Where goods are supplied by a seller who knows or has reason to know that the buyer is purchasing the goods for a particular purpose, and is relying on the seller's skill or judgment in the selection of the goods, the law implies a warranty in the sales transaction that the goods are suitable or fit for the special purpose of the buyer. Fitness of the goods for general purposes will not satisfy this warranty.

c) **Special consumer legislation.**

(1) Some states have expanded the U.C.C. warranties in cases where the transaction involves consumer goods. Typical of such expanded protection is the California consumer protection legislation, which includes within the implied warranty of merchantability attached to the consumer goods the warranty that the goods are free from defects in workmanship and materials, are adequately contained, packaged, and labeled, and conform to the representations on the label. [Cal. Civil Code §1791]

(2) The Consumer Products Safety Act of 1972 provides that the designer, manufacturer, and/or seller of a defective consumer product may be sued in federal court by an injured consumer for recovery of damages. The Act also establishes a Consumer Products Safety Commission charged with protection of the public from "unreasonable risks of injury" from consumer products. The Act, while applicable to consumer products, specifically exempts consumer goods such as tobacco, automobiles, guns, planes, boats, drugs, cosmetics, and food.

(3) The Magnuson-Moss Consumer Warranty Act of 1975 does not pertain to commercial transactions (*i.e.*, those between merchants), which are still governed by the provisions of the U.C.C. However, it significantly alters the law of warranty as applied to the sale of consumer products. Generally, the Act applies only to the sale of consumer products (tangible personal property distributed in commerce and normally used for personal, household, or family use). While the implied warranties of

merchantability and fitness for a particular purpose found in the U.C.C. are left intact, the Act prohibits a disclaimer of an implied warranty whenever an express warranty is given. The Act provides for limited written warranties and permits the supplier of goods under a limited warranty to limit the duration of implied warranties to the duration of the limited warranty. The Act provides a wide range of public and private remedies for the consumer.

3) **Defenses.**

a) **Disclaimers.** Liability based on warranty is generally subject to disclaimer by the seller. Since it arises out of contract conditions (either express or implied in law), the seller may limit or exclude such warranties by use of an appropriate statement in the contract of sale, but only in strict accordance with, and to the extent allowed by, law. U.C.C. section 2-316 permits the seller to disclaim warranties in the sales contract by use of words indicating that the goods are sold on an "AS IS, WHERE IS" basis "WITHOUT WARRANTIES, EXPRESS OR IMPLIED, AS TO MERCHANTABILITY, FITNESS FOR PARTICULAR PURPOSE, OR ANY OTHER MATTER." The U.C.C. requires that the word "merchantability" appear in any disclaimer of that warranty and that disclaimers be conspicuous (typically accomplished by setting out the disclaimer language in all capitals, bold face, different type font, different color ink, or such similar distinguishing device). U.C.C. section 2-719 declares that otherwise valid disclaimers are unenforceable if found to be unconscionable (a disclaimer that attempts to limit the seller's liability for personal injuries arising out of use of consumer goods is prima facie unconscionable). Note also that warranty disclaimers, since they apply in a contract, are effective only between the parties to the contract and have no binding effect on injured third parties who are not purchasers of the goods. The U.C.C. also requires the buyer to timely (promptly) notify the seller of her claims or else they will be barred.

b) **Contributory negligence.** Contributory negligence is not a defense to a warranty action, but assumption of risk may eliminate the "proximate cause" element if the plaintiff knowingly uses a product after discovering a defect and is then injured by reason of such defect.

5. **Strict Liability.**

a. **Introduction.** As stated *supra*, strict liability is liability without fault. The seller is held liable for injuries caused to the plaintiff irrespective of the seller's negligence or even his exercise of all possible care. The rationale of this theory of liability is that the defendant is considered better able to assume the risk of loss through insurance or otherwise than is the innocent consumer.

b. **Notice of breach--Greenman v. Yuba Power Products, Inc.,** 377 P.2d 897 (Cal. 1963).

Greenman v. Yuba Power Products, Inc.

1) **Facts.** Greenman (P) purchased a power tool from Yuba (D) and sustained injuries when the tool malfunctioned. There was a warranty given with the sale, but a state statute required the buyer to give the seller notice of the breach within a reasonable time after discovery, otherwise the seller was relieved of liability under warranty. D claimed that P's failure to promptly notify D of the breach acted as a bar to the warranty action.

2) **Issue.** Does P's failure to meet the statutory requirement of notice of breach of warranty bar P's recovery?

3) **Held.** No. Judgment for P.

a) The notice requirement of the statute is not appropriate in actions by injured consumers against manufacturers with whom they have not dealt. P introduced substantial evidence that his injuries were caused by defective design and construction of the machine. When a manufacturer places an article on the market knowing that it will be used without an inspection for defects, he will be strictly liable in tort if that article proves to be defective and causes injury to human beings.

4) **Comments.**

a) *Greenman* has now been accepted in almost all of the states. A few courts still speak of warranty but it seems that this concept in its traditional context is dying out, though the U.C.C. warranty concept is gaining recognition as an alternative theory of liability. Generally, any kind of product may be covered under a strict liability theory but the product must be defective or unreasonably unsafe or dangerous to the consumer. Note that a "defect" or dangerous condition can arise from improper design or insufficient warning.

b) Note that under a strict liability theory, the contractual waivers or disclaimers that usually appear in warranty actions will not apply. Further, there is usually no problem with timely notice to the seller. However, if the consumer has been fully advised of the risk (*i.e.*, adequate warnings given), her assumption of risk may be a bar to an action based on strict liability.

B. UNSAFE PRODUCTS

Generally, a product can be considered unsafe if it is defective in manufacture (either workmanship or materials) or design, or has a concealed danger, which defect or danger renders it potentially harmful to normal individuals in the foreseeable use of the product.

Rix v. General Motors Corp.

1. **Manufacturing Defect--Rix v. General Motors Corp.,** 723 P.2d 195 (Mont. 1986).

   a. **Facts.** Rix (P) was injured when his truck was hit by a two-ton chassis-cab that was manufactured by General Motors Corporation (D). P, on a theory of strict liability, maintained that the product (the two-ton truck) was unreasonably dangerous because of both manufacturing and design defects associated with the brake system. The trial judge instructed the jury that in order to recover on a strict liability theory for a manufacturing defect, P needed to establish the following three essential elements: (i) D manufactured and sold a product that, at the time sold by D, was defective and unreasonably dangerous to the consumer or user; (ii) the product was expected to and did reach the ultimate consumer without substantial change from its condition at the time of sale; and (iii) the defective condition proximately caused P's injury. The jury reached a verdict for D. P appeals.

   b. **Issue.** Was the jury properly instructed on the issue of strict liability for a manufacturing defect?

   c. **Held.** Yes. Judgment reversed and remanded.

      1) Under a manufacturing defect theory, the essential question is whether the product was flawed or defective because it was not constructed correctly by the manufacturer, without regard to whether the intended design was safe. Such defects result from some mishap in the manufacturing process, improper workmanship, or use of defective materials. The jury instructions were consistent with the *Restatement (Second) of Torts*, section 402A, which has been adopted by this court as the applicable law with regard to strict liability under a manufacturing defect theory. Thus, the jury instructions were proper.

Prentis v. Yale Manufacturing Co.

2. **Negligent Design--Prentis v. Yale Manufacturing Co.,** 365 N.W.2d 176 (Mich. 1984).

   a. **Facts.** While working in a car parts department, Prentis (P) was operating a stand-up forklift by means of a handle that controlled the forklift by being raised or lowered. The forklift's battery was low, and P was trying to start it by moving the handle up and down. The machine had a power surge, allegedly causing P to fall to the ground. P injured his hip in the fall and sued Yale Manufacturing Co. (D), the forklift manufacturer, claiming breach of warranty and negligence due to the defective design. The trial court instructed the jury on negligence and breach of warranty, but not breach of implied warranty. The jury found for D, but the court of appeals reversed and required a new trial. D appeals.

b. **Issue.** In a products liability case involving an alleged design defect, must the jury be instructed about both negligent design and breach of implied warranty?

c. **Held.** No. Judgment reversed.

1) P's theory was that D's design, because it did not provide a seat or platform for the operator, improperly failed to incorporate the operator as a human factor in the machine's function. P requested separate instructions on implied warranty and negligence theories, but the judge instructed the jury on a unified standard of liability, including common elements of proof under both of P's theories. The jury specifically found that the forklift was not defectively designed.

2) Products liability does not equate to absolute liability. Sellers are not insurers of their products. Thus, whether P sued for negligence or implied warranty, he would have to show a defect, *i.e.*, that something was wrong with the forklift that made it dangerous.

3) The term "defective" includes manufacturing defects, in which the product does not meet the manufacturer's own standards, and design defects, which result from the manufacturer's intentional design decisions. In the latter type of defect cases, there are no easy standards against which the product may be judged.

4) Although a variety of approaches to design defects have been used, the negligence or fault system is the best for several reasons: (i) because the manufacturer intentionally designs its products, access to the decisions made are readily discoverable; (ii) the fault system provides more incentive to design safer products, which in turn reduces injuries and claims and produces lower insurance premiums; (iii) a finding that a design is defective applies to an entire product line with potentially enormous consequences, so it is justifiable to give the plaintiff a higher burden of proof; and (iv) the fault system is fairer because the safety-conscious manufacturer does not have to pay for losses caused by negligent product sellers. This approach is also easily understood by juries.

5) The jury was carefully instructed on the necessary elements for determining whether D defectively designed the forklift when it was told to

consider whether D took reasonable care in light of any reasonably foreseeable use of the product that might cause harm or injury. Because this jury was properly instructed on negligent design, there was no need to also instruct on breach of warranty.

O'Brien v. Muskin Corp.

3. **State of the Art Not Dispositive--O'Brien v. Muskin Corp.,** 463 A.2d 298 (N.J. 1983).

a. **Facts.** The Muskin Corporation (D) manufactured an above-ground swimming pool that had a vinyl liner. The outer wall of the pool had a decal on it that warned "DO NOT DIVE" in half-inch letters. O'Brien (P) dove into one of D's pools and struck his head on the bottom when his outstretched hands hit the vinyl bottom and slid apart. P sued for injuries, claiming the pool was defectively designed. P's expert testified that the vinyl was more slippery than the material used in in-ground pools, but admitted that all above-ground pools were made of vinyl. D's expert testified that the slipperiness was actually a safety feature in some situations. The court instructed the jury about strict liability but only permitted them to consider the adequacy of the warning; they were not permitted to decide whether the vinyl was a design or manufacturing defect. The jury found for D, but the court of appeals reversed. The state supreme court granted certification.

b. **Issue.** May a product be defective even if it meets the state of the art in that industry?

c. **Held.** Yes. Judgment of court of appeals affirmed.

1) In a strict liability case, the plaintiff must prove: (i) that the product was defective; (ii) that the defect existed when the defendant released it into commerce; and (iii) that the defect caused injury to a reasonably foreseeable user. Because the defect must be proved, the manufacturer is not an insurer of the product. But the manufacturer has a duty to warn foreseeable users of the risks inherent in the use of the product, as well as a duty not to put defective products on the market.

2) A defect exists when a product fails to meet a particular standard of evaluation. Manufacturing defects are shown by comparison to the manufacturer's own standards. Design defects, however, are shown by comparison with a standard based on a policy judgment that the product is so dangerous that it creates a risk of harm that outweighs its usefulness. This approach to design defects is referred to as "risk-utility analysis."

3) Risk-utility analysis requires consideration of several factors, including (i) the product's utility to the user and to the public as a

whole, (ii) the product's safety aspects, (iii) the availability of a safer substitute, (iv) the feasibility of safety improvements, (v) the user's ability to avoid danger by exercising due care in using the product, (vi) the user's awareness of the product's dangers, (vii) the manufacturer's ability to spread the loss through price or insurance, and (viii) the state of the art at the time the product was manufactured.

4) A manufacturer may not avoid liability by simply meeting the customary standards of the industry; such customs may lack safety features available under the current state of the art. Even a design that meets the state of the art may not be sufficient because the product may be so dangerous, and its utility so small, that the product should not even be on the market.

5) In this case, the jury should have been allowed to apply the risk-utility analysis to D's pool design. If the risks of injury sufficiently outweighed the utility of the pool, it may have been defective even though there was no alternative technology.

4. Concealed Danger. Even though there are no manufacturing or design defects in a product, the manufacturer and seller may be liable for injuries suffered by users of the product if use of the product involves a risk of harm that is not apparent and the manufacturer or seller fails to give adequate warning of the concealed danger.

a. Unavoidably dangerous products. The fact that a product is by its nature unsafe does not necessarily mean that it is "defective." Many useful products, such as drugs, present risks of injury that cannot be reduced or eliminated with current technology.

b. Warnings defect--Anderson v. Owens-Corning Fiberglas Corp., 810 P.2d 549 (Cal. 1991).

Anderson v. Owens-Corning Fiberglas Corp.

1) Facts. Anderson (P) alleged that he contracted asbestosis and other lung ailments through exposure to asbestos and asbestos products while working at the Long Beach Naval Shipyard from 1941 to 1976. After a verdict for Owens-Corning (D), the manufacturer of the asbestos products, the trial court granted a new trial and the parties argued whether state of the art evidence was admissible in a failure to warn case. P contended that D was strictly liable for P's injuries in that D failed to warn P of the risk of harm that ultimately caused P injury. D, on the other hand, argued that in a strict liability action for failure to warn, it should only be held liable if it had knowledge, actual or constructive, of a potential risk or danger. D also argued that evidence of the state of the art is relevant and, subject to the normal rules of evidence, admissible. The court of appeals agreed with D and the California Supreme Court granted review.

2) **Issue.** May a defendant in a strict liability action based upon an alleged failure to warn of a risk of harm present evidence of the state of the art?

3) **Held.** Yes. Judgment affirmed.

a) Knowledge, actual or constructive, of a potential risk or danger is required before a defendant may be held strictly liable for injuries based upon an alleged failure to warn. Evidence of the state of the art, *i.e.*, evidence that the particular risk was neither known nor knowable by application of scientific knowledge available at the time of manufacture and/or distribution of the product, is both relevant and, subject to the normal rules of evidence, admissible.

b) To hold otherwise (*i.e.*, that knowledge or knowability is irrelevant in a failure to warn case) would render the manufacturer the virtual insurer of the product's safe use, which was never the intention of the strict liability doctrine. In strict liability for failure to warn, as opposed to such an action based on negligence, the reasonableness of the defendant's failure to warn is immaterial; the plaintiff need only show that the defendant did not adequately warn of a particular risk that was known or knowable in light of the generally recognized and prevailing best scientific and medical knowledge available at the time of manufacture and distribution.

4) **Comments.**

a) Note that a product defect cannot be overcome by a warning. Also, the determination of whether the warning given was adequate is usually left for the jury to decide, normally in reliance on expert testimony.

b) The "learned intermediary rule" has been applied with regard to warnings associated with harm from pharmaceuticals. Under the rule, the duty to warn of risks associated with a prescription drug is fulfilled by adequate warning to those authorized to prescribe the drug (*i.e.*, by informing the physician who prescribes the drug).

c. **Post-sale duty to warn.** In *Davis v. Wyeth Laboratories, Inc.*, 199 F.2d 121 (9th Cir. 1968), a drug manufacturer was held to have failed to discharge its duty to warn the plaintiff, who contracted polio after taking a vaccine manufactured by the manufacturer. Without the warning that paralysis could result and that the vaccine was dangerous, the dispensing of the drug, even though through a free clinic to the plaintiff, was unreasonably dangerous.

C. PROOF

1. **Introduction.** The plaintiff has the burden of proving that the product was defective when sold by the defendant and that the defect was causally related to his injury. In some cases, however, the mere fact that something went wrong may create an inference that the product was defective when sold; this is similar to giving the plaintiff the benefit of res ipsa loquitur in negligence cases. However, problems often arise in trying to connect the defect with a particular defendant and in trying to eliminate other intervening causes.

2. **Proof Through Circumstantial Evidence--Friedman v. General Motors Corp.,** 331 N.E. 2d 702 (Ohio 1975).

Friedman v. General Motors Corp.

   a. **Facts.** Friedman (P) turned on the ignition key in his auto while the transmission was in "drive" position. The car unexpectedly started, lurched forward, and caused personal injuries to P's family. P sued General Motors (D) for damages, but the court granted D's motion for a directed verdict. The appellate court reversed and D appeals.

   b. **Issue.** May a plaintiff prove a product is defective by relying solely on circumstantial evidence?

   c. **Held.** Yes. Judgment affirmed.

      1) In order to sustain his claim, P had to prove that the auto was defective, that the defect was present at the time the car left the factory, and that the defect was the direct and proximate cause of the injuries. A defect may be proven by a preponderance of circumstantial evidence, and the evidence presented by P establishes a prima facie case of defect.

      2) The expert testimony indicated that P's car did start while the gear shift indicator was in the "drive" position. This could only happen if there was a defect in the vehicle.

   d. **Dissent.** P's evidence would not be enough to establish a prima facie case of defect except in cases analogous to res ipsa loquitur. The instant case is not such a case, because there are several other explanations of how the accident could have happened. The sum of the evidence submitted is only that something unusual happened with the car, and that a possible explanation of that happening is a defect. The same weakness in evidence exists with respect to the issue of whether the claimed defect existed at the time the car left D's factory.

D. THE PLAINTIFF'S CONDUCT

1. **Contributory Negligence.** A plaintiff's failure to exercise reasonable care to discover the defect is no defense when the action is one based on strict liability. But when the user discovers the danger and nevertheless proceeds, contributory negligence or assumption of risk may be asserted as a defense. However, as stated *supra*, contributory negligence is always a defense in an action based on negligence.

Daly v. General Motors Corp.

2. **Comparative Negligence--Daly v. General Motors Corp.,** 575 P.2d 1162 (Cal. 1978).

   a. **Facts.** Daly (P) brought a strict liability action against General Motors (D) when her husband died as a result of being thrown out of a car in an accident because the allegedly defective door latch failed to operate properly. It appeared at trial that the driver was intoxicated and failed to use the available safety devices. The trial court held for D and P appeals.

   b. **Issue.** Do the principles of comparative negligence apply to actions founded on strict product liability?

   c. **Held.** Yes. Judgment reversed for a new trial.

      1) Strict liability is not absolute liability. The injury must result from a defect in the product. Previous cases have recognized assumption of the risk as a complete defense to a strict liability claim.

      2) Although comparative negligence traditionally applies only to actions based on negligence, the concept does not frustrate the purposes of strict liability. Those purposes relate to problems of proof and shifting of the burden of loss. Application of comparative negligence preserves the purposes of strict liability while reducing the manufacturer's liability to the extent P himself caused his injuries.

      3) This result approximates the goal of equitable allocation of legal responsibility for personal injuries.

3. **Misuse.** If the plaintiff misuses the product, or engages in an abnormal use that was not foreseeable, the defendant will not be held liable, even under a strict liability theory. The use becomes abnormal when the plaintiff fails to follow the defendant's directions and instructions. When an unusual or abnormal use should be anticipated by the defendant (*e.g.*, sailor walking over containers used for transoceanic shipping is injured when he falls through a defective container), strict liability may apply.

a. **Foreseeable misuse--Ford Motor Co. v. Matthews,** 291 So. 2d 169 (Miss. 1974). Ford Motor Co. v. Matthews

1) **Facts.** Matthews' (P's) decedent was killed when he was run over by his tractor, which had been manufactured by Ford Motor Co. (D). The decedent, while standing on the ground, had tried to start the tractor. It was alleged that the tractor was in gear at the time, and had a safety switch that should have prevented it from starting, but the safety switch was defective. D appeals from a judgment for P.

2) **Issue.** If a plaintiff's misuse of a product was foreseeable, may the manufacturer be liable for a defect that, when combined with the misuse, produces an injury?

3) **Held.** Yes. Judgment affirmed.

a) If injury results from misuse of a product that is safe if normally handled, the seller is not liable. However, such misuse must not have been reasonably foreseeable. D should have foreseen that P might carelessly crank the engine without first checking to see that it was not in gear, especially if he were aware of the purpose of the safety switch system. Thus, even if P were negligent, such negligence would not be a bar to a strict liability action against D.

E. PREEMPTION

1. **Introduction.** The Supremacy Clause of the Constitution makes federal law controlling over state law. When Congress makes clear its intent to preempt state law, the courts must recognize preemption. Most cases involve attempts to interpret the intent of Congress where it is not clear.

2. **No Preemption of State Tort Remedy--Medtronic, Inc. v. Lohr,** 518 U.S. 470 (1996). Medtronic, Inc. v. Lohr

a. **Facts.** Lohr (P) received a pacemaker manufactured by Medtronic, Inc. (D). Three years after the implant, the pacemaker failed and P needed emergency surgery. P's physician stated that a defect in an electrical lead caused the failure. P sued in Florida state court, alleging negligence and strict liability. D removed the case to federal court and moved for summary judgment on the ground that 21 U.S.C. section 360k(a) preempted state common law claims by stating that no state may establish or continue in effect any requirement that is different from, or in addition to, any requirement applicable to a covered device. That section was part of the Medical Device Amendments to the Food and Drug Act, which regulates the introduction of new drugs and medical devices. New medical devices are subject to premarket approval ("PMA"), except that pre-1976 devices, as well as products that are substantially equivalent to them, are grandfathered in and can be marketed without further regulatory analysis until the Food and Drug Administration ("FDA") initiates a PMA process. As a result, most new devices, including the pacemaker involved in this case, are approved as substantially equivalent. The district court granted D's motion, and the court of appeals affirmed in part and reversed in part. The Supreme Court granted certiorari.

b. **Issue.** Is a state law cause of action based on general tort principles preempted by a federal statute that covers an area generally when there is no evidence of congressional intent to preempt traditional common law remedies?

c. **Held.** No. Judgment reversed regarding any claims that were preempted.

1) The language of section 360k(a) clearly provides for preemption, but the domain expressly preempted by that language must be determined. States are independent sovereigns, so the courts must presume that Congress does not cavalierly preempt state law causes of action. The presumption against the preemption of state police power regulations supports a narrow interpretation of express preemption language in federal statutes.

2) Another fundamental aspect of interpreting preemption language is ascertaining the intent of Congress. With respect to medical devices, if Congress preempted all state law in the area, it would have precluded state courts from giving state consumers any protection from injuries caused by defective medical devices. Because the federal statute does not contain any private right of action, Congress would have barred relief for injured persons. Nothing in the legislative history suggests such a drastic intention, which would have actually granted immunity to an industry Congress expressly believed needed more, not less, regulation to protect public safety.

3) D claims that even if section 360k(a) does not preempt all common law claims, it should apply to P's claims. The language of the statute reflects a concern that preemption occur only when a particular state requirement threatens to interfere with a specific federal interest. State requirements of general applicability are not preempted unless they establish a substantive requirement for a specific device, and even then, the federal requirements must be applicable to the device in question.

4) The preemption issue may be resolved by comparing the allegedly preempting federal requirement with the alleged preempted state requirement. In this case, P's common law claims are not preempted by the federal labeling and manufacturing requirements. The generality of the federal requirements reflect important but generic concerns about device

regulation generally. The state common law requirements were not specifically developed with respect to medical devices and are not the type of requirements that would impede the ability of federal regulators to enforce federal requirements, so they fall outside the category of requirements covered by section 360k.

d. **Comment.** The Court specifically stated that the federal language does not necessarily preclude general federal requirements from ever preempting state requirements, or general state requirements from ever being preempted. Note that the deciding vote for the holding that none of P's claims were preempted was provided by Justice Breyer. He actually agreed with the dissent that more specific FDA requirements could preempt state law claims such as P's.

F. NONMANUFACTURERS

1. **Lessors.** The strict liability theory applicable to sellers of chattels has been held applicable to bailors and lessors of chattels. They are deemed to be under a duty to inspect the chattel to determine that it is safe.

2. **Sellers--Peterson v. Lou Bachrodt Chevrolet Co.,** 329 N.E.2d 785 (Ill. 1975). Peterson v. Lou Bachrodt Chevrolet Co.

a. **Facts.** Lou Bachrodt Chevrolet Co. (D) sold a six-year-old car to a person who loaned it to a third person. The car later struck Peterson's (P's) two children, killing one and severely injuring the other. P brought an action for damages on the theory of strict product liability. The court dismissed the action, and P appeals.

b. **Issue.** Should strict liability be imposed on a retailer who is outside the original producing and marketing chain?

c. **Held.** No. Judgment affirmed.

1) Strict liability is imposed on the manufacturer because losses should be borne by those who have created the risk and reaped the profit by placing the product into the stream of commerce. Those same considerations also account for the imposition of strict liability on wholesalers and retailers. On the other hand, a wholesaler or retailer who neither creates nor assumes the risk is entitled to indemnity. If strict liability were imposed here, D would, in effect, become an insurer against defects that may have come into existence after the chain of distribution was completed, and while the product was under the control of one or more consumers.

d. **Dissent.** Strict liability has been held applicable to the lessor of a motor vehicle. The same reasoning ought to apply to a used car dealer who sells a vehicle with a dangerous but reasonably discoverable defect.

e. **Comment.** In *Price v. Shell Oil Co.*, 466 P.2d 722 (Cal. 1970), a lessor (Shell) was held liable for injuries suffered by an aircraft mechanic as a result of a fall from a defective ladder on a tank truck leased by Shell to the mechanic's employer. A gratuitous bailor is under a duty only to disclose all known defects but is not required to inspect.

3. **Builders and Vendors of Real Property.**

a. **Vendors.** At common law, a vendor of land was not liable to the vendee or third persons for harm resulting from defective conditions that he failed to disclose. Recently, however, several cases have held that there is a duty on the part of the vendor to disclose known dangerous conditions and to discover and repair artificial conditions that involve a risk of harm prior to transferring possession of the land. (*See supra* under **Owners and Occupiers of Land**.)

b. **Builders.** Liability of builders and building contractors based on negligence has developed similar to liability theories applicable to manufacturers of chattels. Today, the principle set forth in *MacPherson* is held to apply to builders and contractors.

4. **Services.** Strict liability does not apply to services rendered, but one must exercise reasonable care in rendering services.

a. **Scope.** Liability extends to all those who may foreseeably be injured by negligence of repairpersons or by those who provide services through the use of a product.

Hector v. Cedars-Sinai Medical Center

b. **Hospital--Hector v. Cedars-Sinai Medical Center,** 225 Cal. Rptr. 595 (1986).

1) **Facts.** Hector (P) sued Cedars-Sinai Medical Center (D) alleging personal injury from the implantation by her physician of a defective pacemaker at D's hospital. The pacemaker was selected by P's physician and purchased from a third-party manufacturer, American Technology, Inc. P's complaint contained three causes of action: negligence, strict liability, and breach of warranty. D moved for partial summary judgment on the second and third causes, alleging that they presented no triable issues of fact as a matter of law. The trial court granted the motion. P then requested dismissal of the negligence cause, which the court granted. P appeals, contending that D was not exempt from the application of the strict products liability doctrine.

2) **Issue.** Does the doctrine of strict liability apply to a hospital whose patient receives a defective product in the course of treatment at the hospital?

3) **Held.** No. Judgment affirmed.

   a) As a provider of ***services*** rather than a seller of a product, D is not subject to strict liability for a defective product provided to the patient during the course of the patient's treatment. The essence of the relationship between hospital and patient is the provision of professional medical services necessary to effect the implantation of the pacemaker—the patient does not enter the hospital merely to purchase a pacemaker but to obtain a course of treatment that includes implantation of a pacemaker.

   b) Unlike the products sold in a hospital gift shop, for which the hospital is strictly liable, the pacemaker provided to the patient is necessary to the patient's medical treatment. The hospital's actions concerning the provision of the pacemaker are "integrally related to its primary function of providing medical services."

XVI. NUISANCE

A. INTRODUCTION

Nuisances are interferences with a person's right to quiet enjoyment of her land. The interference must come from an invasion of the land. In turn, the invasion can be of particles (including gases), noise, vibration, etc. This all stems from the common law principle that held that one must use his land so as not to injure his neighbors. There are two types of nuisances, public and private.

1. **Private Nuisances.** There are three elements to private nuisances: (i) there must be a substantial interference with the plaintiff's use and enjoyment of her land caused by the defendant; (ii) the defendant must act either intentionally (meaning intending to cause the action that produces the offense) or negligently (including wantonly, recklessly, etc.); and (iii) the plaintiff must be entitled to the use and enjoyment of the land; she must be in possession, but need not be the owner.

   a. **Weighing the harm.** From the above rule it is evident that the extent of the harm must be evaluated. This includes looking at the extent and character of the harm, the burden it will cause the defendant to correct the harm, the social value of the land invaded, and the suitability of the invaded land to the locality. See the Restatement (Second) of Torts for more details.

   b. **Nuisances at law.** A nuisance at law (nuisance per se) is one not permitted in the neighborhood in question. Thus, storing highly radioactive atomic wastes in barrels in a residential neighborhood is a nuisance per se.

   c. **Nuisances in fact.** A nuisance in fact (nuisance per accidens) is one that, due to the location or circumstances, is a nuisance. A business that may lawfully be conducted at the particular location is never a nuisance per se. It can only be a nuisance in fact.

2. **Public Nuisances.** This is a nuisance that adversely affects the public as a whole. A public nuisance may be a crime and penal sanctions may be available to curb it. Conversely, if the use is permitted by statute or ordinance, it is not a public nuisance. Private individuals can bring public nuisance suits only in limited circumstances. The private plaintiff must show that the nuisance is especially injurious to her and that the harm she suffers is different from the harm to the public generally. Finally, if the plaintiff meets this criteria, she need not have an interest in adversely affected land.

3. **Unintentional Act.** An unintentional act may be a nuisance. When an unintentional act is involved, the court must take into account not only

the gravity of the harm (as in intentional act cases) but also the degree of fault of the defendant.

4. **Compared to Trespass.** An invasion of a plaintiff's land may be either a trespass or a nuisance. The chief distinction is that a nuisance involves interference with the quiet enjoyment of the land and trespass involves interference with the right to possess the land.

B. BASIS OF LIABILITY

1. **Three Bases.** Liability can rest on any of three bases: (i) ***intentional conduct***; (ii) ***negligence***; or (iii) ***strict liability based on abnormally dangerous activity***.

2. **Substantial Interference.** There must be a substantial interference with the use and enjoyment of land that would be offensive to a reasonable person of ordinary sensibilities.

   a. **Sensitive persons.** The fact that a particular person is unusually sensitive does not make conduct a nuisance as to that person. Thus, it is not a nuisance to ring a church bell merely because it throws a sensitive person into convulsions. [Rogers v. Elliot, 15 N.E. 768 (Mass. 1888)] The fact that people in the vicinity are hardened to unfavorable conditions may bar an action for nuisance. There are some things that the law requires people to put up with, such as smoke and noise from a factory.

   b. **Number of instances.** Older cases held that there had to be a recurring interference, but today this is not required. One occurrence may suffice to create liability for nuisance. However, the duration of the interference is crucial in some cases.

3. **Locality.** The nature of the locality becomes an important factor here. The courts must determine what is a reasonable use within the context of the custom of the community.

C. APPLYING NEGLIGENCE LAW

1. **Persons Protected by Private Nuisance Law--Philadelphia Electric Company v. Hercules, Inc.,** 762 F.2d 303 (3d Cir. 1985).

Philadelphia Electric Company v. Hercules, Inc.

   a. **Facts.** The Pennsylvania Industrial Chemical Corporation ("PICCO") operated a hydrocarbon resin manufacturing plant on property that was sold to Gould. Gould then sold the site to Philadelphia Electric Co. (P), which owned an adjacent site. Hercules, Inc. (D) succeeded to PICCO, assuming all its debts and liabilities. The Pennsylvania Department of Environmental Resources discovered that toxic residue from the site was seeping into a river and P spent about $400,000 to clean it up. P then sued D on theories of private and public nuisance and indemnity for its damages and for an injunction to require D to clean up any further wastes. The district court granted judgment for P and D appeals.

b. **Issue.** May a buyer of real estate force the seller to clean up toxic wastes left on the site on the theory that the wastes constitute a private nuisance?

c. **Held.** No. Judgment reversed.

1) A private nuisance is a nontrespassory invasion of another's interest in the private use and enjoyment of land. Assuming that D created a nuisance and is liable on that basis, the issue is to whom D is liable.

2) The rule of caveat emptor applies to P's purchase of the land because both parties were commercial corporations, there was no misrepresentation or concealment, and P had a full chance to investigate the property's condition. P seeks to circumvent this limitation on a nuisance theory, but there is no case authority for P's proposition that it may recover from D on a private nuisance theory for conditions existing when it bought the land.

3) Private nuisance law is intended to resolve conflicts between neighbors, who, unlike buyers, have no protection through inspection and negotiation. Certainly the price P paid for the land reflected the possible environmental risks. To apply private nuisance law against the seller would undermine the market mechanism.

4) P also seeks recovery under public nuisance law, but P's damages are not the same as those suffered by the public. The public suffers from the interference with its right to pure water. P suffers from the cost of clean up. Because P's harm is different from the public's, P has no standing to bring an individual action for public nuisance.

5) P claims the award should be upheld on the basis of indemnification, but this doctrine applies to jointly liable defendants, not a plaintiff's cause of action against one defendant.

d. **Comment.** The court noted that D might be liable to its neighbors for a private nuisance, or to users of the river water for a public nuisance. In addition, a governmental agency could possibly take action against D on statutory or public nuisance grounds.

Morgan v. High Penn Oil Co.

2. **Negligence Is Not an Element if the Act Is Intentional--Morgan v. High Penn Oil Co.,** 77 S.E.2d 682 (N.C. 1953).

a. **Facts.** Morgan (P) lived on nine acres about 1,000 feet from High Penn Oil Co.'s (D's) refinery since 1945. Since 1950, for several hours a week,

D dumped large quantities of nauseating gases and odor into the air. These nauseating gases invaded P's land. The gases were highly noticeable for up to two miles away. P sued to recover temporary damages for a private nuisance. P won $2,500 and D appeals.

b. **Issue.** Is negligence a necessary element for a private nuisance?

c. **Held.** No. Judgment affirmed.

1) A nuisance per se (nuisance at law) is an act, occupation, or structure that is a nuisance at all times and under any circumstances regardless of location or surroundings. A nuisance per accidens (nuisance in fact) is that which becomes a nuisance by reason of its location or by reason of the manner in which it is constructed.

2) An oil refinery is a lawful business and hence cannot be a nuisance per se. However, D errs in contending that an oil refinery cannot be a nuisance per accidens, absent it being constructed or operated in a negligent manner.

3) Negligence and nuisance are two distinct fields of tort liability. While the same act or omission that results in negligence may also result in nuisance liability, such is not always the case.

4) Basically a private nuisance is (i) any substantial nontrespassory invasion of another's interest in the private use of land, (ii) whether intentional or unintentional.

a) If the invasion is unintentional, the defendant's conduct must be negligent, reckless, or ultrahazardous (*e.g.*, blasting with dynamite).

b) If an intentional invasion is involved, then the defendant's conduct must be unreasonable under the circumstances.

5) Conduct is "intentional" if the defendant acts with the purpose of causing it or knows that it results from its conduct or knows that it is substantially certain to result from its conduct. Anyone who creates or intentionally creates or maintains a private nuisance is liable regardless of the degree of care or skill exercised to avoid such injury.

6) D intentionally and unreasonably caused noxious gases and odors to escape onto P's land to such a degree as to substantially impair P's use and enjoyment of the land. Thus, D is liable in nuisance. D also intends to operate the refinery in the future in the same manner it has in the past. Thus, P is entitled to an injunction as part of its remedy.

Carpenter v. The Double R Cattle Company, Inc.

3. **Balancing Utility and Harm--Carpenter v. The Double R Cattle Company, Inc.,** 701 P.2d 222 (Idaho 1985).

a. **Facts.** The Double R Cattle Company, Inc. (D) operated a feedlot near the home of the Carpenters (Ps). D expanded the feedlot to handle 9,000 cattle, and Ps filed suit claiming the odor, pollution, dust, and noise from the feedlot constituted a nuisance. The jury found for D, but the court of appeals reversed because the trial court did not instruct the jury according to the new version of section 826 of Restatement (Second) of Torts. The Idaho Supreme Court granted review.

b. **Issue.** May a nuisance exist even if the utility of the conduct outweighs the harm, so long as the harm is serious and payment of damages is feasible without requiring the business to cease?

c. **Held.** No. Judgment reversed.

1) The traditional rule in Idaho is that the utility of the conduct must be considered in determining whether a nuisance exists. The new Restatement approach would change this rule by permitting a finding of nuisance even when the utility of the conduct outweighs the harms it produces. The new approach has not been adopted in Idaho.

2) The economy of Idaho relies on agriculture, lumber, mining, and industrial development. The new approach would unreasonably burden these industries and is therefore against public policy.

d. **Dissent.** The traditional rule is outdated. D's feedlot is clearly a nuisance. The new approach would permit D to stay in business so long as it compensates P for the harms imposed on P. This approach prevents a neighboring landowner from incurring all the external costs of D's operation. Idaho's businesses will not be eliminated if they have to pay for the nuisances they create.

D. LAND USE REGULATION THROUGH NUISANCE

Winget v. Winn-Dixie Stores, Inc.

1. **Zoning--Winget v. Winn-Dixie Stores, Inc.,** 130 S.E.2d 363 (S.C. 1963).

a. **Facts.** Winget (P) brought an action for damages alleged to have been sustained as a result of the location and operation, by Winn-Dixie Stores, Inc. (D), of a supermarket on land adjacent to P's home. D appeals from a judgment entered in P's favor.

b. **Issue.** May the location and operation of a supermarket, by itself, constitute a nuisance?

c. **Held.** No. Judgment reversed and remanded.

1) The evidence shows that in locating the building, in terms of zoning and construction, D did not create a nuisance. If a lawful business is operated in an unlawful or unreasonable manner, so as to interfere with the proper use and enjoyment of the property of others, such will constitute a nuisance.

2) People who live in organized communities must, of necessity, suffer some inconvenience and annoyance consequent upon the reasonable use of the property of others.

3) P's allegation that the increased congestion and noise that resulted from the operation of D's store constituted a nuisance is without foundation. However, disturbance from odors, escaping garbage, floodlights, and air conditioning may well, as P claims, constitute nuisance, because they raise an inference that such acts are not normal or necessary incidents to the operation of the store. Those issues must be submitted to the jury for determination.

E. REMEDIES

There are basically two types of remedies. One is an injunction forbidding the activity that causes the nuisance. The other is damages. A court may refuse to grant an injunction and instead award damages, as the next case indicates. An aggrieved party is also entitled to use reasonable self-help to abate the nuisance. The party can use only reasonable force in doing this. Sometimes a party can bring a summary proceeding to abate the nuisance.

1. **Weighing the Value of the Offending Conduct.** Courts must weigh the value of the offending conduct. If the offending conduct is of good social value and may suitably be conducted at the particular location, and it is impractical to prevent the invasion, the court may award the plaintiff damages instead of abating the nuisance.

2. **Economic Considerations--Boomer v. Atlantic Cement Co.,** 257 N.E.2d 870 (N.Y. 1970).

Boomer v. Atlantic Cement Co.

a. **Facts.** Atlantic Cement Co. (D) was operating a large cement plant near a large community. Suit was brought by Boomer and others (Ps), as neighboring landowners, for injury to land due to smoke, dirt, and vibration. A nuisance was found at trial, with temporary damages, but the lower courts refused to enjoin continued operation of the plant because of the large disparity in economic consequences between the nuisance and an injunction. This left Ps with the option of bringing successive suits as further damage occurred.

The court also found an amount of permanent damages to guide a settlement. Ps appeal.

b. **Issue.** Where a nuisance is shown with substantial damages, must an injunction be allowed as a matter of course, regardless of economic consequences?

c. **Held.** No. Judgment reversed on other grounds.

1) The general rule adhered to with great consistency has been that where damages are substantial, injunction will lie to abate a nuisance. However, to grant injunction in the instant case would require the court to close down a business that is important to commerce and that cannot at present be operated in a different manner.

2) The drastic remedy of closing down D's plant can be avoided in various ways. One way would be to grant the injunction but make the effective date far enough in the future to allow technological development sufficient that D could eliminate the nuisance. Another way would be to grant the injunction conditioned on D's payment to Ps of permanent damages.

3) To grant permanent damages in lieu of injunction would more justly balance the equities in this case. D will be required to pay the damages, or an injunction will lie.

d. **Dissent.** We should not change the longstanding rule that an injunction should issue to stop a nuisance that causes substantial continuing damage. This approach licenses a continuing wrong and impairs the incentive for D to eliminate the nuisance. The holding of the majority also imposes a servitude upon Ps' lands without their consent and is unconstitutional.

Spur Industries, Inc. v. Del E. Webb Development Co.

3. **Preexisting Lawful Industries--Spur Industries, Inc. v. Del E. Webb Development Co.,** 494 P.2d 700 (Ariz. 1972).

a. **Facts**. Spur Industries, Inc. (D) had owned and operated a cattle feedlot for a number of years prior to the development of the housing subdivisions owned by Del E. Webb Development Co. (P). P began constructing retirement villages and other housing units a couple of miles away from D's cattle feedlot, and as the housing units began to spread in the direction of the feedlot, a problem began to develop because of the noxious odor and flies around the feedlot. P began to encounter strong sales resistance to those houses that were closest to the cattle yard. Therefore, P brought suit to enjoin the operation of the feedlot because it constituted a public nuisance. The trial court held that the cattle feedlot was a public nuisance and issued an injunction. D appealed, claiming that it should not be required to close down, and that if it is required to close down it should be indemnified by P.

b. **Issue.** When the operation of a lawful business becomes a nuisance by reason of the encroachment of a nearby residential area, may the business operation be enjoined?

c. **Held.** Yes. Judgment affirmed in part.

1) A change in the surrounding area can make a preexisting lawful use into a nuisance. A state statute provides that anything that constitutes a breeding ground for flies and is injurious to the public health is a public nuisance. A business that is not a public nuisance per se may become such by being carried on at a place where the health, comfort, and convenience of a populous neighborhood begins to be affected.

2) A party that "comes to the nuisance" usually cannot get an injunction against any prior use, on the theory that he knows of the nuisance and accepts the area as it is. But in this case, because the nuisance was injurious to the public health, an injunction is appropriate.

3) Because P brought people to the nuisance, to the foreseeable detriment of D, P must indemnify D for the reasonable expense of moving or shutting down.

F. DEFENSES

The defenses available to the defendant are dependent upon whether his conduct has been intentional or negligent, or whether he is deemed strictly liable for the interference.

1. **Contributory Negligence.** Contributory negligence is available only in situations where the nuisance is based on the negligent acts of the defendant.

2. **Assumption of Risk.** Assumption of risk is available in situations where the nuisance is based on the negligent conduct of the defendant and where the nuisance is based on strict liability.

XVII. DEFAMATION

A. INTRODUCTION

At common law, every element of the prima facie case of defamation was based on strict liability except that of publication. Publication had to be intentional or negligent. Substantial changes in the proof requirements have occurred due to modern constitutional decisions. The chapter is organized to present the common law principles first, with the impact of the constitutional decisions later. The common law elements of defamation are:

1. **Defamatory.** The matter published must be capable of a defamatory meaning.

2. **Referring to Plaintiff.**

   a. **Identification required.** One of the basic elements of defamation is that the statement be "of and concerning" the plaintiff. If the plaintiff is clearly identified in the statement, such as having his name mentioned, proof of this element is easy. When additional facts are necessary to indicate that the plaintiff is the one intended, this additional area of proof is referred to as "colloquium."

   b. **Group libel.** When a defamatory statement attacks members of a group generally, it is difficult for any one member of the group to seek a remedy. In order for any one member of such a group to recover, certain requirements must ordinarily be met. First, the statement must be understood to include all or, in some cases, most of the people in a group. It would be difficult, for example, for a member of a group to recover if the statement included only "some" or "a few" of the group. Success would be more likely for the plaintiff, however, if the statement referred to "all" of the group. Secondly, the size of the group must be small. As the size of the defamed group increases, there is less chance for any one member of the group to recover. A defamatory statement about "all lawyers" would not be the basis for a claim by any one lawyer.

3. **Defamatory of the Plaintiff.**

4. **Publication.** In order to hold the defendant liable, the plaintiff must show either that the defamatory matter was intentionally communicated by the defendant to some third person who understood it, or that the communication to the third person was made through the defendant's failure to exercise due care (*i.e.*, done negligently).

5. **Causation.**

6. **Damages.**

B. DETERMINING WHAT IS DEFAMATORY

Most courts have adopted the rule that matter communicated to others is defamatory if it tends to lower the reputation of the party about whom it refers, in the eyes of the community (a substantial minority of those in the locality where the matter is published is sufficient), or if it causes others to refrain from associating with the party about whom it refers.

1. **Ambiguous Statements for Jury to Decide--Belli v. Orlando Daily Newspaper, Inc.,** 389 F.2d 579 (5th Cir. 1967).

Belli v. Orlando Daily Newspaper, Inc.

   a. **Facts.** The Orlando Daily Newspaper, Inc. (D) printed false information concerning Belli's (P's) alleged misuse of Florida Bar Association funds. The court found, as a matter of law, that D's publication was not libel per se, and dismissed P's claim. P appeals.

   b. **Issue.** May the court rule, as a matter of law, whether a statement open to two meanings is defamatory?

   c. **Held.** No. Judgment reversed and remanded.

      1) A libel per se is any publication that exposes a person to distrust, hatred, contempt, ridicule, or obloquy. Both judge and jury play a part in determining whether language constitutes libel. First, the court determines whether D's words are reasonably or necessarily capable of a particular defamatory interpretation. Then, the jury must decide whether the words were in fact understood as defamatory.

      2) D just barely makes a case that its article is nondefamatory and merely recounts how P "put one over" on the bar association. On the other hand, the bare bones of the article are capable of carrying the meaning that P tricked the bar out of hundreds of dollars. Thus, since the publication is capable of carrying a defamatory meaning, the jury should have been allowed to determine whether it was so understood by the common mind.

2. **Minority Rule.** Matter communicated to others is defamatory if it arouses hatred, contempt, or ridicule for the party about whom it refers, or causes him to be shunned by others.

3. **Colloquium.** Published matter may be defamatory of someone, but not specifically mention the plaintiff. However, if it could reasonably be in-

terpreted by those receiving the communication as referring to the plaintiff, he will have a cause of action. In *Youssoupoff v. Metro-Goldwyn-Mayer Pictures, Ltd.* (Eng. 1934), the defendant made a movie dealing with the alleged circumstances in which the influence of Rasputin on the Czar and Czarina brought about the destruction of Russia. In the film, Rasputin, who was portrayed to be the basest of characters, ravishes a princess called Natasha. The plaintiff was Princess Irina, a member of the Russian Royal House, and claimed that, though the name of the character was changed to Princess Natasha, it was intended to refer to her, and was so understood by those viewing the film, all of which lowered her reputation, held her up to contempt, etc. The jury agreed and awarded her damages in the amount of £25,000.

Grant v. Reader's Digest Association

4. **Innuendo or Implication--Grant v. Reader's Digest Association,** 151 F.2d 733 (2d Cir. 1945).

   a. **Facts.** Reader's Digest (D) published an article stating in part that Grant (P) had recently acted as the legislative representative of the Communist Party. The statement did not say that P was a Communist (which, at the time, would have caused him to be shunned by others, etc.) but P claimed that such a conclusion could be reasonably drawn from the statement—the party would not hire someone to represent them who was not also a "fellow traveler." The trial court dismissed the complaint for insufficiency in law.

   b. **Issue.** Was the matter defamatory?

   c. **Held.** Perhaps. Judgment reversed and remanded.

      1) The fact that "right-thinking people" would not find the matter defamatory is not determinative; if a substantial number of people would think less of P, shun him, etc., this is sufficient for taking the case to trial. Liability is not a question of majority vote.

      2) Further, the fact that the statement did not directly state that P was a Communist or a "fellow traveler" (which might lower his reputation in the community, etc.), is not material, as this was certainly implied.

   d. **Comment.** The form of the statement is not the determining factor. If a third person receiving the communication could reasonably interpret it as defamatory of the plaintiff, the plaintiff will have a cause of action.

Kilian v. Doubleday & Co., Inc.

5. **Fabrication Similar to Fact--Kilian v. Doubleday & Co., Inc.,** 79 A.2d 657 (Pa. 1951).

   a. **Facts.** Doubleday (D) published a story in which Kilian (P) was said to have been reprimanded and fined for mistreatment of American soldiers. P had in fact been disciplined for similar misbehavior, but had not participated in the incidents described. P brought an action for libel, and the jury decided for D. P appeals.

b. **Issue.** May D avoid liability for its libelous statements merely because it proved that P had in fact been guilty of similar misconduct?

c. **Held.** No. Judgment reversed.

1) The fact that P was found guilty of similar misconduct does not support D's attempt to use truth as an affirmative defense. The misconduct relied on in justification of the publication must be as broad as the charge, and proving the truth of one of many charges does not constitute a justification.

2) There was not a shred of evidence that the author saw any of the events, or that those events or even substantially similar ones occurred, or that P was aware of such happenings, or that he sanctioned them. The court erred, therefore, in submitting to the jury the question of whether the publication was substantially true.

6. **Group Defamation--Nieman-Marcus v. Lait,** 13 F.R.D. 311 (S.D.N.Y. 1952).

Nieman-Marcus v. Lait

a. **Facts.** Lait (D) wrote a book in which he claimed that unnamed models and saleswomen employed by Nieman-Marcus (P) were prostitutes. D also claimed that most of P's salesmen were homosexual. P and three groups of its employees, including all of its models, 15 out of 25 of its salesmen, and 30 out of its 382 saleswomen, sued D, claiming libel and defamation. D moves to dismiss.

b. **Issue.** When a publication libels some or less than all of a designated small group, do the individuals in the group have a cause of action?

c. **Held.** Yes. Motion denied.

1) When a large group is libeled, none of the individuals in the group may sue. If the group is small and each member is referred to, any individual member can sue. This is because a defamation of a small class affects each individual in the class. However, when a small group is libeled and not all members are included, some courts hold that no individual member has a cause of action while other courts would permit such a suit.

2) In this case, D claimed that most of P's salesmen were "fairies." This is a small group and suit is permissible.

3) D's book refers to P's saleswomen generally, but the group of 382 members is large and no specific individual is named. No reason-

able person would identify a particular member of this class with the publication's allegations.

4) The models clearly have a cause of action.

Bindrim v. Mitchell

7. **Mixing Fiction with Fact--Bindrim v. Mitchell,** 92 Cal. App. 3d 61, 155 Cal. Rptr. 29, *cert. denied*, 444 U.S. 984 (1979).

a. **Facts.** Mitchell (D), a novelist, registered in Bindrim's (P's) group therapy program, which involved nude encounters. P was a psychologist. D promised not to disclose the activities, but she soon wrote a novel about the technique, using a Dr. Herford as a psychiatrist who conducted the sessions. Dr. Herford had a different appearance than P, but the evidence showed that the novel was based substantially on P's conduct observed by D. P sued for libel against D and her publisher. The jury found for P, but the trial court granted a new trial unless P agreed to a remittitur of damages. Both parties appeal.

b. **Issue.** Does publication of a book based on P's conduct, but also including fictional and derogatory accounts, constitute libel?

c. **Held.** Yes. Judgment affirmed as modified.

1) The test for libel is whether a reasonable person, reading the book, would understand that the fictional character described therein was actually P.

2) Here, the only differences between Dr. Herford and P were the respective physical descriptions and the degrees held. The narrative was closely parallel to actual real life events. Whether the reader would have considered the defamatory passages as mere fictional embroidering or as reporting of actual conduct was a jury question, which was resolved in P's favor.

3) Although only those persons who were involved in the therapy groups would recognize P, publication to only one person other than P constitutes libel.

d. **Concurrence.** D would not have committed libel if she had written a factual account or an entirely fictional one. The vulgar language attributed to the novel's therapist is clearly defamatory. The fact that one person reasonably understood the defamatory effect of the novel suffices to show what readers generally would reasonably understand.

e. **Dissent.** The only similarity between Dr. Herford and P is that they both practice nude encounter therapy. Those actions in the novel that are similar to P's are classified as identifying, while those that are different are libelous because they are false. Thus, a novel is libelous because it is fictional, and malice is inferred from the fact that the publisher knew it was not a true representation of P.

C. LIBEL AND SLANDER

1. **Defined.** Traditionally, libel was defined as defamation by written or printed word whereas slander was defamation by word of mouth. As other forms of communication became available (radio and television), a modification of definitions became necessary. The modern definitions are found in the Restatement of Torts, section 568:

   a. Libel consists of the publication of defamatory matter by written or printed words, by its embodiment in physical form, or by any other form of communication that has the potentially harmful qualities characteristic of written or printed words.

   b. Defamation other than that defined above is slander.

   c. The area of dissemination, the deliberate and premeditated character of its publication, and the persistence of the defamatory conduct are factors to be considered in determining whether a publication is a libel rather than a slander.

2. **Radio and Television Broadcasts.**

   a. A broadcast of defamatory words read from a manuscript has been held to be libel.

   b. Defamatory matter not reduced to writing, but broadcast by radio or television is libel rather than slander. For example, in *Shor v. Billingsley*, 158 N.Y.S.2d 476 (1956), the defendant, in a television appearance, said, "I wish I had as much money as [the plaintiff] owes." The court held the rules of libel, rather than slander, should apply because the exhibition leaves a lasting impression similar to that of written words.

   c. A few states have statutes making such broadcasted material slander.

   d. To decide whether a publication is libel or slander in difficult cases (*e.g.*, defamations contained on a phonograph record, or in a television or radio program), courts generally consider these factors: (i) permanence or nonpermanence of form; (ii) area of dissemination; and (iii) deliberate or premeditated character of the publication. The greater the permanency and possible area of dissemination, and the more willful the publication, the more likely the courts are to call it libel.

3. Damages for Slander.

a. **Actual damages.** Care must be used in reviewing the damage principles applicable to libel and slander. The constitutional decisions now require proof of actual damages in many defamation cases in order to recover damages.

b. **Nominal damages.** At common law, proof of a libel or a slander per se would, in the absence of proof of damages, entitle the plaintiff to at least nominal damages.

c. **Compensatory damages.** Compensatory damages are of two types:

1) **General damages.** General damages are available when the words are actionable per se and the plaintiff prevails. At common law these were presumed to be the natural or probable consequence of the defendant's conduct, and the plaintiff did not need to prove actual damages. Under modern constitutional decisions, however, the plaintiff must prove actual damages in many cases.

2) **Special damages.** Special damages must be alleged in the pleadings and proven by the evidence. These damages are usually to recover pecuniary losses and generally have to be proven at common law for an action in slander to lie.

d. **Punitive damages.** Punitive damages are given only when claimed in the pleadings and the evidence shows actual malice.

e. **Slander per se—damages.** Special damages do not have to be proven for an action in slander in four (and only four) situations:

1) Where the defendant charges that the plaintiff has committed a serious, morally reprehensible crime, or that the plaintiff has been incarcerated for such a crime;

2) Where the defendant imputes to the plaintiff a presently existing, loathsome, communicable disease (venereal disease, leprosy, etc., but not tuberculosis or insanity);

3) Where the defendant imputes to the plaintiff conduct, characteristics, etc., incompatible with the proper performance of the plaintiff's business, trade, office, or profession; and

4) Where the defendant imputes unchastity to a female plaintiff.

Terwilliger v. Wands

4. Imputing Unchastity to a Man--Terwilliger v. Wands, 17 N.Y. 54 (1858).

a. **Facts.** Terwilliger (P) sued Wands (D) for slander. D told several people that P, a man, committed adultery. P learned of this, took ill because of it, and consequently could not do his farm work. P brought an action for slander per se. The trial court granted a nonsuit for D at the end of P's case. P appealed to the court of general term, which affirmed the trial court ruling. P appeals.

b. **Issue.** Is it slander per se to impute unchastity to a man?

c. **Held.** No. The nonsuit for D is affirmed.

1) It is not slander per se to impute unchastity to a man; therefore, to recover for slander, P must prove special damages.

2) Slander actions are given by law to remedy a damaged reputation. Generally, this reputation injury is shown through proving special damages. Loss of marriage or of customers or the prevention of receiving some other benefit that the plaintiff normally would receive is sufficient damage.

a) Slander actions are not available to heal wounded feelings.

b) The words must be defamatory in their nature. They must disparage a plaintiff's character. Here, the words could have had that effect if believed.

c) Harm caused by a third person's repetition of slander is deemed remote and is not actionable (*i.e.*, A slanders B, and C repeats A's comments).

d) In this case, apparently no one believed the slander, hence there was no damage to reputation.

e) P tried to show damage through loss of health caused by the apprehension of damage to reputation. Even if P could have shown his illness was directly the result of the defamation, the nonsuit would have been affirmed since fear of harm is not sufficient.

d. **Comment.** The court bases its holding in part on the consideration that any loss of health (such as occurred with P) is not a "natural, ordinary" consequence of P's character being damaged. Also, the imputation of unchastity to a woman is slander per se (so no special damages need be shown), but this rule has not generally been extended to men.

5. **Damages Rule for Libel.** If the defamation is in the form of libel and is clear on its face, most jurisdictions ***presume general damages*** from the fact that it was published. The plaintiff need not show special damages to recover, although if he can show some, he can recover these also. The rationale is that because of the permanency of form, possible extent of dissemination, etc., of

a libel, there is greater likelihood of harm, so general damages may be presumed.

a. **Libel per quod.** There is less agreement when the matter published is innocent on its face, but becomes defamatory when linked up with certain extrinsic facts. Some follow the general libel rule and never require special damages. A few states presume general damages only if the libel would be actionable as one of the four types of "slander per se." About 20 states require proof of special damages in every case of libel per quod.

b. **Retraction statutes.** Several states have "retraction statutes," the effect of which is to limit the damages recoverable against specified media that publish defamations. Typically, these statutes provide that the named defendant cannot be held liable for general damages resulting from a defamatory publication unless it has failed to fairly and promptly make a retraction of such defamation, after demand upon it by the injured party. Special damages may be recovered, however, regardless of the plaintiff's demand or the defendant's retraction.

D. PUBLICATION

In defamation, "publication" means the communication by the defendant of defamatory matter to a party other than the plaintiff.

1. **Manner of Publication.** The plaintiff must prove that the defendant intentionally communicated the defamatory matter to some third person who understood it, or that the defendant failed to exercise due care in communicating it to the third person and was therefore negligent. Words communicated only to the plaintiff are not actionable. Similarly, defamatory words that a third party does not understand are not actionable. In *Economopoulos v. A.G. Pollard Co.*, 105 N.E. 896 (Mass. 1914), only the plaintiff heard the defamatory words in English, and no one else (besides the plaintiff) understood the defamatory words spoken in Greek ("You have stolen a handkerchief from us and have it in your pocket"). Note, however, that under certain circumstances, the publication may be effected through the plaintiff; *e.g.*, the plaintiff is a minor or blind (third party must read it to the plaintiff).

2. **Common Law Rule.** The common law rule was that every delivery of libelous matter was itself a new publication that gave rise to a new and separate cause of action. This is still the general rule except with regard to books, periodicals, and newspapers.

   a. **Single publication rule.** The modern "single publication" rule holds that the publication of a book, periodical, or newspaper gives rise to but one cause of action. When a book is printed containing a libel, the statute of limitations begins to run from the date of its first publication. In *Ogden v. Association of the United States Army*, 177 F. Supp. 498 (D.C. 1959), the defendant published a book about Korea, which contained a passage critical of the plaintiff's handling of a platoon, that the plaintiff claimed was defamatory. The court held the plaintiff's action barred by the statute of limitations on the basis of the single publication rule.

E. BASIS OF LIABILITY

1. **Malice.** In the early development of the law of defamation, "malice" had to be pleaded and proved for there to be recovery. Though malice may still be important with regard to punitive damages, malice (in the sense of ill-will) is no longer necessary to a cause of action for defamation, though it often poses a difficulty for the courts. Courts sometimes confuse common law malice with "actual malice" (the defendant's knowledge of the falsity of his defamatory communication or his reckless disregard of the truth, which is discussed below). Many courts now require actual malice instead of ill-will malice whenever malice is required (*e.g.*, recovery of punitive damages and loss of qualified privilege).

2. **Constitutional Privilege.** In order to protect freedom of speech and freedom of the press, a constitutional privilege has been developed with regard to statements that concern public officials or public figures, or that are on matters of legitimate public interest. Matter that is otherwise defamatory and that relates to public officials or public figures or to matters of legitimate public interest is not actionable unless the plaintiff can show that the defendant published the defamatory matter with knowledge of its falsity or in substantial disregard thereof. The plaintiff's right to be free from defamation must be balanced against the right of the people to receive information of public interest.

3. **Public Officials and Actual Malice--New York Times Co. v. Sullivan,** 376 U.S. 254 (1964).

New York Times Co. v. Sullivan

   a. **Facts.** New York Times (D) published an advertisement that criticized the action of officials in Montgomery, Alabama, with regard to their treatment of civil rights workers. The advertisement stated that the treatment violated constitutional rights of blacks through intimidation and violence. It was uncontroverted that many facts asserted in the advertisement were false. Commissioner Sullivan (P) was responsible for the police department. P sued D. The trial court awarded P $500,000 in damages. The trial court held that a false publication is libelous per se if it injures an official in his public office or imputes misconduct to his office. The award was sustained by the Alabama Supreme Court. D appeals.

b. **Issue.** May a public official recover damages for a defamatory falsehood relating to his official conduct if he does not prove that the statement was made with actual malice?

c. **Held.** No. Judgment reversed.

1) The advertisement was an expression of protest on a major public issue and hence clearly qualifies for First Amendment protection. The constitutional guarantees of free speech and press require a federal rule that prohibits a public official from recovering damages for defamation unless the statements were made with actual malice.

2) Protection of statements made in the exercise of a First Amendment freedom has never depended upon the truth of the statement. Injury to official reputation affords no more excuse for repressing otherwise free speech than does factual error.

3) The fact that the Alabama law allows the defense of truth does not save the law from unconstitutionality. A rule compelling a critic of official conduct to guarantee the truth of his statements on pain of a libel judgment imposes self-censorship and a dampening of free choice.

4) The rule created by this case is analogous to that which protects federal officials from libel suits for their nonmalicious statements about private citizens.

5) "Actual malice" means with knowledge that the statement is false or making the statement with a reckless disregard of the truth or falsity. P's case lacks proof of actual malice.

6) Prosecutions for libel of the government cannot be brought even by an official who insists that they are a reflection on his conduct.

7) There was no reference to P in the advertisement either by name or position, and there was no basis suggested at trial to justify P's belief that he was personally attacked by references in the advertisement to the police.

d. **Comment.** This case holds, in effect, that the news media (and private citizens) can defame public persons as long as the publication occurs without the defendant's knowledge that the statement is false or with reckless disregard of the truth on the defendant's part.

St. Amant v. Thompson

4. **"Reckless Disregard" as Malice--St. Amant v. Thompson,** 390 U.S. 727 (1968).

a. **Facts.** St. Amant (D) made a political speech on television and read the statements of a third party, which falsely accused Thompson (P), a deputy sheriff, of criminal conduct. The Supreme Court of Louisiana affirmed for P on a finding that D acted in "reckless disregard" of the truth so as to constitute the malice necessary under *New York Times*. The Supreme Court granted certiorari.

b. **Issue.** May negligence alone constitute recklessness?

c. **Held.** No. Judgment reversed for D.

1) Recklessness is not measured by the reasonable person standard, as mere negligence is never sufficient to show "actual malice."

2) The test is whether the defendant in fact entertained serious doubt as to the truth of his publication. Publishing with such doubts would be reckless disregard for truth or falsity and would demonstrate actual malice.

5. **False Quotes--Masson v. New Yorker Magazine,** 501 U.S. 496 (1991).

Masson v. New Yorker Magazine

a. **Facts.** New Yorker Magazine (D) published an article by Janet Malcolm, an author and contributor to *The New Yorker*, concerning Masson (P), a well-credentialed scholar, psychoanalyst, former director of the Sigmund Freud Archives, and acknowledged public figure. In the article, Malcolm enclosed lengthy passages in quotation marks, indicating that these were statements made by P. During D's editorial fact checking process, P was contacted by one of D's editors and, according to P, he advised the editor that there were a number of errors in the few passages discussed. The article was nonetheless published as a two-part series and later republished in book form by Alfred A. Knopf, Inc. in spite of, and with knowledge of, P's claim that the article published by D contained defamatory material. P filed an action for libel in United States District Court in San Francisco. In support of his claim, P offered several passages that were purported to be direct quotes from the author's interviews with P, but were unsupported by either the author's tapes or her contemporaneous notes. D's motion for summary judgment was granted, and the Ninth Circuit Court of Appeals affirmed. The United States Supreme Court granted certiorari.

b. **Issue.** Are false quotes that are either substantially true or are one of a number of possible "rational interpretations" of an ambiguous conversation or event entitled to constitutional protection?

c. **Held.** No. Judgment reversed.

1) Since P is a public figure, he must prove that D published the defamatory statement with actual malice, *i.e.*, with "knowledge that it was false or with reckless disregard of whether it was false or not."

However, we reject the idea that any alteration beyond correction of grammar or syntax in an alleged quotation proves its falsity for determining "actual malice."

2) Instead, we conclude that the deliberate alteration of words uttered by a plaintiff only equates with knowledge of falsity when the alteration results in a material change in the meaning conveyed by the statement. Further, an altered quotation is not protected even if it is a "rational interpretation" of an actual statement.

Gertz v. Robert Welch, Inc.

6. **Private Individuals--Gertz v. Robert Welch, Inc.,** 418 U.S. 323 (1974).

a. **Facts.** Gertz (P), a reputable attorney, represented the family of a youth who had been shot and killed by a police officer in a civil action against the officer. Robert Welch, Inc. (D), published an article in its magazine accusing P of participation in a Communist conspiracy against the police and membership in two Marxist organizations. P sued D for libel and the trial court directed a verdict on the liability issue in P's favor because the statements were admittedly false and libelous per se. The jury returned a verdict of $50,000, but the trial judge entered a judgment n.o.v. for D on the ground that the article was about a matter of public interest and protected by the *New York Times* rule, absent a showing of actual malice. An appeals court affirmed. The Supreme Court granted certiorari.

b. **Issue.** May a private individual who sues for defamation be awarded punitive damages when liability is not based on knowledge of falsity or reckless disregard of the truth?

c. **Held.** No. Judgment for D is reversed and the case is remanded for a new trial.

1) An erroneous statement of fact is not worthy of constitutional protection but it is inevitable in free debate. Some falsehood must be protected in order to protect important speech and avoid media self-censorship that results when the media are required to guarantee the accuracy of their factual assertions. Nevertheless, there is a legitimate state interest underlying the law of libel, which is the compensation of the victims of defamation.

2) The balance of freedom of speech and the state's interest in protecting its citizens from libel requires that a different rule be applied to private individuals than that stated in *New York Times*.

3) A private individual does not have the access to the media that is available to public officials and public figures to contradict the libel and minimize its impact.

4) Public officials and public figures, by their involvement in public affairs, accept the risk of close public scrutiny. Private individuals who are defamed are thus more deserving of recovery.

5) So long as they do not impose liability without fault, the states may define the appropriate standard of liability for defamation of a private individual.

6) P, although he had been active in civic and professional organizations, was not a public figure. He had not sought public notoriety. Furthermore, he never discussed the case with the media.

7) Because of the competing interest of the First Amendment, state remedies for defamation must only compensate the actual injury, unless actual malice is proven.

8) States may not presume damages in this type of case. Actual injury must be shown by competent evidence.

9) The awarding of punitive damages must necessarily be carefully limited; otherwise, juries have the power to punish the expression of unpopular views.

d. Comment. This case created the following rules: Liability without fault cannot be imposed on the news media defendant. The plaintiff must prove that the publisher either knew the statement was false or was at least negligent in ascertaining the truth. In addition, in order to recover damages, actual damages must be proved. Only if actual malice can be shown can damages be presumed.

7. Public-Private Distinction. As noted above, the proper basis of liability in a defamation case depends on a determination of whether the plaintiff is a public or private figure. If the plaintiff is a public figure, actual malice is the appropriate standard. If the plaintiff is a private figure, at least negligence is required. The courts have developed two tests to determine whether a plaintiff is a public figure:

a. A plaintiff is a public figure for all purposes if she has assumed a role of special prominence in the affairs of society.

b. A plaintiff is a public figure for the limited purposes being reported if she thrust herself to the forefront of a particular public controversy in order to influence the resolution of the issues involved.

8. The Media-Nonmedia Question--Dun & Bradstreet, Inc., v. Greenmoss Builders, Inc., 472 U.S. 749 (1985).

Dun & Bradstreet, Inc., v. Greenmoss Builders, Inc.

a. Facts. Dun & Bradstreet (D) provided to five of its customers a credit report indicating that Greenmoss Builders, Inc. (P) had filed for bankruptcy. In fact, P had not filed for bankruptcy and the mistake was made by a high school student employed by D. The bankruptcy had been by a former employee of P. D notified the five customers but refused to give P the names of those who received the report. P sued and, although the trial court had not instructed the jury on the requirements of actual malice, the jury awarded punitive damages. The trial judge ordered a new trial, but the Vermont Supreme Court reversed. The United States Supreme Court granted certiorari.

b. **Issue.** Do the constitutional standards apply to all defamation cases regardless of the identity of the defendants or the type of issues involved?

c. **Held.** No. Judgment affirmed.

1) The constitutional protections granted by the First Amendment apply when there are matters of public concern. Here there was merely the private reporting of credit ratings by a nonmedia defendant. P will not be required to meet the constitutionally mandated element of actual malice in order to recover punitive damages.

d. **Dissent** (Brennan, Marshall, Blackmun, Stevens, JJ.). The opinion of the majority should not be read too broadly. The only issue is whether punitive damages should be allowed in the absence of proof of actual malice. Trying to distinguish between media and nonmedia defendants is not workable. In addition, there is nothing in the First Amendment that indicates that the press is entitled to greater rights than nonpress. The attempt to distinguish between private and public concerns is also not workable. The majority gives no guidance as to the test to apply. P should be able to recover actual damages, but should not recover punitive damages unless actual malice is proven.

e. **Comment.** Justices Burger and White concurred. A majority of the Court in this case rejected the media-nonmedia distinction, and the plurality opinion interpreted the *Gertz* rules as only applying to defamation on matters of "public concern."

Philadelphia Newspapers, Inc. v. Hepps

9. **Private Figure Must Prove Falsity--Philadelphia Newspapers, Inc. v. Hepps,** 475 U.S. 767 (1986).

a. **Facts.** Philadelphia Newspapers, Inc. (D), published an article containing charges that Hepps (P) and his business had links to organized crime and influenced the government through those links. P sued for defamation. Under state law, a private plaintiff had to prove negligence or malice, and then the defendant had to prove the defamatory statement was true. The jury found for D, but the Pennsylvania Supreme Court reversed and ordered a new trial. The Supreme Court granted certiorari.

b. **Issue.** When a newspaper publishes speech of public concern, may a private-figure plaintiff recover damages without proving that the statements are false?

c. **Held.** No. Judgment reversed.

1) The accommodation between defamation and freedom of speech and of the press varies according to the nature of the speech and the status of the plaintiff. If the speech is of public concern, a public official or public figure must prove more than the common law requirements before he can recover from a media defendant. If the speech is of public concern but the plaintiff is a private figure, the constitutional requirements are less stringent but still more demanding than the common law rule. When the speech is of exclusively private concern, a private figure may essentially follow the common law rule.

2) It may not be possible in all cases to prove conclusively whether particular speech is true or false, and in such cases the burden of proof is dispositive. The common law rule requires the defendant to prove truth as a defense. This rule must yield to the First Amendment when, as in this case, the newspaper articles are of public concern, even though the plaintiff is a private figure. The Constitution favors protecting true speech, and this allocation of the burden of proof is the best means to avoid deterring true speech on matters of public concern.

d. **Dissent** (Stevens, J., Burger, C.J., White, Rehnquist, JJ.). A private individual should not be forced to bear the risk that a defamatory statement, made out of malice or careless indifference, cannot be proven false. The majority has given no weight to the state's interest in protecting a private individual's reputation. Deliberate libels contribute little to the marketplace of ideas. D in this case would only have to prove the truth of its statements if P first proves D was at fault. The First Amendment certainly does not protect deliberate defamation through unprovable facts. Even if the majority's rule should apply to attacks on public figures, it should not apply when a private individual is the subject of the attack.

10. **No Constitutionally Protected Opinion--Milkovich v. Lorain Journal Co.,** 497 U.S. 1 (1990).

Milkovich v. Lorain Journal Co.

a. **Facts.** Milkovich (P) was the coach of a high school wrestling team that was involved in a brawl with a competing team and placed on probation by the Ohio High School Athletic Association. Parents of some team members sued to enjoin the association from enforcing the probation. At a court hearing, P and the school superintendent denied that P had incited the brawl. A sports columnist wrote a column indicating that P had lied under oath, thereby preventing the team from receiving just punishment. P and the superintendent sued the newspaper (D) separately. After 15 years of litigation, the court held that the column was constitutionally protected opinion and granted D's motion for summary judgment. The Ohio Court of Appeals affirmed. The United States Supreme Court granted certiorari.

b. **Issue.** Is there a First Amendment-based protection for defamatory statements categorized as "opinion"?

c. **Held.** No. Judgment reversed and remanded.

1) At common law, the privilege of "fair comment" developed as an affirmative defense to an action for defamation, affording immunity for the honest expression of opinion on matters of legitimate public interest when based upon a true or privileged statement of fact.

2) Here, D argues that we should establish another First Amendment-based protection for defamatory statements that are characterized as "opinion" as opposed to fact, relying on dictum in *Gertz v. Robert Welch, Inc.* (*supra*). However, we do not think that *Gertz* was intended to create such a privilege. To do so would ignore the fact that an expression of "opinion" may often imply an assertion of objective fact.

3) Under our current law, a statement on matters of public concern must be provable as false before there can be liability for defamation, at least when a media defendant is involved. Next, statements that cannot reasonably be interpreted as stating actual facts are protected. Thus, we are not persuaded that an additional separate constitutional privilege for "opinion" is required to ensure freedom of expression.

4) The dispositive question in this case then is whether a reasonable fact finder could conclude that statements in D's column imply that P perjured himself. We think the answer is yes. The language in the article is not the loose, figurative, or hyperbolic language that would negate the impression that the writer was seriously maintaining that P committed the crime of perjury. Also, the connotation that P committed perjury is sufficiently factual to be proved true or false.

F. PRIVILEGES

Although a statement may be defamatory, a defendant may escape liability by proving that she had a privilege to speak. These privileges are in the nature of true defenses and must be pleaded and proven by the defendant. The privileges are creations of public policy and are usually intended to protect some important public interest. These public interests may include protecting the rights of people in certain positions to speak or protecting the right of people in certain relationships to exchange information. It is important to note that privileges may be either absolute or qualified.

1. **Absolute Privileges.** These privileges are a complete defense to any action for publication of a defamation. They are not affected by the showing of malice, excessive publication, or abuse.

   a. **Governmental privileges.**

      1) **Judicial.** Witnesses, attorneys, judges, jurors, and the parties in an action are privileged to utter defamations that have some relevancy to the matter at hand.

      2) **Legislative.** All federal and state legislative members are absolutely privileged to utter defamations while on the floor or in committee. The utterances need not be relevant.

      3) **Executive.** Top cabinet-grade executives of state or federal government are absolutely privileged. This includes the President, Cabinet officers, and department heads. Relevancy is a requirement, however.

   b. **Domestic.** Spouses may utter defamations of third persons to each other. Some courts extend this privilege to utterances among members of the immediate family.

2. **Qualified Privileges.** Under certain conditions, a speaker may have a qualified privilege to speak. Although privileged to speak, the defense may be lost if the statements were the result of excessive publication. By this, the court usually means either revealing more information than necessary or telling more people than necessary. Some courts have indicated that the privilege may be lost by a showing of malice. There is, however, some confusion as to how malice is defined. Some courts hold the privilege lost under this concept by a showing of ill will, while others (probably a majority) require proof that the statement was made when the speaker knew that the statement was false. Still others allow the privilege to be defeated by a showing that the speaker had no reasonable belief in the truth of the statement. These qualified privileges may arise in one of several ways.

   a. **Protect personal interest.** Where the speaker seeks to protect some interest personal to herself, the statements may be privileged.

   b. **Common interest.** Where the speaker seeks to protect some interest common to her and the listener, the statement may be privileged.

c. **Third party interest.** Where the speaker seeks to protect some interest of the listener or some other third party, the statement may be privileged.

d. **Other.** Other qualified privileges exist for such activities as credit reporting or fair comment on newsworthy events.

Sindorf v. Jacron Sales Co., Inc.

3. **Employer Privilege--Sindorf v. Jacron Sales Co., Inc.,** 341 A.2d 856 (Md. Ct. Spec. App. 1975).

a. **Facts.** Jacron Sales Co. (D), Sindorf's (P's) former employer, had a discussion with P's new employer in which he made false accusations suggesting that P might be a thief. P sued D for slander, but the court granted D's motion for a directed verdict on the basis of conditional privilege. P appeals.

b. **Issue.** If D acts with malice, or in reckless disregard of the truth, does he lose his conditional privilege to defame?

c. **Held.** Yes. Judgment reversed and remanded.

1) When a former employer communicates with a new or prospective employer about a former employee, a conditional privilege arises from a discharge of a duty owed to the new or prospective employer. Such immunity is forfeited when the former employer acts with malice, in reckless disregard for the truth, or in a manner motivated by ill will.

2) Here, D patently went beyond the requirements of the duty owed to P's new employer, in misrepresenting facts as to P's honesty. Thus, since reasonable minds could differ as to whether D acted with actual malice, the question should go to the jury on remand.

d. **Appeal.** On appeal, the court held that *Gertz* applied to this case. Even though P might be able to satisfy the *Gertz* requirements, D would still be entitled to assert conditional privilege. If privilege is successfully asserted, P would have to prove malice to overcome the privilege.

4. **Exceeding Privilege.** A conditional privilege will be destroyed by the following:

a. Excess publication;

b. Publication for an improper purpose;

c. Publication not bearing on the interest to be protected;

d. Actual malice; or

e. Lack of belief in the truth of the statement.

G. DEFENSES

1. **Truth.** At common law, truth was an absolute defense. The defendant could avoid liability by proving that the statements sued on were true. Modern constitutional decisions still recognize that truth defeats liability, but the burden of proof on that issue has changed. In order to recover, the plaintiff must now prove that the statements were false.

2. **Consent.** Although rarely raised, consent is a defense to an action for defamation. It may arise when a plaintiff asks for information and receives a defamatory report.

3. **Retraction Statutes.** Many jurisdictions provide statutes allowing the defendant to retract defamatory statements. If these statutes are followed, the publisher will not be liable for general damages, although special damages may still be recovered upon sufficient proof.

4. **Right of Reply.** Some jurisdictions have passed statutes requiring a media defendant to give plaintiffs the right to reply. Although upheld as they apply to television, these statutes have been held unconstitutional when applied to newspapers.

H. REMEDIES

1. **Constitutional Limitations on Damages.** The interests of free press and debate, guaranteed by the First Amendment, limit damage recoveries against the mass media. The Constitution protects speakers by limiting the kinds of damages recoverable, and by prohibiting any recovery unless specific standards of liability are met. The constitutional rules limiting damage recoveries are discussed *supra.*

2. **Punitive Damages.** Formerly, most states allowed punitive damages if the defamation could be shown to have been uttered with common law malice, such as hatred, ill will, or spite.

   a. Some states disallowed punitive damages entirely under state law.

   b. Although lower courts have expressed some question about the continuing legitimacy of punitive damages in defamation cases, the Supreme Court has indicated that states may award such damages when the defendant knew his statement was false or was reckless in not recognizing its falsity *(i.e.*, actual malice).

3. **No Injunctions.** Courts traditionally have refused to permit defamatory speech to be enjoined. [Willing v. Mazzacone, 393 A.2d 1155 (Pa. 1978)]

XVIII. PRIVACY

A. INTRODUCTION

The focus of this tort is not injury to reputation, but interference with the "right to be let alone" that results in injury to feelings, without regard to any effect on property, business, or reputation. Most states recognize this tort by case law, and some do by statute; a few states do not recognize it at all.

1. **The Prima Facie Case.** The elements of a privacy cause of action are:

   a. **Act by the defendant.** The act may consist of words or any type of affirmative conduct.

   b. **Serious and unreasonable invasion of the plaintiff's privacy.** This is the crux of most invasion of privacy suits.

   c. **Intent, negligence, or strict liability.** Most invasion of privacy suits involve intentional acts, but this is not essential. Liability may be imposed for negligent invasions and, at common law, even for invasions based on strict liability. Constitutional privileges may affect this element of the case.

   d. **Causation.**

   e. **Damages.**

2. **Types of Action.** There are four types of actionable invasions of privacy:

   a. Appropriation of another's name or likeness (publicity);

   b. Unreasonable intrusion upon the seclusion of another (intrusion);

   c. Unreasonable publicity given to another's private life (public disclosure); and

   d. Publicity that unreasonably places another in a false light before the public (false light).

Flake v. Greensboro News Co.

3. **Commercial Appropriation of One's Likeness--Flake v. Greensboro News Co.,** 195 S.E. 55 (N.C. 1938).

   a. **Facts.** Greensboro News (D) was found liable by the trial court for mistakenly publishing Flake's (P's) picture (in an advertisement for bread) as that of the leading lady of the Paris Follies. When D was notified of the mistake it apologized and printed a complete retraction and explanation. P won at trial and D appeals.

b. **Issue.** Does a person whose likeness is used in an advertisement without her permission have a cause of action for invasion of privacy?

c. **Held.** Yes. Judgment reversed and new trial ordered.

1) P may recover, but only nominal damages. D retracted and apologized and the act was a mistake. There is case law recognizing protection from authorized use of letters, literary work, or artwork, and therefore, by analogy, one should have a right not to have her picture published without consent.

B. INTRUSION ON SECLUSION

1. **Physical Solitude.** Similarly, invasion of one's physical solitude, as by a peeping tom, is an actionable invasion of privacy, as is searching another's handbag or spying with high-powered binoculars, or a motion picture camera.

2. **Receipt of Information Obtained by Intrusion--Pearson v. Dodd,** 410 F.2d 701 (D.C. Cir.), *cert. denied*, 395 U.S. 947 (1969).

Pearson v. Dodd

a. **Facts.** Certain former and current staff members of Senator Dodd (P) entered P's office and copied documents from P's files. The information was given to Pearson (D), who knew how it was obtained. D published the information in a newspaper column. P sued for invasion of privacy and conversion. The trial court denied partial summary judgment for P on the privacy issue but granted it on the conversion claim. Both parties appeal.

b. **Issue.** May a reporter be liable for invasion of privacy when he merely receives information obtained through intrusion?

c. **Held.** No. Judgment reversed in part.

1) Invasion of privacy through intrusion occurs when a party obtains information by improperly intrusive means. Here, D did not intrude into the protected sphere of privacy of P in obtaining the information. D merely received it. Thus, D was not liable for intrusion.

2) The other aspect of invasion of privacy involves publication. The information published by D related to P's qualifications to serve as United States Senator, and therefore is protected speech. Publication of matters of general public interest is a proper defense to a claim of invasion of privacy.

3) There was no conversion of the physical contents of P's files.

d. **Concurrence.** The irony of the case is that the press is enabled to obtain information by means that would shock the press if used by the government.

C. PUBLIC DISCLOSURE OF PRIVATE FACTS

1. **Elements.** If a reasonable person would find the disclosure of the private facts highly objectionable, then the plaintiff has a cause of action.

2. **Private Facts.** Matters to be distinguished here are:

   a. **Matters of public record.** Matters of public record are not actionable since they are already public.

   b. **Public occurrences.** Public occurrences are not actionable since anyone present would have seen them. They also are already public.

Cox Broadcasting Corp. v. Cohn

3. **Constitutional Privilege--Cox Broadcasting Corp. v. Cohn,** 420 U.S. 469 (1975).

   a. **Facts.** Cohn (P) brought an action for damages against Cox Broadcasting (D), claiming that his right of privacy had been invaded. D, during the course of a television broadcast, revealed the name of P's daughter, who had been a rape victim. Relying on a statute that made such publication a misdemeanor, the state supreme court upheld a lower court decision for P. The Supreme Court granted certiorari.

   b. **Issue.** May a state extend a cause of action for damages for invasion of privacy caused by the publication of the name of a crime victim, which is a matter of public record?

   c. **Held.** No. Judgment reversed.

      1) Clearly the First and Fourteenth Amendments protect the right to publish materials that are already of public record. There can be no invasion of privacy by a defendant when the matter has already been made public. To allow such actions would result in the news media being forced to engage in self-censorship.

D. PUBLICITY

Cantrell v. Forest City Publishing Co.

1. **Placing One in a False Light--Cantrell v. Forest City Publishing Co.,** 419 U.S. 245 (1974).

   a. **Facts.** Mrs. Cantrell's (P's) husband, the father of four, was killed along with some 40 other people when a bridge collapsed. Forest

City (D) assigned a reporter to do a feature story focusing on the husband's funeral and the impact of the death on the Cantrell family. Five months later, the reporter returned to the Cantrell home to write a follow-up story. P was not home but her children were interviewed and photographed. The story stressed the family's poverty, the house's deterioration, and the children's poor clothing. It was conceded that the story had a number of inaccuracies and falsehoods. The case went to the jury on the "false light" theory of invasion of privacy. The district judge, on D's motion, struck the claims relating to P's three youngest children. P and her eldest son received a judgment. D appealed. The sixth circuit held that D's motion for directed verdict should have been granted as to all of the Cantrells and set aside the verdict. The Supreme Court granted certiorari.

b. **Issue.** Is a newspaper's reckless disregard for the truth, which sheds false light on a plaintiff, actionable?

c. **Held.** Yes. Judgment reversed and case remanded.

1) The jury was properly instructed that D was liable only if it was shown that D published the article with knowledge of its falsity or reckless disregard of the truth. This is the constitutional "actual malice" standard used in defamation cases.

2) The district court dismissed the demand for punitive damages on the grounds that common law malice was not proven by P. There was, however, a finding of actual malice.

3) There was sufficient evidence for the jury to find that the reporter knew of the falsity of the story. D can be held on the basis of respondeat superior since it approved and published the story.

2. **Parody of Public Figures--Hustler Magazine v. Falwell,** 485 U.S. 46 (1988). Hustler Magazine v. Falwell

a. **Facts.** Hustler Magazine (D) published a parody of an advertisement in which Falwell (P), a nationally known minister, is depicted as describing a drunken incestuous rendezvous with his mother in an outhouse. The ad contained a disclaimer at the bottom. P sued for invasion of privacy, libel, and intentional infliction of emotional distress. After a directed verdict on the privacy claim, the jury found for D on the defamation claim, on the ground that it contained no assertion of fact. The jury awarded P $200,000 on the emotional distress claim, however. The court of appeals affirmed. The Supreme Court granted certiorari.

b. **Issue.** May a public figure recover damages for emotional harm caused by the publication of an offensive parody intended to inflict emotional injury, but which could not reasonably have been interpreted as stating actual facts?

c. **Held.** No. Judgment reversed.

1) Although the First Amendment promotes political debate by protecting even vigorous criticism of public officials, not all speech about a public figure is protected. A public figure may hold a speaker liable for damages to reputation caused by publication of a defamatory falsehood if the statement was made with knowledge that it was false or with reckless disregard of whether it was false.

2) P claims a different rule should apply here, where the state has sought to prevent emotional distress instead of damage to reputation. While an intent to cause emotional distress may be determinative in tort law, the First Amendment disregards the speaker's intent in the area of public debate about public figures. The alternative would deter political satire.

3) While D's parody may be more outrageous than normal political cartoons, there is no principled standard for distinguishing between more and less outrageous expression. Speech may not be suppressed for the sole reason that it offends society.

XIX. CIVIL RIGHTS

A. INTRODUCTION

The problem of official violation of civil rights has confronted the courts for years. These rights are now protected by statute in most cases, but the scope of protection is determined by the courts. 42 U.S.C. section 1983 imputes liability to any person who, under color of law, deprives another of his civil rights.

1. **Right to Vote--Ashby v. White,** 92 Eng. Rep. 126 (K.B. 1702). Ashby v. White

   a. **Facts.** P was illegally denied his right to vote by D, a public official. P's action for damages was dismissed because there was no common law or statutory remedy to cover it. P appeals.

   b. **Issue.** In denying P his right to vote, did D commit an actionable offense?

   c. **Held.** Yes. Judgment reversed.

      1) P's right to vote is derived from the common law, and consequently he may maintain an action for the destruction of it. If P has a right, he must also have a means to vindicate and maintain it. Otherwise, a right exists without a remedy. If the creation of such a cause of action produces a multiplicity of actions, so be it, for every person who is injured ought to have his recompense.

      2) As to the argument that Parliament should decide the issue, the obvious answer is that Parliament would undoubtedly say, take your remedy at law. The adoption of this action will make public officers more careful to observe the rights of citizens.

2. **Due Process Rights--Camp v. Gregory,** 67 F.3d 1286 (7th Cir. 1995).

   a. **Facts.** The Department of Children and Family Services ("DCFS") became the legal guardian of Anthony, a minor, once Camp (P), his aunt and former guardian, became unable to care for him because of her health. Gregory (D) was assigned as Anthony's caseworker. Despite knowing that P could not provide the degree of supervision and care that Anthony needed, D returned him to P's care. D failed to follow up on Anthony's progress and neglected to make appropriate referrals. D made false representations to the state court regarding Anthony's situation. P notified D that Anthony was not attending school and was putting himself in dangerous situations, yet D left Anthony in P's care. Anthony died on his 16th birthday upon being shot away from home. P sued, claiming that D denied

Anthony substantive due process by failing to place him in a safe living environment. The district court dismissed the suit under *DeShaney v. Winnebago County Department of Social Services*, 489 U.S. 189 (1989). P appeals.

b. **Issue.** May a social worker be held liable for placing a child in a home where he knows or has reason to know the child will not receive adequate supervision for activities outside the home and the child is later murdered outside the home by a third party?

c. **Held.** Yes. Judgment affirmed under qualified immunity.

1) *DeShaney* held that because the Due Process Clause does not confer an affirmative right to government aid, the state cannot be held liable for injuries that could have been averted had it chosen to provide the aid. That case involved a child who had been repeatedly abused by his father, to the point of becoming permanently retarded. Local officials had investigated and determined that there was insufficient evidence to permit them to retain custody. The Court there did note that once the government takes a person into custody, it assumes responsibility for his safety and general well-being. But that responsibility goes away when the government releases the person.

2) In this case, it is significant that DCFS had become Anthony's guardian, because at that point it assumed a role that made it constitutionally liable for Anthony's well-being. Several cases hold government officials liable for placing minors in foster homes where they suffered abuse or neglect. The government may return a child to her parents without violating her rights, but when it places a child in a foster home, it may be liable for damages.

3) P does not allege that D placed Anthony in an abusive home or that anyone in P's household abused or neglected him. However, supervision is also an important part of child care, and a child such as Anthony has a due process right not to be placed with a custodian whom the state knows will fail to exercise the requisite degree of supervision.

4) While normally when the state returns a child to its home there is no liability, this case is different because P specifically asked to terminate her guardianship because she could not provide the necessary supervision and because D retained responsibility after placing Anthony in P's home. In effect, D resurrected the danger that had motivated P to surrender guardianship in the first place. In addition, if D in fact misled the court about Anthony's situation, he may have frustrated the efforts of other private persons and the government to improve Anthony's situation.

5) While public officials cannot be constitutionally obligated to protect a child from all dangers outside the home, any more than parents them-

selves could be, a parent does not relinquish all responsibility once a child leaves the house. Accordingly, the government has a duty not to place one of its charges with an adult that it knows will not or cannot exercise supervision outside the home. In that situation, a caseworker such as D may be held liable for a deprivation of liberty if the caseworker fails to exercise bona fide professional judgment, the caretaker fails to exercise reasonable supervision, the injury suffered is reasonably foreseeable to the caseworker, and there is a causal link between the lack of supervision and the injury.

6) A public official who deprives someone of his constitutional rights may be immune if his actions were objectively reasonable, meaning that his conduct does not violate clearly established statutory or constitutional rights a reasonable person would have known. In this case, although P did allege facts sufficient to state a claim for violation of substantive due process, D has qualified immunity. P did not argue that her complaint alleged a separate procedural due process claim so that issue was not considered.

3. **Punitive Damages--Memphis Community School District v. Stachura,** 477 U.S. 299 (1986).

Memphis Community School District v. Stachura

a. **Facts.** Stachura (P) was suspended from his tenured teaching position in response to parents' complaints about the way P taught science with sexually explicit films. P sued the Memphis Community School District (D) and others under 42 U.S.C. section 1983, claiming the suspension deprived him of liberty and property without due process. The district court instructed the jury on compensatory and punitive damages and told them they could award additional compensatory damages depending on the value of the constitutional rights violated. The jury awarded compensatory and punitive damages. The court of appeals affirmed and the Supreme Court granted certiorari.

b. **Issue.** May a plaintiff recover punitive damages under section 1983 for violations of constitutional rights?

c. **Held.** No. Judgment reversed and remanded.

1) Under section 1983, a plaintiff is entitled to damages as determined by the common law of torts. Except for punitive damages, tort damages are intended to provide compensation for the plaintiff's injury. Such damages may be awarded for mental anguish and suffering as well as out-of-pocket losses. Compensatory damages also provide a measure of deterrence.

2) Contrary to the compensatory purpose of section 1983, the jury in this case was instructed that it could compensate P depending on

the money value of the rights' importance in our system of government. This detracts from P's provable injury and focuses on the abstract importance of the constitutional rights involved. The abstract value of a constitutional right is not a proper basis for damages under section 1983.

3) P claims the instructions authorized a form of presumed damages, but presumed damages are a substitute for compensatory damages, not an addition to such compensatory damages. The erroneous instructions are not harmless error, because it is impossible to determine how the jury arrived at its award. On remand, the jury should be instructed as to compensatory damages for P's injury and punitive damages only.

XX. ABUSE OF LEGAL PROCEDURE

This section covers several distinct torts involving the plaintiff's interest in freedom from unjustifiable legal proceedings.

A. MALICIOUS PROSECUTION

The tort of malicious prosecution concerns the wrongful institution of criminal proceedings by one private citizen against another, resulting in damage.

1. Prima Facie Case.

a. **Instigation of proceedings by the defendant.** Criminal proceedings are initiated by a charge made to the police or other public officials in such form as to cause the issuance of a warrant or indictment against the accused.

b. **Proceedings terminated favorably to the plaintiff.** The plaintiff must allege and prove that the criminal proceeding was terminated in a manner indicating his innocence.

c. **Lack of probable cause.** The plaintiff must also show that the defendant instituted the proceedings without probable cause—*i.e.*, that the defendant had no honest or reasonable belief in the truth of the charge. This is an objective test, but it is also a good faith requirement. Thus, the defendant may be held liable even where there are sufficient facts to indicate to a reasonable person that the plaintiff was guilty, if the defendant himself knows better. Because of its complex nature, the question of probable cause is usually decided by the judge.

d. **Improper purposes.** It must appear that the defendant instituted the proceeding for some improper purpose, meaning some motive other than bringing a guilty person to justice. This is sometimes called "malice." Lack of probable cause must be proved independently from the improper purposes requirement because even a person acting from improper motives may know of facts that give rise to a reasonable and honest belief of guilt. While lack of probable cause cannot be inferred from improper purpose, improper purpose ***may*** be inferred from lack of probable cause.

e. **Causation and damages.** The plaintiff may recover all expenses incurred in defending against the criminal prosecution (*e.g.*, attorneys' fees, investigative expenses, court costs). He may also recover damages for mental suffering and embarrassment, harm to reputation, damage to business, etc., as well as punitive damages in appropriate cases.

f. **Defenses.**

1) **Plaintiff's guilt.** Notwithstanding the termination of criminal proceedings favorable to the plaintiff, the defendant may show as a defense that the plaintiff really was guilty of the crime. The acquittal in the criminal proceedings only establishes that the state could not prove the plaintiff's guilt "beyond a reasonable doubt," whereas in the civil tort proceedings, the standard of proof is only a preponderance of the evidence.

2) **Privilege.** Judges, prosecutors, and various other law enforcement officers are absolutely privileged and immune from charges of malicious prosecution.

Texas Skaggs, Inc. v. Graves

2. **Knowledge that the Plaintiff Lacked Intent to Commit Crime--Texas Skaggs, Inc. v. Graves,** 582 S.W.2d 863 (Tex. 1979).

a. **Facts.** Graves (P), a former employee of Texas Skaggs, Inc. (D), wrote two checks for a total of $34.70 at D's store for groceries. P's husband, from whom P had separated, had withdrawn all of P's money from her checking account without telling P. Consequently, the checks bounced. Once P found out, she agreed to cover the checks as soon as she could get the money from her credit union. The day after P paid the money, D's manager reported P's bad checks to the local police. He later filed an affidavit for P's arrest. P was arrested but released when her claim that she had paid the checks was verified. P was given the checks that had been attached to the arrest affidavit. D insisted on prosecuting P and P hired a defense attorney. The judge dismissed the case because the prosecution did not have the checks. P then sued for malicious prosecution. The jury found for P and awarded her $20,000. D appeals.

b. **Issue.** May a person who seeks criminal prosecution for apparently proper reasons be held liable for malicious prosecution if the person actually had knowledge to indicate the accused did not have the necessary intent to commit the crime charged?

c. **Held.** Yes. Judgment affirmed.

1) To support a claim for malicious prosecution, P would have to prove: (i) that D instituted or continued a criminal prosecution against P; (ii) that the proceedings terminated in P's favor; (iii) that there was no probable cause for the proceeding; (iv) that D acted with malice; and (v) that P suffered damages.

2) There is no question that D initiated and continued the prosecution of P. However, D claims that the dismissal for failure of evidence was not a termination in favor of P. The proper rule is that any ter-

mination that concludes the proceeding so that it cannot be revived is sufficient for a malicious prosecution suit. The prosecution of P was abandoned because conviction became impossible or improbable; it was not dismissed on technical or procedural grounds. Had the prosecutor pressed for a full trial, P would have been found not guilty. By finding for P, the jury rejected D's defense that P was in fact guilty of the charge.

3) The probable cause element is based on an objective reasonable person standard, but it also includes a subjective element. If, despite facts that would lead a reasonable person to believe that P was guilty, D actually knew better, then D may have lacked probable cause. To be guilty, P must have had the intent to defraud. However, D knew that the checks were small and were used only to buy groceries, that P immediately agreed to make restitution, and that she did in fact make restitution. P could have written many more checks had she intended to defraud D. Under the circumstances, the jury could reasonably conclude that D had no probable cause to institute or continue the prosecution. D's knowledge created a duty to investigate further before prosecuting.

4) Malice is shown by evidence that D had a wrongful or improper motive, but lack of probable cause may permit an inference of malice. D's continued prosecution after P was released, with the statement that it did not care whether P had paid the checks, indicates a malicious intent on the part of D.

5) The evidence supports the verdict. P was arrested in front of her friends and former fellow employees. She was taken to the police station and booked. Her criminal record interfered with her ability to obtain employment elsewhere. There is no indication that the jury acted improperly in making the award, and the award is not so excessive that it shocks the sense of justice.

B. MALICIOUS INSTITUTION OF CIVIL PROCEEDINGS

Many states extend the concept of malicious prosecution to civil proceedings as well. The basic elements are the same as those in actions based on malicious criminal proceedings, and the same types of damages may be recovered.

1. **Nature of Proceedings.** The tort extends to any form of noncriminal proceeding—including administrative hearings, insanity or narcotics commitment proceedings, etc.

    a. An action may be maintained for malicious institution of civil proceedings where the damage complained of results solely from the recordation of a lis pendens—even though the notice itself would be absolutely privileged insofar as slander of title is concerned.

b. However, a small claims court proceeding, even if maliciously instituted, may not be the basis of a suit. Such proceedings are too inexpensive and informal to cause any real damage.

2. **Effect of Prior Verdict.** Unlike the criminal acquittal in malicious prosecution cases, a verdict for the plaintiff in the prior civil proceedings cannot be questioned in a subsequent action for malicious institution of those proceedings; *i.e.*, all material issues decided in the first suit are res judicata between the parties.

3. **Special Injury Requirement.** The tort of malicious prosecution originated in England, where costs are awarded to the prevailing party. When the costs remedy was deemed inadequate because of the aggravated nature of the case, extra damages for malicious prosecution were permitted to compensate for: (i) injury to the defendant's fame; (ii) injury to the defendant's person or liberty; and (iii) injury to the defendant's property. This English rule requiring special injury has been followed by many American courts. However, most jurisdictions do not require proof of special injury.

Friedman v. Dozorc

4. **Attorney's Duty--Friedman v. Dozorc,** 312 N.W.2d 585 (Mich. 1981).

a. **Facts.** Serafin died from a fatal blood disease shortly after surgery for removal of a kidney stone. Her husband hired Dozorc (D), an attorney, to bring a malpractice action against Friedman (P), the urologist who recommended the surgery. At the malpractice trial, D did not call any expert witnesses to show that P had breached professional standards. The judge directed a verdict for P and the other defendants in that trial. P then sued D for the negligent instigation of a lawsuit, abuse of process, and malicious prosecution. The trial court granted summary judgment for D. The court of appeals affirmed in part but reversed the dismissal of P's claim for malicious prosecution. Both parties appeal.

b. **Issue.** Does an attorney owe a duty of care to prospective adverse parties in a lawsuit?

c. **Held.** No. Judgment affirmed.

1) P claims that an attorney who brings civil suit owes a duty under the Code of Professional Responsibility to his client's adversary. This duty requires that the attorney have a good-faith belief that his client has a tenable claim, based on a reasonable investigation of the facts and law.

2) While an attorney may have an obligation to investigate, this duty extends to his client, not to the client's adversary. A duty toward the

adversary would constitute a conflict of interest as the attorney would have a duty towards both sides of the lawsuit. It would also deter attorneys from bringing close cases and from suing those who would likely retaliate.

3) P's claim for abuse of process requires proof of (i) an ulterior purpose and (ii) an act in the use of process that is improper in the regular prosecution of the proceeding. In this case, P could not show that D had committed any irregular act. The mere issuance of a summons and complaint is not abuse of process.

4) An action for malicious prosecution is permitted in Michigan, but only upon proof of special injury. The English rule is better than the American rule because it limits the circumstances in which malicious prosecution suits may be brought. The remedy for excessive litigation is not more litigation.

5) The arguments against the English rule are not persuasive. Another tort action is not the best means of deterring meritless litigation. Under the American rule, an action for malicious prosecution could be brought by any former defendant in a civil case who prevailed at trial. This remedy is too strong. Adding the prospect of retaliatory malicious prosecution suits to the existing problems of delays and expenses in bringing suits would too strongly favor the defense.

6) Besides special injury, a suit for malicious prosecution must prove (i) favorable termination of prior proceedings, (ii) absence of probable cause for those proceedings, and (iii) malice. The fact that a defendant prevailed is insufficient to prove that the case was maliciously prosecuted. To establish a case of malicious prosecution against an opposing attorney, the plaintiff must prove that the attorney had an improper purpose, independent of any improper purpose of the client's of which the attorney was unaware. It is not enough to show that the attorney did not make an adequate investigation because of time constraints imposed by statutes of limitation and because of lack of power to compel discovery before suit is filed.

5. Cause of Action Arises Before Actionable Suit Is Complete--Grainger v. Hill, 132 Eng. Rep. 769 (1838). Grainger v. Hill

a. Facts. Grainger (P) owned a ship, which he mortgaged to Hill (D) for £80, promising to repay a year later. P was to continue using the vessel for his own profit. However, before the due date, D threatened to arrest P for not paying, unless P agreed to give up his ship. P refused to pay and D, knowing P could not make bail, had him arrested and imprisoned until he gave up the ship. As a result, P lost four voyages. P sued, and D moved for a dismissal on the ground that D's suit was not yet terminated.

b. **Issue.** May a suit for abuse of process be commenced before the process is completed?

c. **Held.** Yes. Judgment for P.

1) In an action for malicious arrest or malicious prosecution, the proceeding must be terminated before the injured party may sue, because the injured party must show absence of reasonable and probable cause.

2) P here is proceeding on a theory that D abused the process of the law, which is a new type of case. As his claim is based on D's using the process of law for a purpose not within the scope of the process, it does not matter whether D had reasonable or probable cause, so the process does not have to be terminated before P can sue.

d. **Comment.** In modern times, unreasonable use of the subpoena power may constitute abuse of process. [*See, e.g.*, Board of Education v. Farmingdale Classroom Teachers Association, 343 N.E.2d 278 (N.Y. 1975)—teachers association used subpoenas to require all teachers to appear in court at the same time, effectively closing down the schools]

XXI. MISREPRESENTATION

A. INTRODUCTION

1. **Definition.** Misrepresentation is a specialized area of the law where the plaintiff is seeking damages for some economic loss suffered because of reliance on a false statement. Although some recovery for a negligently made false statement is allowed, the traditional common law action for fraud or deceit required a knowingly made false statement.

2. **Basic Elements for Fraud.** The basic elements for fraud are:

   a. A false representation of a material fact;

   b. Scienter or knowledge that the statement is false;

   c. Intent to induce reliance;

   d. Justifiable reliance on the statement; and

   e. Damages.

3. **Basic Elements for Negligence.** A negligent misrepresentation occurs when there is:

   a. A false representation of a material fact;

   b. Failure on the part of the defendant to use reasonable care to determine the truth of the statement;

   c. Duty to the plaintiff who relied;

   d. Justifiable reliance; and

   e. Damages.

4. **Deceit Actions Based upon Innocent Misrepresentations.**

   a. **Majority rule of no liability.** Under the majority rule, if the defendant innocently misrepresents a material fact by mistake, she will not be liable. The maker of the statement must have actual knowledge of its falsity, or negligent ignorance as to its truth or falsity.

   b. **Minority rule: liability.** However, a growing minority position in cases involving the sale of land or chattels is that the good faith of the maker is immaterial. All that need be shown is that the statements were false and intended to induce reliance and that damages resulted from the plaintiff's justifiable reliance thereon.

B. CONCEALMENT AND NONDISCLOSURE

Swinton v. Whitinsville Savings Bank

1. **Failure to Disclose--Swinton v. Whitinsville Savings Bank,** 42 N.E.2d 808 (Mass. 1942).

   a. **Facts.** Whitinsville Savings Bank (D) sold a house to Swinton (P) knowing it to be infested with termites, but made no mention of the fact to P. P could not readily ascertain the condition and later incurred considerable expense for termite control. P brought suit against D for fraudulent concealment. D demurred, and the court sustained the demurrer. P appeals.

   b. **Issue.** Does a seller's mere nondisclosure of a known defect in a home constitute fraudulent concealment?

   c. **Held.** No. Judgment affirmed.

      1) A vendor who fails to disclose a latent defect is not liable therefore. Mere nondisclosure when dealing at arms length is no basis for an action for misrepresentation.

      2) There was no fiduciary relation between the parties. D did nothing to prevent P from discovering the defect. The law does not require sellers to disclose every known nonapparent defect any more than it requires buyers to disclose every known nonapparent virtue.

   d. **Comments.**

      1) This rule has been changed in most jurisdictions by case law or statute, at least where a home sale is involved.

      2) When the plaintiff seeks equitable relief (*e.g.*, rescission of contract), courts have been much more liberal and often grant relief. When the parties stand in some confidential or fiduciary relationship, the defendant may be liable for nondisclosure. Also, a confidential relationship may be found to have been created by certain types of contracts (*e.g.*, suretyship, joint adventure, insurance), such that the defendant will have a duty to make a full and fair disclosure of all the material facts.

2. **Incomplete or Ambiguous Statement.** Courts often allow a deceit action for nondisclosure of basic facts going to the essence of the transaction. However, it is difficult to set out definite rules or principles in this area; in large part, recovery depends on the degree of the half-truth.

3. **Persons to Whom Duty to Disclose Extends--Griffith v. Byers Construction Co. of Kansas, Inc.,** 212 Kan. 65 (1973).

Griffith v. Byers Constuction Co. of Kansas, Inc.

a. **Facts.** Griffith and others (Ps) discovered that the new homes they had purchased were built on highly saline soil, which was impossible to landscape. Alleging that Byers Construction Co. (D) graded the land to prevent discovery of the defective soil, Ps sued D on the alternative theories of breach of implied warranty of fitness, and fraud in the concealment of a material matter. D was granted summary judgment on the first theory and a dismissal on the latter. Ps appeal.

b. **Issue.** Does a real estate developer have a duty to disclose known defects in a manner sufficient to apprise the ultimate buyers?

c. **Held.** Yes. Judgment affirmed as to implied warranty; reversed as to fraud.

1) By subdividing and offering lots for sale, D did not, by implication, warrant the fertility of the soil, nor could liability on an implied warranty be reasonably imposed on him.

2) As to D's argument of lack of privity, since, as the evidence shows, Ps were within a class of persons D intended to reach, the doctrine of privity provides no defense. One who makes a fraudulent misrepresentation or concealment is subject to liability for pecuniary loss to persons whom he intends or has reason to expect to act in reliance on the misrepresentation or concealment.

3) Where a vendor has knowledge of a defect in property that is not within the fair and reasonable reach of the vendee and that could not be discovered by the exercise of reasonable diligence, the silence of the vendor constitutes fraudulent concealment. To be actionable, the fraudulent concealment must be material to the transaction. The soil condition of a new residential building site is clearly material.

d. **Comment.** There has been little tendency to require the buyer with special knowledge to disclose it to the seller.

C. BASIS OF LIABILITY

1. **To the Recipient.** A tort action for misrepresentation is fundamentally different from a suit for rescission of a contract based on misrepresentation of a material fact. A contract claim merely requires proof of misrepresentation, whether made intentionally or innocently. A tort claim

requires more; *i.e.*, the plaintiff must prove wrongdoing on the part of the defendant.

Derry v. Peek

a. **Scienter--Derry v. Peek,** [1889] 14 A.C. 337.

1) **Facts.** Derry and other directors of a railway company (Ds) issued a prospectus stating that their charter gave the company the right to use steam power instead of horses. Ds honestly believed this to be the truth, but later the Board of Trade refused to consent to the use of steam and the company folded. Peek (P) had invested in the company in reliance on the representation that it had the right to use steam as stated in the prospectus. The trial court dismissed the suit, the appellate court reversed, and Ds appeal to the House of Lords.

2) **Issue.** May an action for deceit be maintained against one who makes a false statement in the honest belief that it is true?

3) **Held.** No. Judgment reversed.

a) One must establish scienter on the part of the defendant in order to sustain an action for deceit. Scienter may be defined as knowledge of the falsity of the representation made, or knowledge that one has no knowledge one way or the other as to the truth or falsity of the representation made (*i.e.*, recklessness).

4) **Comment.** This is known as the English rule and is followed by about half of the American jurisdictions. [*See also* Restatement (Second) of Torts §526] However, in many of these states one can maintain a negligence action to recover any pecuniary loss sustained.

b. **Reasonableness of belief.** The plaintiff may be able to prove by inference that the defendant did not entertain an honest belief from the fact that the belief is unreasonable.

c. **Motive.** Motive does not play a part in an action for deceit, at least as far as liability is concerned. Therefore, an asserted good motive on the part of the defendant cannot provide a defense.

d. **Representation of mere belief as knowledge.** When a party represents a material fact to be true to her personal knowledge, the other party is entitled to rely on the representation. When knowledge is possible, one who represents a mere belief as knowledge misrepresents a fact. Therefore, when a party represents a material fact to be true to her personal knowledge, and it is actually untrue, there is an actionable fraud if the other party acts on it to her injury. However, if the plaintiff knows that the representations of the defendant are indeed false, her actions (reliance) based on them will be unjustified and the defendant will not be liable.

e. **Negligence in making a statement.**

1) **English rule.** The English rule is that the plaintiff may have no relief from the defendant's negligently spoken or written word—negligence must be based upon an act.

2) **American rule.** American courts, on the other hand, have adopted a contrary rule and allow recovery where there is a duty, if one speaks at all, to give the correct information. However, for this rule to apply, there must be knowledge or its equivalent: (i) that the information is desired for a serious purpose; (ii) that the recipient will rely and act upon it; and (iii) that the recipient will be injured in some way if the information is false.

   a) In addition, there must be a relationship between the parties such that one has a duty to give the information with care and the other has a right to rely on it.

3) **Duty to give correct information--International Products Co. v. Erie Railroad Co.,** 155 N.E. 662 (N.Y. 1927).

International Products Co. v. Erie Railroad Co.

   a) **Facts.** International Products (P) imported certain goods for resale, which Erie Railroad (D) agreed to store in D's warehouse. On August 17, P, in order to obtain insurance on the goods, inquired where the goods were stored and was informed that they were at Dock F. P told this to the insurer. In fact, the goods had not yet arrived, and when they did arrive, part of them were stored in Dock D. Several months later, when the goods in Dock D were destroyed by fire, P was unable to collect from the insurer because of the misdescription in the policy. P successfully sued D for the insurance it would have been entitled to but for D's negligent misinformation. D appeals.

   b) **Issue.** May damages be recovered for negligent misrepresentation where there is a duty to give correct information?

   c) **Held.** Yes. Judgment for P affirmed.

      (1) Where there is a duty to give correct information, the negligent giving of false information is actionable.

      (2) Although the English rule as given in *Derry v. Peek* is that no cause of action is maintainable for a mere statement unless the maker knows it to be false, American courts have found liability for negligent statements where there is a duty to be correct.

      (3) For the misrepresentation to be actionable, the maker must have known that the information was requested for a serious purpose, would be relied upon, and that damage would result if it

was incorrect. Furthermore, the relationship between the parties must justify reliance upon the information.

(4) D was about to become bailor of P's goods, and knowing that P sought to insure its goods, owed a duty to P to provide accurate information.

4) **Scope of duty in negligence cases.** When the action is one in negligence, the defendant must have contemplated the reliance of a particular plaintiff or group of persons to which the plaintiff belongs, whereas in a deceit action, liability extends to all those whose reliance was reasonably foreseeable.

f. **Products.**

Winter v. G.P. Putnum's Sons

1) **Books--Winter v. G.P. Putnam's Sons,** 938 F.2d 1033 (9th Cir. 1991).

a) **Facts.** Winter (P) purchased a book distributed by G.P. Putnam's Sons (D) in the United States to help in the collection and eating of wild mushrooms. The book contained errors, and P became critically ill after picking and eating some wild mushrooms, requiring a liver transplant. P sued D, alleging products liability, breach of warranty, negligence, negligent misrepresentation, and false representation. D was granted summary judgment and P appeals.

b) **Issue.** May a book publisher be liable for damages for the accuracy of the material contained in the book published?

c) **Held.** No. Judgment affirmed.

(1) The information contained in a book is not a product for purposes of strict liability under products liability law. Because a publisher has no duty to investigate the accuracy of the text it publishes, it has no liability for breach of warranty, negligence, negligent misrepresentation, or false representation.

Hanberry v. Hearst Corp.

2) **Endorsements--Hanberry v. Hearst Corp.,** 81 Cal. Rptr. 519 (1969).

a) **Facts.** Hanberry (P) purchased a pair of shoes, which Hearst Corporation (D's) publication had given the Good Housekeeping seal of approval, and was injured because of alleged slipperiness of the soles. P sued D, claiming *inter alia*, that D had negligently misrepresented the quality of the shoes. P's appeal follows a dismissal of P's claim.

b) **Issue.** May D be held liable to a purchaser, who, relying on D's endorsement of a product, buys the product and is injured because it is defective?

c) **Held.** Yes. Judgment reversed as to negligent misrepresentation.

(1) P may recover damages if she can prove that D violated its duty of care by failing to test and examine the shoes, or by conducting the testing in a negligent manner. D's argument that it made a mere expression of opinion is not persuasive because, by the very procedure and method it used, D represented to the public that it had superior knowledge about the product it endorsed. The seal itself promises replacement or refund, if the consumer good proves defective.

(2) As to the alternative theories of strict liability or breach of warranty, it is clear that they are neither supported by the authorities nor warranted by the circumstances.

g. **Gratuitous statements.** One who is under no duty to furnish information cannot be held liable for its falsity if there has been no intent to deceive, *e.g.*, where a person volunteers information through an act of courtesy.

h. **Deceit actions based upon innocent misrepresentations.**

1) **Majority rule of no liability.** Under the majority rule, if the defendant innocently misrepresents a material fact by mistake she will not be liable. The maker of the statement must have actual knowledge of its falsity, or no knowledge as to its truth or falsity.

2) **Minority rule: liability.** However, a growing minority position is that the good faith of the maker is immaterial. All that need be shown is that the statements were false and that damages resulted therefrom. The minority position was adopted in section 552C of the Restatement (Second).

3) **Application of minority rule--Richard v. A. Waldman and Sons, Inc.,** 232 A.2d 307 (Conn. 1967).

Richard v. A. Waldman and Sons, Inc.

a) **Facts.** A. Waldman and Sons, Inc. (D) mistakenly represented to the purchaser of a home, Richard (P), that the home was built 20 feet within the boundary, when in fact it was only 1.8 feet from the boundary. P recovered damages for false representation, and D appeals.

b) **Issue.** Does the fact that D's misrepresentation was "innocent" bar P from recovery?

c) **Held.** No. Judgment affirmed.

(1) An innocent misrepresentation may be actionable if the declarant has the means of knowing, ought to know, or has the

duty of knowing the truth. D, as a real estate developer, has special means of knowledge, and had a duty to know where the boundary was located.

(2) Moreover, P was entitled to rely on D's representations. D's argument that the terms of the sales contract were merged into and superceded by the deed is irrelevant, because an action for misrepresentation may be brought in tort.

(3) Thus, the evidence shows that P should recover damages for the difference between the actual value of the property and the value as it has been represented.

2. To Third Persons.

a. **Class of plaintiffs.** The defendant must have intended to induce the reliance of the plaintiff, or a class of persons to which the plaintiff belongs, in a particular transaction.

Credit Alliance Corp. v. Arthur Andersen & Co.

b. **Specific plaintiff identified--Credit Alliance Corp. v. Arthur Andersen & Co.,** 483 N.E.2d 110 (N.Y. 1985).

1) **Facts.** Arthur Andersen & Co. (D) supplied audited financial statements for L.B. Smith. Smith used these statements to obtain loans from Credit Alliance Corporation (P). Although the statements showed Smith to be solvent as late as 1979, Smith filed for bankruptcy in 1980. As a result of the insolvency of Smith, P had several million dollars in loans default. P sued D, claiming that they were negligent and fraudulent in the preparation of the statements. In a companion case, European American Bank lost money because of defaults by Majestic Electro. European American had relied on statements prepared by Strauhs & Kaye. The appellate division had permitted each complaint to stand and Ds appeal.

2) **Issue.** May a plaintiff recover for economic losses caused by a defendant, when that defendant knows that a specifically identified plaintiff will rely on the defendant's work?

3) **Held.** Yes. Judgment in Credit Alliance's case is reversed but judgment in European American's case is affirmed.

a) When a defendant is on notice that the information it supplies is to be used by one clearly identified plaintiff, and, in fact, the defendant was hired specifically to provide that information to that plaintiff, the defendant owes a duty to use reasonable care towards that plaintiff. The "directly transmitted" information is close to a privity relationship.

b) When the defendant realizes that the information supplied may be relayed to others but is not on notice of the specific plaintiff, no duty exists as to that plaintiff. Under such circumstances, the defendant's duty runs to the party with which it contracted and not the plaintiff.

c) In this case, D was supplying information for Smith and owed no duty to P. Strauhs & Kaye, however, were hired specifically to provide information to European American Bank. Strauhs, therefore, owed a duty and may be liable to European Bank.

c. **Comment.** In *Glanzer v. Shepard*, 135 N.E. 275 (N.Y. 1922), a public weigher had been contacted to weigh beans and supply the weight ticket to the buyer. Since the weigher was conducting a public calling and knew the specific use of the ticket, the weigher was liable to the buyer for an economic loss. (*See also Ultramares Corp. v. Touche, Niven and Co., infra.*)

d. **Third party not in privity--Citizens State Bank v. Timm, Schmidt & Co.,** 335 N.W.2d 361 (Wis. 1983).

Citizens State Bank v. Timm, Schmidt & Co.

1) **Facts.** Timm, Schmidt & Co. (D) was an accounting firm that prepared financial statements for a client who later obtained a loan from Citizens State Bank (P). P relied on the financial statements to approve the loan of $380,000. Later, D discovered over $400,000 worth of mistakes in the statements. As a result, the client was eventually liquidated and P was unable to recover over $150,000. P sued D. The trial court granted D's motion for summary judgment, and the appellate court affirmed. P appeals.

2) **Issue.** May an accounting firm be held liable for negligence in preparing financial statements when a third party not in privity relies on the statements?

3) **Held.** Yes. Judgment reversed.

a) The traditional rule has been that accountants are not liable to third parties not in privity who rely on financial statements negligently prepared by the accountants. The modern trend favors holding accountants liable, however.

b) The rationale for holding professionals liable to third parties is that such liability promotes care in performance of professional duties. Third parties would have no alternative means of recovery. The professionals may spread the risk through liability insurance. Accordingly, privity alone is not a bar to suits by third parties against accountants.

c) Some courts restrict this type of liability to the class of persons who might reasonably be expected to rely on the information. However, tort law generally holds tortfeasors fully liable for all foreseeable consequences of negligent acts and this rule applies here.

d) Public policy may impose limits on the scope of liability. The following factors may limit liability if they apply in a particular case: (i) an injury remote from the negligence; (ii) an injury out of proportion to the culpability of the negligent tortfeasor; (iii) an unreasonable burden on the negligent tortfeasor; (iv) a likelihood that fraudulent claims would be filed; (v) no sensible or fair limit on recovery.

e) In this case, the facts must be fully developed before the application of the various policy factors may be made.

Ultramares v. Touche, Niven and Co.

e. **Fraud action--Ultramares v. Touche, Niven and Co.,** 174 N.E. 441 (N.Y. 1931).

1) **Facts.** Touche, Niven and Co. (D), a firm of public accountants, was hired by Stern to prepare and certify a balance sheet exhibiting the condition of the business. D knew that the balance sheet would be used by banks and creditors who dealt with Stern, and so presented Stern with 32 originals. Although the sheet showed a net worth of over $1 million, the business was actually insolvent. Further, D certified that in its opinion, the balance sheet presented a true view of the financial condition of Stern. Ultramares (P) loaned Stern money in reliance on the audit certified by D and suffered losses when Stern went into bankruptcy. P brought suit against D for negligence and fraud. A jury awarded P damages, but the trial judge granted D's motion to dismiss without entering the judgment. An appellate court dismissed the fraud action but not the negligence claim. D appeals. P cross-appeals the dismissal by the trial court of the cause of action for fraud.

2) **Issues.**

a) Can P recover based on the negligent misstatement of D even though P has no contractual relationship with D?

b) Can P recover under a fraud action by showing that it was one of the class that D should have foreseen would receive D's statements?

3) **Held.** a) No. b) Yes. Case remanded for trial as to the fraud action and dismissed as to the negligence action.

a) Liability for negligent misstatement extends only to the other parties to the contract pursuant to which the statement was given. To allow recovery without privity would expand liability for negligent speech to that of liability for fraud.

b) This holding does not limit liability for misstatements that are reckless or insincere, but only means that liability for honest blunders is bounded by contract.

c) Here, D certified as true something about which it had no knowledge because it did not properly investigate. Thus a jury might infer fraud.

f. **Scope of liability.** The scope of liability for negligent misrepresentation is much more limited than the scope of liability for deceit.

1) When the action is for deceit, the defendant will be liable to any person whose reliance on his representation was intended by him and he will be deemed to have intended the reliance of all those who were substantially certain to be exposed to the information. However, when the action is for negligent misrepresentation, the defendant will be liable only if there was a contemplation of reliance by the particular plaintiff.

2) Mere reasonable anticipation that a statement will be communicated to others, or even knowledge that the recipient intends to make a commercial use of it in dealing with unspecified strangers, may be sufficient to impose liability for deceit (if the statement is made without knowledge of the subject and is represented as one's own knowledge) but not for negligent misrepresentation.

3) The Restatement (Second) of Torts deals with this problem by stating that if the person who makes the fraudulent misrepresentation intends or has reason to believe that the information will be repeated or communicated to a third person, and that it will influence the third person's conduct, then liability may extend to that third person.

D. NECESSITY OF RELIANCE

1. **Justifiable Reliance Required.** In order for there to be liability for deceit or negligent misrepresentation, there must be justifiable reliance by the plaintiff on the representation, which must be a representation of a material fact. The plaintiff's unconditional reliance on misrepresentation of a material fact is almost always justified. The one exception to

this is that one cannot justifiably rely on obviously false statements (no one can rely on a known falsity).

Williams v. Rank & Son Buick, Inc.

2. **Reliance Unjustified--Williams v. Rank & Son Buick, Inc.,** 170 N.W.2d 807 (Wis. 1969).

a. **Facts.** Williams (P) bought a car from Rank & Son Buick, Inc. (D) in reliance on the false representation of D's salesman that the car had air conditioning. P brought an action for fraud and was awarded damages. D appeals.

b. **Issue.** May P recover damages for misrepresentation, when the falsity of D's statement could have been detected by ordinary observation?

c. **Held.** No. Judgment reversed.

1) One cannot justifiably rely on an obviously false statement. Because of the obvious falsity of D's statement, the court finds as a matter of law that P's reliance was unjustified.

2) Although this rule provides an unsavory defense for a defendant, when the plaintiff acts in reliance on such statements, in blind disregard of the exercise of ordinary care, the court will refuse to intervene. Otherwise, a party could enter a contract with no intent to perform unless the contract ultimately proved profitable, or could lose the benefit of a contract by an inadvertent slip of the tongue.

3) Here, P was a high school graduate of reasonable intelligence and business acumen and had ample time to determine whether the car was air conditioned.

d. **Dissent.** The falsity of the statement was not so obvious that this should be decided as a matter of law.

E. OPINION

1. **Performance, Value, and Quality.** Usually a person is not justified in relying on misrepresentations of opinion as the value or quality. A misrepresentation must be of an existing fact, not the mere expression of an opinion. When a buyer and seller are on equal footing, and the buyer has ample opportunity to examine the goods to be purchased, general statements by the seller as to the performance (*e.g.*, "performs well," etc.) or value of the goods that are false will not give rise to an action for fraud and deceit. A reasonable amount of "puffing" is tolerable and to be expected, especially when the parties stand on equal footing.

2. **Quantity and Price of Timber--Saxby v. Southern Land Co.,** 63 S.E. 423 (Va. 1909). Saxby v. Southern Land Co.

a. **Facts.** Saxby (P) brought an action to recover damages from Southern Land Co. (D) for alleged misrepresentations made in connection with the sale of a farm. D gave its opinion as to how much timber the land contained, how much timber had been burned off, what price P could sell the wood for, and how fertile the soil was. All of D's figures were high. D's demurrer was sustained and P appeals.

b. **Issue.** May P recover damages for misrepresentation that is based on the mere expression of an opinion?

c. **Held.** No. Judgment affirmed.

1) The mere expression of an opinion, no matter how strong and positive the language may be, is not fraud. An indefinite expression ought to put the person to whom it is made on inquiry. The expressions P relied on as grounds for fraud cannot be regarded as other than speculative expressions of opinion, and should have put P on his guard to make further inquiry.

3. **Sales Talk--Vulcan Metals Co. v. Simmons Manufacturing Co.,** 248 F. 853 (2d Cir. 1918). Vulcan Metals Co. v. Simmons Manufacturing Co.

a. **Facts.** Vulcan (P) bought the machinery and patents necessary to produce Simmons's (D's) vacuum cleaners. Subsequently, P sued D, claiming that D misrepresented the quality and performance of the machine, and lied about the fact that it had never been put on the market. P appeals from a directed verdict for D.

b. **Issue.** May a buyer sue the seller if the seller's representations about its product prove to be exaggerated?

c. **Held.** No. Judgment affirmed in part and reversed on other grounds.

1) There are some statements that no person takes seriously, unless he suffers from credulity. Some statements, like the claims of campaign managers before elections, are rather designed to allay the fear that would attend their absence. It makes much difference whether the parties stand on equal terms.

2) In the case at bar, since P was allowed full opportunity to examine and test the cleaner, the parties must be considered equal in bargaining power. P has no right to treat statements like these as material in his determination, since D justifiably should have expected P to make an independent and adequate inquiry. As to the representa-

tion that the cleaners had never been put on the market, the question of its materiality is unsettled enough to put to the jury.

4. **Analysis.** When analyzing "opinion" problems, one must look at the following:

   a. Form of the statement;

   b. The subject matter (is it common or specialized knowledge);

   c. The relationship of the parties;

   d. The margin of error; and

   e. Whether the parties were on an equal footing.

F. LAW

Misrepresentations as to law or matters of law are not actionable under the general rule, since everyone is presumed to know the law and such misrepresenations are thus treated as opinions only. However, a plaintiff's reliance on the defendant's representations of law is usually justified when the representation is factual in nature.

1. In *Sorenson v. Gardner*, 334 P.2d 471 (Or. 1959), the court held that a misrepresentation that a house conforms to the provisions of a building code (being a representation of facts not disclosed to the recipient) is a misrepresentation that the facts (*i.e.*, vents, plumbing, wiring, etc.) constitute compliance with the law, and is therefore actionable. However, the court pointed out that reliance may not be justified if the representation as to law is more of an opinion; *i.e.*, if the defendant would have advised the plaintiff of all of the facts (vents, plumbing, wiring, etc.) and then stated that these comply with the law.

2. Representations as to the law of a foreign state are generally treated as statements of fact upon which the plaintiff may justifiably rely.

G. PREDICTION AND INTENTION

McElrath v. Electric Investment Co.

1. **Future Intention--McElrath v. Electric Investment Co.,** 131 N.W. 380 (Minn. 1911).

   a. **Facts.** Electric Investment Co. (D) told McElrath (P) that a transit company intended to build a line to D's hotel in the future. P leased the hotel from D, relying on this statement. D also told P that P would clear $1,500 per year in profit. P later sued, claiming D's statements were false. The court overruled D's demurrer and D appeals.

b. **Issue.** Do false representations give rise to a cause of action when they have reference to future intentions of the defendant?

c. **Held.** Yes. Judgment affirmed.

1) While mere promises or conjectures as to future events do not constitute a cause of action, D intended to create in P the belief that D had a particular present intention to do something in the future. A statement of present intention to make future improvements, when no such intention exists, is actionable as a false representation.

2. **Statute of Frauds--Burgdorfer v. Thieleman,** 55 P.2d 1122 (Or. 1936).

Burgdorfer v. Thieleman

a. **Facts.** Burgdorfer (P) brought an action for deceit (misrepresentation) against Thieleman (D), alleging that D had induced him to purchase property from D, by promising to pay the mortgage on the land, when he really had no intention to do so. D appeals a judgment for P.

b. **Issue.** Is P's action barred by the Statute of Frauds?

c. **Held.** No. Judgment affirmed.

1) Although an oral agreement not to be performed within a year is usually invalid under the Statute of Frauds, an exception arises when, at the time D makes the promise, he has the intent to never fulfill it. Evidence of such misrepresentation is not for the purpose of establishing an agreement, as per the Statute of Frauds, but to prove fraud. The cases that apply the Statute of Frauds to oral agreements of this type either rest upon the absence of fraudulent intent or else completely disfavor the rule that the intention of the defendant not to perform constitutes fraud.

3. **Note.** One may prove an oral promise by oral testimony. This does not violate the Statute of Frauds if it is not being used to establish the agreement but rather to prove fraud.

H. DAMAGES

Actual damage is an essential element in order for the plaintiff to succeed in an action for fraud and deceit. Nominal damages are not awarded, but punitive damages may be if the conduct is sufficiently culpable.

Hinkle v. Rockville Motor Co., Inc.

1. **Failure to Prove Value--Hinkle v. Rockville Motor Co., Inc.,** 278 A.2d 42 (Md. 1971).

   a. **Facts.** Rockville Motor Co. (D) sold Hinkle (P) a car, which was fraudulently represented as being new, when in fact it was used, and had been previously wrecked. At trial, the court directed the verdict for D, on the ground that P had not presented enough evidence of the car's value at the time of sale for the jury to determine damages. P appeals.

   b. **Issue.** Did P's failure to prove the value of the car at the time of sale deprive the jury of the only permissible standard by which to determine damages?

   c. **Held.** No. Judgment reversed and remanded. The court follows the "flexibility theory" of damage determination, which includes the following elements:

      1) If he wishes, the plaintiff may recover only the amount he actually lost.

      2) If damages are proved with sufficient certainty, the "benefit of the bargain" rule will be employed.

      3) In instances where the evidence casts virtually no light on the value of the property had it conformed to the defendant's representations, damages will be awarded only for the loss sustained. Since, in every case, the plaintiff should be able to recover "out of the pocket" losses, there should never be an instance where the plaintiff is denied recovery for failure to prove the value of the chattel at time of sale.

XXII. INTERFERENCE WITH ECONOMIC RELATIONS

A. BUSINESS RELATIONS

1. **Injurious Falsehood.** "Injurious falsehood" covers the torts commonly known as "disparagement," "slander of title," and "trade libel." The gist of this tort is interference with the prospect of sale or some other advantageous relationship with respect to the plaintiff's property. The property involved may be real or personal, tangible or intangible (cases frequently involve the goodwill of the plaintiff's business).

   a. **Prima facie case.**

      1) **False statement.** First, the plaintiff must always prove that the defendant published a statement that was in fact false and untrue, or a dishonest expression of the defendant's opinion.

      2) **Publication to third person.**

      3) **Statement disparaging plaintiff's business, property, etc.** A statement is "disparaging" if it is reasonably likely to discourage others from dealing with the plaintiff, or otherwise interferes with the plaintiff's relations with others to her disadvantage.

         a) **Statements denying plaintiff's ownership ("slander of title").** A statement that casts reasonable doubt on the validity or extent of the plaintiff's title is clearly a disparagement. These are the cases commonly known as "slanders of title."

         b) **Statements denying quality of plaintiff's property ("trade libel").** Statements attacking the quality of the plaintiff's property (land, chattels, etc.), such that they would reasonably deter another from dealing with her, may be actionable as a disparagement whether the statement is of fact or opinion.

         c) **Statements derogatory of plaintiff's business in general ("trade libel").** Cases often involve statements (again of fact or opinion) that are derogatory of the plaintiff's business or the manner in which it is conducted, without necessarily reflecting on the title or quality of any particular property (*e.g.*, statements that service in the plaintiff's restaurant is "poor," that its customers are "ruffians").

         d) **Statements need not be defamatory.** The statement need not be defamatory as long as it is false. For example, a false statement made to a potential customer that "the plaintiff is dead (or out of business) so buy your goods from me" is not defamatory of the plaintiff, but certainly is a trade libel—an "injurious falsehood."

4) **Intent.** The general view requires simply an intent to disparage, *i.e.*, to cast doubt upon the plaintiff's property.

a) **Motive immaterial.** It is not necessary to show that the defendant was motivated by malice or ill will toward the plaintiff, or that he was in fact attempting to discourage some third person from dealing with the plaintiff.

b) **Scienter.** Most courts do not require a showing that the defendant knew or should have known that his statements were false, or that he did not have enough knowledge either way to make the statement.

5) **Causation and damages.** The usual requirement of actual and proximate causation exists. However, unlike defamation, where general damages are sometimes recoverable without a showing of pecuniary loss, the plaintiff here must always prove proximately caused special damages (actual, out-of-pocket, pecuniary damages).

a) **Slander of title.** The usual damages in slander of title cases are loss of profits on a contemplated sale of property, and costs of legal proceedings to remove the cloud on the plaintiff's title.

b) **Trade libel.** Typical damages in trade libel cases are loss of profits from existing or prospective sales to customers. Traditionally, however, it is not enough to show a general decline in business resulting from the falsehood. Only the loss on specific sales can be recovered (*i.e.*, as to the particular customers who have refrained from dealing with the plaintiff).

(1) Under modern business circumstances, it is often difficult to establish loss of specific customers. Recognizing this, courts are tending to back away from such a rigid rule. Thus, if the plaintiff cannot reasonably be expected to identify the particular persons who have refrained from dealing with him, she may be able to recover on a showing of general decline in business.

(2) In most states, consequential damages (*e.g.*, loss of business that forced the plaintiff to close her doors or go into bankruptcy) are not recoverable.

Ratcliffe v. Evans

b. **Proof of damages--Ratcliffe v. Evans,** 2 Q.B. 524 (1892).

1) **Facts.** Ratcliffe (P) carried on a business with his father by the name of Ratcliffe & Sons. After the father died, P continued the business, but

Evans (D), publisher of a local paper, published statements that the firm no longer existed and that P no longer was in the business. P sued for damages resulting from the injurious falsehood, and proved only general damages. P recovered and D appeals.

2) **Issue.** May an action for injurious falsehood lie if the plaintiff can only prove general damages?

3) **Held.** Yes. Judgment affirmed.

   a) P could not prove the loss of any particular customers. The only proven damages were general, of the type allowed in a libel action. To deny P recovery because he cannot prove special damages would be a denial of justice since the general damages suffered are precisely those which D intended to inflict. Therefore, P may recover general damages.

4) **Comment.** Although proof of special damages is an essential element of this tort, a modern tendency allows recovery for a general loss of business if all other causes for the decline may be excluded. However, the prevailing view requires proof of the identity of particular lost customers and transactions.

c. **Slander of title--Horning v. Hardy,** 373 A.2d 1273 (Md. Ct. Spec. App. 1977).

Horning v. Hardy

1) **Facts.** The Hornings (Ds) were developing land and had a house for sale thereon. A buyer was ready to purchase the house. The Hardys (Ps) claimed that they owned the land involved, and sued for trespass and ejectment. Ps' attorney told Ds' prospective buyer of the suit and the deal collapsed. Ds were unable to sell anything after that time. Ds counterclaimed alleging slander of title and tortious interference with contract. The trial court denied recovery to either party and both appeal.

2) **Issue.** Does an honest claim to the land in question constitute a privilege sufficient to defeat an action for slander of title?

3) **Held.** Yes. Judgment affirmed.

   a) Ps failed to establish ownership and the trial court correctly found for Ds on that claim.

   b) The tort of slander of title may be more accurately stated as the tort of "injurious falsehood." This consists of publication of a matter derogatory to P's business affairs calculated to prevent others from dealing with him, or to otherwise interfere with his relations with others. It is similar to defamation but requires proof of falsity, special damages, and causation.

c) Negligence may suffice to support a claim for injurious falsehood where the defendant, knowing that the statement is false and defamatory, acts in reckless disregard of these matters, or acts negligently in failing to ascertain them.

d) A qualified privilege may exist where the defendant has a present economic interest to protect. The defendant must be able to protect his interest without fear of liability before the plaintiff's transaction is accomplished. The privilege may be lost only upon proof of malice; mere negligence does not defeat the privilege.

e) Here, the question of whether Ps abused their privilege by malice was one for the trial court, which found for Ps. Ps' failure to adequately investigate their claim does not satisfy the test for malice.

d. Privileges. Common law privileges that apply to defamation, whether absolute or qualified, also apply to injurious falsehood.

1) Improper motives. A ***rival claimant*** to property has a conditional privilege to protect his interest in that property by making a bona fide claim to it. However, this conditional privilege offers no defense when the defendant operated under bad motives, or in the absence of a good faith belief in the truth of the assertions. In *Gudger v. Manton*, 134 P.2d 217 (Cal. 1943), the court held that the defendant lost such a conditional privilege when the defendant attempted to execute against property of the plaintiff, knowing that it was not subject to the defendant's judgment against the plaintiff's wife. The court awarded the plaintiff $16,000 in damages caused by his inability to sell his property due to the defendant's disparagement of his title.

2) Excessive publication. Excessive publication likewise may defeat a conditional privilege.

Testing Systems Inc. v. Magnaflux Corp.

3) Unfavorable comparison--Testing Systems, Inc. v. Magnaflux Corp., 251 F. Supp. 286 (E.D. Pa. 1966).

a) Facts. Testing Systems (P) and Magnaflux Corp. (D) manufacture the same type of products. D stated that the United States government found P's products to be 40% less effective than D's, and told P's prospective customers that P's "stuff is no good." P sued for trade libel or disparagement of property.

b) Issue. Is there a cause of action for trade libel based upon D's statements, or was D privileged to make an unfavorable comparison between P's and D's products?

c) Held. D's statements are actionable.

(1) D is not simply saying that his products are better than P's by stating that P's products are 40% less effective. To say that one's product is better than another's is to state mere opinion, which is not really amenable to proof. But here D's statement is one of fact, the truth of which can be ascertained.

d) Comments.

(1) It is generally recognized that competitors have the privilege of "puffing" about their own products and asserting that their products are the best on the market. A person can partake of some boasting and exaggeration even though he knows what he is saying is false. However, statements that amount to unfair competition are not privileged—*e.g.*, intentional false statements of fact concerning a competitor's business or products.

(2) Under the Restatement (First) of Torts, absence of privilege (like falsity) was part of the prima facie case, and had to be proved by the plaintiff to establish the tort. [Restatement §624] However, the Restatement (Second) of Torts and many cases state the opposite, treating the existence of privilege as a defense to be proved by the publisher of the disparagement.

2. Interference with Contractual Relations.

a. Introduction. Tort liability has been imposed for intentional interference with the plaintiff's existing or prospective economic relationship with third persons, thereby protecting the plaintiff's interest in stabilizing her contract relations and expectations. This is an area of still-emerging principles; most of the cases are of recent origin, reflecting development of social and economic policies in these areas.

b. Nature of contract. Historically, this tort was first recognized in the master-servant relationship—*i.e.*, a third person who induced a servant to quit his master's employ might be held liable to the master in tort for loss of the servant's services. Today, the tort can apply to any type of valid contract, except a contract to marry.

1) Inducing breach--Lumley v. Gye, 118 Eng. Rep. 749 (1853). Lumley v. Gye

a) Facts. Lumley (P) contracted for the exclusive services of a certain opera singer. Gye (D), knowing of the contract, induced the singer to break the contract and perform for him. P sued for damages and D demurred.

b) **Issue.** Is there an action for interference with contract?

c) **Held.** Yes.

(1) An action will lie against a person who maliciously procures a breach of contract, resulting in loss to the plaintiff. D, by procuring a violation of P's rights, has harmed P.

d) **Comment.** This was the first case that set out the general principle of liability based upon interference with contract. Subsequent cases have extended this principle to cover interference with advantageous relations of pecuniary value.

2) **Preventing performance.** In *Bacon v. St. Paul Union Stockyards*, 201 N.W. 326 (Minn. 1924), Bacon was employed as a livestock dealer. The St. Paul Union Stockyards ("St. Paul") prevented Bacon from entering the stockyard. The court held that Bacon stated a cause of action because St. Paul wrongfully prevented Bacon from continuing in his employment, although the court recognized that St. Paul might have a valid justification for its conduct.

3) **Illegal contracts.** Contracts that are illegal or contrary to public policy do not qualify, since the law will not aid in upholding them.

c. **Prima facie case.**

1) **Contractual relation.** There must be some contractual relationship, either existing or prospective.

2) **Defendant's interference.** The defendant must play some active role in causing the interference. For example, it is not enough that he accepted an offer from the party with whom the plaintiff had been dealing, even if he had knowledge of the plaintiff's relationship with that party. The defendant does not have to be shown to have induced a breach of the plaintiff's contract. All that must appear is that he has prevented performance or made the performance more difficult and onerous, as in *Bacon v. St. Paul Union*, *supra*.

3) **Intent.** It must be shown that the defendant acted with an awareness of the existing contract, and that he intended to cause the interference therewith that proximately resulted from his conduct.

4) **Causation and damages.** There is the usual requirement of actual and proximate causation and damages.

a) **Types of damages recoverable.** The cases are far from uniform as to what types of damages are recoverable (probably because this tort is more frequently asserted as a basis for injunctive relief). The better view seems to allow recovery for all actual damages, consequential damages (unforeseen expenses), mental suffering, damage to reputation, and punitive damages, in appropriate cases.

b) **Offset recovery for breach of contract.** The fact that the plaintiff may have an action against the party who breaches the contract does not mitigate the plaintiff's claim against the defendant for inducing the breach. The two are joint wrongdoers, and each is liable for the loss (the defendant in tort, and the other in contract). However, any recovery against the breaching party must be offset against the damages recoverable from the defendant who induced the breach.

5) **Defenses—privilege.** The principal defense to this tort is one of privilege; *i.e.*, the defendant will not be liable if there was proper justification for the interference and only reasonable methods were employed. This requires proof that both the ends and the means were justifiable.

a) **Purpose.** The interference may be privileged by the interests served by the defendant's conduct. This is generally true even if the defendant harbored ill will toward the plaintiff.

(1) **Furtherance of nonpersonal interests.** Claims of privilege are generally upheld where the defendant was acting for a social good (*e.g.*, attempting to exclude a diseased youngster from school that the defendant's child attends); or to protect a third person's interest (*e.g.*, attorney's sincere advice to client not to deal with the plaintiff).

(2) **Furtherance of the defendant's own financial interest.** If the defendant is acting to further his own interests, any claim of privilege will turn on whether he is seeking to protect existing economic interests or merely a prospective advantage.

(a) **Protecting present interest.** If the defendant has a present contract of his own with one of the parties, he is privileged to prevent the performance of another that threatens it. For example, if the defendant induces a debtor to pay off the bills he owes the defendant, thereby rendering the debtor unable to perform his contract with the plaintiff, the defendant is not liable for inducing breach of the plaintiff-debtor contract.

(b) **Protecting prospective advantages.** If the defendant has no existing relationship with either of the contracting parties and induces the breach solely to further his own business—*e.g.*, hiring away the plaintiff's best employees, inducing the plaintiff's suppliers not to supply, etc.—his purpose is not protected, and generally no privilege is recognized.

b) **Means.** Even if the interference is for a justifiable purpose, the defendant is never privileged to use unethical or wrongful means. Thus, violence, lies, bribery, or extortion will defeat the privilege.

c) **Prospective relationship.** When the interference involves a prospective relationship, courts recognize a more extensive privilege.

(1) The defendant is privileged to use any bona fide competitive means to solicit the customers for himself before they enter into a contract with the plaintiff. However, to the extent that he uses unlawful methods, he loses the privilege—and may also be liable for unfair competition.

(2) Courts recognize the privilege of labor organizations to boycott their employers, and by peaceful picketing or other peaceful means, to induce others not to deal with their employers.

Della Penna v. Toyota Motor Sales, U.S.A., Inc.

d. **Wrongfulness element--Della Penna v. Toyota Motor Sales, U.S.A., Inc.,** 902 P.2d 740 (Cal. 1995).

1) **Facts.** Toyota Motor Sales, U.S.A., Inc. (D) required dealers for its Lexus brand to agree not to re-export the vehicles to Japan, where there was demand for such cars. D was concerned that re-exporting the Lexus cars, which were in short supply, would impair its dealers in the United States. Della Penna (P), an auto wholesaler, purchased Lexus cars from United States dealers and exported them for resale to Japan. P's suppliers appeared on D's offenders list, which subjected them to sanctions from D. As a result, P could no longer purchase the cars. P sued for antitrust violations and for interference with his economic relationship with Lexus retail dealers. At trial, the trial court dismissed the antitrust claim and granted D's motion to include a jury instruction that P must prove that D's alleged interfering conduct was "wrongful." The jury found for D. P appealed. The court of appeal reversed, holding that wrongfulness is not an element of interference with economic relations. The California Supreme Court granted D's petition for review.

2) **Issue.** Is wrongfulness an element of the tort of interference with business relations?

3) **Held.** Yes. Judgment reversed and the trial court judgment affirmed.

a) *Lumley v. Gye, supra*, dealt with inducement to breach an existing contract. The tort of interference with prospective economic relations was first recognized in *Temperton v. Russell*, 1 Q.B. 715 (1893), a secondary boycott case. The *Temperton* court reasoned that there was no distinction between inducing persons to break a contract and inducing persons not to enter into a contract, because there is the same wrongful intent in both cases.

b) The keystone of liability was the malicious intent of the defendant and the damage to the plaintiff's business. Eventually the development of the tort led to a prima facie case that required only the defendant's awareness of the economic relation, a deliberate interference with it, and the plaintiff's resulting injury. This approach has been widely criticized for being too easy for the plaintiff, putting a burden on the defendant to show justification. Most courts now require the plaintiff to show that the alleged interference was wrongful, improper, or illegal.

c) The courts should recognize a distinction between disruption of existing contractual relations and interference with economic relationships short of contractual. If the plaintiff seeks to recover for alleged interference with prospective economic relations, he has the burden of pleading and proving that the defendant's interference was wrongful beyond the fact of the interference itself. The use of the term "wrongful" in the jury instruction in this case was therefore appropriate. The precise meaning of the term "wrongful" will need to be determined in future cases.

4) **Concurrence.** The court takes the proper approach to reformulating this tort, but the term "wrongfulness" is inherently ambiguous and should be avoided. The court should adopt a clear standard, and make it clear that the interfering party's motive is not determinative.

e. **Taking business from one's employer--Adler, Barish, Daniels, Levin and Creskoff v. Epstein,** 393 A.2d 1175 (Pa. 1978).

Adler, Barish, Daniels, Levin and Creskoff v. Epstein

1) **Facts.** Epstein (D) and other associates of the law firm of Adler, Barish, Daniels, Levin and Creskoff (P) terminated their employment with P. D continued to use P's offices for about a week, during which time D solicited business from P's clients. D contacted the clients and sent form letters by which the clients could discharge P and retain D as their counsel. P brought suit for an injunction against interference with the existing contractual arrangements between P and its clients. The trial court granted relief, but the superior court reversed. P appeals.

2) **Issue.** May a former associate of a law firm use his knowledge of the firm's clients to directly solicit the clients' business and interfere with existing contractual relationship?

3) **Held.** No. Judgment reversed.

a) The Code of Professional Responsibility, DR 2-103 (A), states that "A lawyer shall not recommend employment, as a private practitioner, of himself . . . to a non-lawyer who has not sought his advice regarding employment of a lawyer."

b) D claims that his conduct was protected under the First Amendment because it was speech. States may not prohibit all truthful advertising of legal services, because it is protected commercial speech. However, commercial speech is not absolutely protected by the First Amendment. *Ohralik v. Ohio State Bar Association*, 436 U.S. 447 (1978), indicated that the states may regulate speech that violates the disciplinary rules. Since the solicitation that D used could have the effect of frustrating informed and reliable decision-making by P's clients, it is not protected.

c) P is entitled to relief if the elements of the tort of intentional interference with existing contractual relations are met.

d) Since D did interfere with P's contractual relations, the only element that might not have been met is the requirement that the interference be "improper." Many factors must be considered in determining whether conduct is improper, but the primary factor here is the violation of a recognized ethical code. Therefore, D's action was improper and all the elements of the tort are satisfied.

e) D claims he was free to engage in his own business venture, but in so doing, he may not take advantage of a confidential relation created while employed by P. Since D used his knowledge acquired while working for P, P is entitled to relief.

Brimelow v. Casson

f. **Well-being of employee as a privilege--Brimelow v. Casson,** [1923] 1 Ch. 302.

1) **Facts.** Arnold, the manager of a burlesque troupe, underpaid the chorus girls, who were therefore forced to resort to prostitution to survive. The actors' association persuaded the theatre owners to breach their contracts with Arnold unless Arnold would pay higher wages. The owners of the troupe brought suit against the actors' association for the interference.

2) **Issue.** Is protection of the well-being of the employees a sufficient justification for interfering with the contractual relations of the relations of the employer?

3) **Held.** Yes. Case dismissed.

a) The only way the association could protect the interests of the women was to induce the theatres to not accept the performances unless the women were adequately paid. The nature of the harm to the women is such that if the interference here was not justified, no interference could be. Therefore, no cause of action exists.

g. **Interference with noncommercial expectancy--Harmon v. Harmon,** 404 A.2d 1020 (Me. 1979).

Harmon v. Harmon

1) **Facts.** Harmon (P) was told by his mother that he would receive a one-half interest in certain property, and her will reflected this desire. However, P's mother became ill in her old age, and she transferred the property to P's brother and sister-in-law (Ds). P sued, claiming Ds used fraud and undue influence to induce his mother to make the transfer. The trial court dismissed the complaint and P appeals.

2) **Issue.** May a person whose expected legacy is interfered with have a cause of action for tortious interference with an advantageous relationship?

3) **Held.** Yes. Judgment reversed.

a) Prior cases recognized an interest in employment at will sufficient to support a cause of action for interference when the employee is discharged. An action for wrongful interference with an expected legacy has also been recognized.

b) When a will is executed, the legatees have an expectancy interest. Even though the testator could later change the will, if she does so due to wrongful conduct by a third party, the expectation is lost and the legatees have an injury. This is a natural extension of the rule applied to commercial interests.

c) In this case, P's mother is still alive. However, he has still lost his expectancy and should not have to wait until his mother dies before he can bring this action. Important evidence, including the mother's testimony, would be lost if P were required to wait until her death before he could sue.

3. **Tortious Breach of Contract.**

a. **Forced contracting--Neibuhr v. Gage,** 108 N.W. 884 (Minn. 1906).

Neibuhr v. Gage

1) **Facts.** Gage (D) threatened Neibuhr (P) that, unless P transferred to D certain shares of stock in a corporation, D would accuse him of grand larceny and have him convicted. P understood that D would use false testimony to fulfill his threat and P transferred the stock. P sued for damages, and recovered a favorable verdict. The trial court granted a new trial. Both parties appeal.

2) **Issue.** May a party who is forced to enter a contract under duress recover damages instead of seeking rescission?

3) **Held.** Yes. Judgment reversed with directions to enter judgment on the verdict.

a) A party who has been induced by fraud to enter a contract may keep what he has received and sue for damages, or may rescind and sue for what he gave up or seek rescission by the court in equity.

b) P has chosen the first alternative. D claims that such an alternative is not available where no fraud is involved. However, the remedies should not be more restricted where the wrongdoing is more serious. Therefore, a party injured by duress is entitled to the same remedies as a party injured by deceit.

Freeman & Mills, Inc. v. Belcher Oil Company

b. **Denial of contract--Freeman & Mills, Inc. v. Belcher Oil Company,** 900 P.2d 669 (Cal. 1995).

1) **Facts.** Belcher Oil Company (D) retained a law firm to defend it in a Florida lawsuit. D was to pay fees for accountants. The law firm hired Freeman & Mills (P) to provide a financial analysis and litigation support for D. P signed an agreement with the law firm. D's general counsel left and his replacement fired the law firm and told them to have P stop their work. P billed the law firm, but did not get paid. P then billed D directly. After a year, P directly asked D about the bill. D suggested that it has not been consulted about the scope of P's services and that P should get paid by the law firm. P sued D for breach of contract, bad faith denial of contract, and quantum meruit. P's statements showed a bill of $77,583. The jury found that D had authorized the law firm to retain P, that P had performed under the contract, that D had breached the contract, and that P suffered damages of $25,000. The jury also found that D had denied the contract with oppression, fraud, or malice and awarded P $477,583 in punitive damages. The trial court corrected the judgment to award $131,614 in compensatory damages, including the $25,000, the $77,538, and prejudgment interest, and $400,000 in punitive damages. The court of appeal reversed on the ground that there was no special relationship between the parties to justify a denial of contract claim, and ordered a retrial for the issue of damages under the breach of contract claim only. The California Supreme Court granted review.

2) **Issue.** May a party to a contract recover in tort for another party's bad faith denial of the contract's existence?

3) **Held.** No. Judgment affirmed.

a) The court recognized a tort of bad faith denial of contract in *Seaman's Direct Buying Service, Inc. v. Standard Oil Co.*, 686 P.2d 1158 (Cal. 1984). In that case, Seaman's was put out of business when Standard Oil refused to stipulate to the existence of a letter of intent between the parties that had led to Seaman's signing a 40-year lease.

The court held that a party to a contract may incur tort remedies when, in addition to breaching the contract, it seeks to avoid liability by denying, in bad faith and without probable cause, that the contract exists. The trial court in that case had failed to instruct the jury on the bad faith requirement, so the judgment was reversed.

b) The *Seaman's* tort raised considerable confusion in the lower courts. In addition, there are public policy reasons for not recognizing this tort. Among these is recognition that the goal of contract remedies is compensating the promisee for the breach, not to compel the promisor to perform his promises. *Seaman's* also raises a risk of converting every contract breach into a tort with accompanying punitive damage recovery. For these and other reasons, *Seaman's* should be overruled.

c. **No tort recovery for breach of performance bond--Cates Construction, Inc. v. Talbot Partners,** 980 P.2d 407 (Cal. 1999).

Cates Construction, Inc. v. Talbot Partners

1) **Facts.** Talbot Partners (P) hired Cates Construction, Inc. (D) to build a condominium project on property P purchased for $1 million. The contract required D to have the project ready for occupancy in eight months. D furnished a performance bond from Transamerica, issued in favor of P. The project was delayed, which triggered the performance bond. P sued for breach of contract and tort. The court found that Transamerica had breached the bond in various ways, which led to the loss of the project. The parties tried P's tort cause of action before a jury, with stipulated compensatory tort damages of $1. The jury awarded P $28 million in punitive damages based on its finding that Transamerica breached the implied covenant of good faith and fair dealing and was guilty of malice and oppression. The court of appeal reduced the punitive damages to $15 million. The California Supreme Court granted review.

2) **Issue.** May a developer recover in tort for his surety's breach of the covenant of good faith and fair dealing implied in a performance bond?

3) **Held.** No. Judgment reversed.

a) A surety promises to answer for the default of another, and is only liable if the principal defaults. In this case, Transamerica was properly held liable for delay damages flowing from the project delay caused by D.

b) Every contract includes an implied covenant of good faith and fair dealing, which means that neither party will do anything to injure the right of the other to receive the benefits of the contract. Breach of this implied covenant is limited to contract instead of tort remedies, except in cases involving insurance policies. An insured may recover damages such as emotional distress damages or punitive damages if the insurer is guilty of oppression, fraud, or malice.

c) The insurance exception reflects the elements of adhesion, public interest, and fiduciary responsibility that are typical of insurance policies. Insurance polices are not purchased for profit or advantage, but for peace of mind and security. Insured parties cannot find another insurance company to pay for a loss already incurred, so they face a unique economic dilemma when the insurer breaches.

d) Tort recovery in the insurance context is a major departure from traditional principles of contract law and has not been extended beyond that arena. P claims that performance bonds are essentially a form of insurance so that tort recovery should apply in this case.

e) By statute, surety is recognized as a class of insurance, but sureties have rights and defenses that do not apply to the typical insurance relationship. Sureties are also exempt from the regulations that apply to insurers pertaining to settlement of claims. The policies that justify tort recovery in insurance cases do not apply to sureties, where there is no adhesion or disparate bargaining power. Sureties also do not protect against calamitous or catastrophic events, but instead involve a commercial advantage for the obligee. A surety does not have a fiduciary relationship with the obligee.

f) Tort remedies are not necessary to compel commercial sureties to handle claims responsibly. The parties can include a liquidated damages provision to discourage nonperformance. Contract remedies adequately compensate for all damages within the contemplation of the parties when they enter the contract. Allowing tort remedies could lead to additional litigation and increase the cost of obtaining bonds and would give obligees additional leverage with sureties that they do not have in contract disputes.

g) For these reasons, tort recovery should not be allowed in cases involving a construction performance bond. The legislature may permit such recovery if it deems it appropriate.

B. INTERFERENCE WITH FAMILY RELATIONS

1. **Introduction.** Tort law provides some protection for relationships that the plaintiff has with others. Interference with family relationships has

produced a significant amount of litigation. Alienation of a spouse's affection has been the most common claim, but there have been claims for alienation of affection between parents and children. The basic requirement is that the third person's conduct must alter the spouse's mental attitude, shifting affection from the plaintiff spouse toward the defendant third party.

2. **Alienation of Affections--Nash v. Baker,** 522 P.2d 1335 (Okla. Ct. App. 1974). Nash v. Baker

   a. **Facts.** Nash (P) on behalf of herself and her children, brought an action against Baker (D) for alienation of P's husband's affections, after her husband, allegedly as a result of the sexual and material enticements of D, left home to cohabit with D. The court sustained D's demurrer as to each of the children, and the jury rendered a verdict for D as to the wife's action. P appeals.

   b. **Issue.** Does a minor child have a common law right to sue a third person whose actions break up the parents' marriage, depriving the child of parental society and guidance?

   c. **Held.** No. Judgment affirmed.

      1) The common law recognized no such right in the child, and a majority of the jurisdictions that have ruled on the question have also denied the child an action.

      2) Modern statutes abolishing causes of action for alienation of affections and related injuries, and other related trends evidenced by an increase in the incidence of divorce and a liberalization in the laws relating thereto, all indicate that Prosser's prediction, that this action will be allowed in an increasing number of jurisdictions, may never be realized.

      3) In addition, there may be a growing feeling that the "fault" leading to the breakup of a marriage may not be readily determinable in court.

XXIII. MISCELLANEOUS TORTS

A. IMPLIED TORTS

1. **Introduction.** Statutes and constitutions may create rights without specifying how the rights are to be enforced. When such rights are violated, the courts are left to determine whether, and how, the rights may be enforced.

Burnette v. Wahl

2. **Comprehensive Legislative Scheme--Burnette v. Wahl,** 588 P.2d 1105 (Or. 1978).

   a. **Facts.** Five minor children under state custody brought actions through Burnette and their other guardians (Ps) against Wahl and their other mothers (Ds) for failure to perform parental duties. Among other things, Ps alleged that Ds failed to provide parental affection and contact, failed to support their children, abandoned them, negligently left them unattended, and alienated their affection. Four allegations involved violations of statutory duties. The only injuries claimed were emotional and psychological. No physical abuse was involved. The trial court dismissed the complaints and Ps appeal.

   b. **Issue.** May children bring suit against their parents for emotional and psychological injuries caused by the parents' neglect and failure to perform parental duties?

   c. **Held.** No. Judgment affirmed.

      1) The legislature has enacted numerous statutes aimed at remedying situations in which children become victims. This includes a range of civil and criminal procedures designed to make sure children receive proper nurturing, support, and physical care. These procedures do not include a cause of action against parents for emotional injuries resulting from parents' failure to provide these services.

      2) As the common law did not recognize a cause of action such as Ps', and as the legislature did not create one, Ps are asking the court to create a new type of tort liability. While courts have authority to create a cause of action when deemed necessary for policy reasons, they should exercise restraint when the legislature has adopted a comprehensive scheme for dealing with the same problem. Otherwise, the courts might interfere with the legislative purpose.

      3) Under the legislative scheme, when the biological family cannot be reestablished, the parental rights may be terminated so a new family unit may be formed. This step has not been taken

in this case. Ps' tort action is inappropriate because of the potential interference with any plans the designated state agencies may have for these children.

4) Tort law is not an appropriate means of addressing problems between mother and child. Few if any parents can completely meet the physical, emotional, and psychological needs of their children, and a tort action would not solve the problem, nor does a theory of infliction of emotional harm apply between parents and children.

d. **Concurrence.** The doctrine of intrafamily tort immunity still applies to this type of claim, even though it has been abolished as to intentional torts resulting in physical injuries.

e. **Concurrence and dissent.** The cause of action for alienation of affection was properly dismissed, and the pleadings fail to allege outrageous conduct. However, a civil cause of action for damages should be recognized. Only about five percent of abandoned children are adopted and placed in permanent families. The monetary cost to society of providing foster care is huge, and the indirect costs are even more serious. These "orphans of the living" should be able to force their parents to accept the financial burden of raising the children.

f. **Dissent.** Ds' conduct as alleged by Ps constitutes a crime. Civil damages for criminal conduct have been awarded in other contexts.

1) If the statute does not indicate whether the legislature intended to permit or deny a civil remedy, then the availability of civil damages depends on (i) whether the plaintiff is within the class for whose special protection the statute was enacted and (ii) whether the civil remedy would contribute to or detract from achieving the statute's objective. Legislative silence alone is not determinative. Ps' claim is not a new common law theory but a civil claim based on a statute.

2) Criminal laws express different kinds of policy: (i) redefinitions of common law crimes with related common law torts; (ii) regulatory laws, which do not usually by themselves create tort liability; and (iii) governmental sanctions intended to enforce obligations existing independent of the legislation. The child protection laws are the third type of crime and simply enforce recognized parental duties. Parents have a duty not to abandon their children not merely because it is a crime; the criminal statute reinforces the parents' existing duty.

3) The majority's concern for interfering at this stage with the family relationship is inconsistent with the legislative judgment that abandonment such as Ps allege may be prosecuted as a felony. Ds intentionally breached a specific duty towards Ps and Ps should have a cause of action.

Neering v. Weaver

3. Knowing Failure to Arrest--Neering v. Weaver, 670 P.2d 137 (Or. 1983).

a. **Facts.** The Abuse Prevention Act was adopted to strengthen legal protection for persons threatened with assault by a present or former spouse or cohabitant and provided for restraining orders and mandatory arrest and custody. Nearing (P) was separated from her husband. He later entered P's home and struck her. P reported this to Weaver and other police officers (Ds), and P's husband was arrested and charged with assault. The court imposed a restraining order, which was served on P's husband. He thereafter entered P's premises again, damaged them, and tried to remove their two minor children. P reported the incidents to Ds, but Ds declined to arrest P's husband because no officer had seen him on the premises. P reported her husband's next three violations, but Ds failed to arrest him. Finally, P's husband came to the home, threatened to kill P's friend, and assaulted him. P sued, claiming Ds' failure to arrest her husband was the proximate cause of P's severe emotional distress and physical injuries. Ds pleaded affirmative defenses of immunity and discretion. The trial court granted summary judgment to Ds, and the court of appeals affirmed. P appeals.

b. **Issue.** May police officers who knowingly fail to enforce a judicial order be held liable for resulting harm to the psychic and physical health of the intended beneficiaries of the judicial order?

c. **Held.** Yes. Judgment reversed.

1) The law does allow recovery for damages for a plaintiff's psychic or emotional harm when the defendant's conduct infringes a legal right of the plaintiff's independent of an ordinary tort claim for negligence. In this case, P claims that Ds violated their statutory duty under the Abuse Prevention Act, which specifies that an officer "shall arrest" a person when the officer has probable cause to believe that the person has violated an order. This statute, combined with the court order, gave rise to a duty toward P.

2) The duty owed to P does not create absolute liability for any resulting harm. Ds may have a defense of a good faith effort to perform, or prevention. But Ds have a duty to do what the statute requires. The widespread refusal or failure of police officers to remove persons involved in domestic violence was what led to the statute requiring mandatory arrest.

3) Ds claim that their determination of probable cause is a discretionary function or duty, but an officer is not engaged in a discretionary function or duty whenever he must evaluate and act upon a factual judgment. The purpose of the Act was to negate discretion of that kind. The affirmative defense of discretion should have been stricken.

4) Ds also claim immunity under a statute that protect officers from liability for making good faith arrests, but this does not apply to a failure to make arrests.

5) The dissent claims that this decision creates strict liability, but Ds still have defenses available. The policy arguments against this decision were made by the legislature, and there is no liability if the statute is followed.

d. **Dissent.** The majority has created a strict tort liability. In addition, the statute does not contemplate creation of a civil cause of action against the police for failure to arrest.

4. **Nonstatutory Remedy for Violation of Constitutional Rights--Bivens v. Six Unknown Named Agents of Federal Bureau of Narcotics,** 403 U.S. 388 (1971).

Bivens v. Six Unknown Named Agents of Federal Bureau of Narcotics

a. **Facts.** Six unknown named agents of the Federal Bureau of Narcotics (Ds) entered Bivens's (P's) apartment, searched it, arrested P and threatened his family, all without a warrant and without probable cause. P sued in federal court. Finding that no statute was applicable, P based his claim on the Fourth Amendment. The district court dismissed the complaint. P appeals.

b. **Issue.** May federal courts award monetary damages for violation of constitutional rights by federal agents in the absence of a controlling statute?

c. **Held.** Yes. Judgment reversed.

1) Ds assert that P's only remedy is in state courts, and that if they violated the Fourth Amendment, the only effect is that Ds must be treated as having acted as private individuals. This assertion is unduly restrictive.

2) The constitutional protections must be observed by the federal courts. Since P has stated a cause of action under the Fourth Amendment, he is entitled to recover money damages for any injuries suffered as a result of the violation of his rights. It is not necessary to have a federal statute to provide for such relief.

d. **Concurrence** (Harlan, J.). P's interest in freedom from official contravention of the Fourth Amendment is a federally protected interest. Since federal courts may grant equitable remedies, they may also grant a traditional remedy at law. The Bill of Rights was intended to vindicate individual rights in the face of legislative action. The basic question is whether compensatory relief is "necessary" or "appropriate" to vindicate P's interest. The status of our Constitution in our legal system requires that courts vindicate the interests therein protected by whatever effective means are available.

e. **Dissent** (Burger, C.J.). An appropriate remedy should be fashioned by Congress, not the courts.

f. **Dissent** (Black, J.). The creation of judicial remedies for particular wrongs is the duty of the legislatures, not the courts. Judicial economy may require that the courts attend to other legitimate grievances, and allocation of judicial resources is a legislative duty.

Transamerica Mortgage Advisors, Inc. (TAMA) v. Lewis

5. **Implied Remedies--Transamerica Mortgage Advisors, Inc. (TAMA) v. Lewis,** 444 U.S. 1 (1979).

a. **Facts.** Transamerica Mortgage Advisors, Inc. (D) was the investment advisor for the Mortgage Trust of America. Lewis (P), a shareholder of the trust, brought suit against D alleging that P had violated the Investment Advisors Act of 1940 by not registering the trust and by violating its fiduciary duties as outlined in the Act. P sought injunctive relief, rescission of D's contract with the trust, restitution of fees paid to D by the trust, and damages. The trial court ruled that the Act did not confer a private right of action and dismissed P's complaint. The court of appeals reversed, and D appeals.

b. **Issue.** May implied private remedies be found in a federal statute in the absence of any indication that Congress intended to create such private rights?

c. **Held.** No. Judgment reversed in part.

1) Section 206 of the Act broadly proscribes fraudulent practices by investment advisors. Section 215 provides that contracts whose formation or performance would violate the Act are "void."

2) Under section 215, a contract is "void," so Congress must have intended that the legal consequences of voidness could be litigated by private parties. Therefore, a private party may bring an action for rescission and restitution, or for an injunction against continued performance of the contract.

3) Section 206 does not create any civil liabilities. Nothing in the legislative history of the Act indicates any intent to create a general private cause of action. Congress provided for private actions in other securities laws, and could have done so here. In the jurisdictional section of the Act, Congress expressly deleted a provision that referred to "actions at law" and "liability." The mere fact that the Act was intended to protect victims such as P does not require

implication of a private cause of action. Therefore, P may not recover for violations of section 206.

d. **Dissent** (White, Brennan, Marshall, Stevens, JJ.). The approach for determining whether P has a private right of action involves consideration of four factors, all of which would, on balance, tend to favor P.

1) Is P one of the class for whose special benefit the statute was enacted? Here it is clear that P was in such a class.

2) Is there any indication of legislative intent, explicit or implicit, either to create such a remedy or to deny one? Here, there is no indication of legislative intent. In the absence of any contrary indication, however, the courts may provide litigants exercising implied rights of action whatever relief is consistent with the congressional purpose. The majority has confused the question of whether a cause of action exists with the question of the nature of relief. The majority has allowed rescission, but not recovery of damages for breach of fiduciary duty.

3) Is the private action consistent with the underlying purposes of the legislative scheme? Here, the answer is clearly yes.

4) Is the cause of action one traditionally relegated to state law, so that it would be inappropriate to infer a cause of action based solely on federal law? The states have not traditionally regulated the activity of investment advisors.

B. EXPRESS RIGHTS OF ACTION

1. **Civil RICO--Reves v. Ernst & Young,** 507 U.S. 170 (1993).

Reves v. Ernst & Young

a. **Facts.** Reves (P) was trustee in bankruptcy for a bankrupt Farmers Cooperative ("Co-op"). The former manager, White, embezzled funds from the Co-op to build a gasohol plant, which the Co-op acquired after White was indicted for federal tax fraud. Ernst & Young (D), successor to the Co-op's auditors, Arthur Young, reported to the Co-op's board that the gasohol plant had a value of $4.5 million when in fact the actual value was far less, and if so reported, would have caused the Co-op to be insolvent. After a run on the Co-op's demand notes, it filed for bankruptcy. P then sued D under the federal Racketeer Influenced and Corrupt Organizations chapter of the Organized Crime Control Act of 1970 ("RICO"). [18 U.S.C. §1962(c)] The district court found for D and the Eighth Circuit Court of Appeals affirmed, except that it reversed the damage award and remanded for a new trial. P appeals.

b. **Issue.** Do outside auditors who review completed transactions and certify financial records fall within the coverage of section 1962(c) for purposes of establishing civil RICO liability?

c. **Held.** No. Judgment affirmed.

1) To fall within the coverage of section 1962(c), which makes it unlawful "to conduct or participate, directly or indirectly, in the conduct of such enterprise's affairs through a pattern of racketeering activity," one must participate in the operation or management of the enterprise itself. Auditing does not rise to such a level.

C. PREEMPTION

New York Central Railroad Company v. Winfield

1. **Basic Rules Regarding Preemption--New York Central Railroad Company v. Winfield,** 244 U.S. 147 (1917).

a. **Facts.** Winfield (P) worked for the New York Central Railroad Company (D). While tamping a cross-tie on D's main track, P struck a pebble that rebounded and hit his eye, causing blindness in that eye. P sought compensation under the state's worker's compensation law. D objected that its liability and P's rights as an employee were governed exclusively by the Employers' Liability Act of Congress, which provided for awards in cases involving employer negligence. The commission granted him an award, and the state court upheld the award. D appeals.

b. **Issue.** When Congress provides a remedy in a field, are state remedies within that field preempted?

c. **Held.** Yes. Judgment reversed.

1) Under the Commerce Clause, Congress may regulate the obligation of common carriers and the rights of their employees for injuries sustained in interstate commerce. When Congress acts upon a subject, all state laws covering the same field are necessarily superseded by the federal law. Because Congress acted upon the subject here, the issue is only the extent to which the Act covers the field.

2) Some states have adopted P's position that the Act only relates to injuries resulting from D's negligence. Other states followed D's position, that negligence is not relevant to the applicability of the Act, but only to D's obligation to pay for the injury. The latter position is more consistent with the Act, because Congress wanted to create uniform rules for compensating em-

ployees for injuries suffered while working for railroads in interstate commerce.

3) The Act does not require D to pay for injuries that occur without D's negligence, because Congress determined that carriers should only be liable for injury resulting from negligence. There is nothing in the Act that would leave the states free to require compensation where the Act withholds it. Congress did consider providing a remedy regardless of negligence, but never adopted that provision.

4) If the various states were allowed to require carriers to compensate their employees for injuries in interstate commerce that occurred without negligence, it would disturb the uniformity that Congress sought. The Act prevents the states from providing compensation both where the Act requires it and where it withholds or excludes it.

d. **Dissent** (Brandeis, Clarke, JJ.). Congress could have done what the majority claims they did, but the Act does not express such an intention. The Act was intended to end the widespread practice of denying employees compensation for injuries due to the railroads' negligence. Congress legislated on one branch of the subject, but did not preclude the states from providing methods of compensating employees for accidents not caused by the employer's negligence. The field for this type of injury does not require uniformity because of the different conditions in the various states.

2. **No Preemption of Uncovered State Tort Remedies--English v. General Electric Company,** 496 U.S. 72 (1990).

English v. General Electric Company

a. **Facts.** English (P) was employed by the General Electric Company (D) as a lab technician at a nuclear-fuels production facility. P complained to D about violations of nuclear-safety standards at the facility, including her co-workers' failure to clean up radioactive material spills. On one occasion, she deliberately failed to clean a work table that had been contaminated during a preceding shift, instead marking it. A few days later, she pointed out to her supervisor that the area had not been cleaned up. Work was then halted for a clean up. D charged P with a knowing failure to clean up radioactive contamination. D told P to find another job within the facility that did not involve nuclear materials. When she was unable to do so, she was terminated. P filed a complaint under section 210(a) of the Energy Reorganization Act that protected employees against discharge for discrimination. The administrative law judge found that D had violated section 210(a), but dismissed the complaint because P filed it too late. P then sued in federal court for wrongful discharge and intentional infliction of emotional distress. The district court held that P had stated a valid claim, but granted D's motion to dismiss on the ground that the claim fell within a field that had been preempted by the federal government in the Act. The court of appeals affirmed. The Supreme Court granted certiorari.

b. **Issue.** Does the federal government preempt state tort remedies when it adopts a regulatory plan for governing employer-employee relationships regarding one type of employer discrimination, but not the type claimed in the state law claim?

c. **Held.** No. Judgment reversed.

1) State law is preempted under the Supremacy Clause in three circumstances:

a) Congress explicitly defines the extent to which its enactments preempt state law.

b) The state law regulates conduct in a field that Congress intended the federal government to occupy exclusively, even though Congress did not explicitly state the scope of the federal regulation. Congressional intent may be inferred from a pervasive scheme of federal regulation, but when the field allegedly preempted includes areas traditionally occupied by the states, the congressional intent to preempt must be clear.

c) The state law actually conflicts with federal law.

2) In this case, the Act does not explicitly preempt P's claim. The lower courts did not hold that Congress preempted the field, either. Instead, they held that there was an actual tension between P's cause of action and the congressional goals.

3) The Court has previously held that Congress has occupied the entire field of nuclear safety concerns, except the limited powers expressly ceded to the states. It is unlikely, however, that Congress has preempted all state law claims arising from conduct covered by section 210. For example, an employer who hired thugs to assault an employee whistleblower on the job would have retaliated under section 210, but D's position would preclude action by the state even under the state criminal code.

4) The real field-preemption issue is whether P's tort claim is so related to the radiological safety aspects involved in the operation of a nuclear facility that it falls within the preempted field. While a claim for intentional infliction of emotional distress may have some effect on an employer's decisions and make retaliation more costly, this effect is neither direct nor substantial enough to bring P's claim within the preempted field.

5) P's claim could still be preempted if it conflicts with particular aspects of section 210. The district court found that P did not deliberately com-

mit a safety violation within the meaning of section 210, so that section's exemption for such cases does not apply. D claims that because Section 210 lacks a general authorization for exemplary damages, it should bar a state action that would permit such an award. But state causes of action are not preempted solely because they impose liability over and above that authorized by federal law. D finally claims that the availability of state law actions would give whistleblowers less incentive to use Section 210 procedures, with the result that federal regulatory agencies may not be made aware of some violations. This is too speculative to be a basis for preemption, and anyway, most retaliation occurs after a safety complaint has already been registered.

3. **Compliance with Regulations--Ramirez v. Plough, Inc.,** 863 P.2d 167 (Cal. 1993). Ramirez v. Plough, Inc.

a. **Facts.** Ramirez (P), a four-month-old baby, had cold symptoms and his mother gave him St. Joseph Aspirin for Children ("SJAC"), a product manufactured and distributed by Plough, Inc. (D). D's packages of SJAC contained a warning that aspirin could increase the risk of developing Reye's syndrome and that a doctor should be consulted before use in children with flu or chicken pox. The label also described the symptoms of Reye's syndrome. All of this was printed in English on the label as required by the Food and Drug Administration ("FDA"). P's mother was born in Mexico and did not read English. She did not ask anyone to translate the label and did not ask her doctor about giving P aspirin. P developed Reye's syndrome resulting in severe physical and mental damages. P sued D for fraud, negligence, and product liability due to D's alleged failure to warn about the dangers of Reye's syndrome by not printing the instructions in Spanish. The district court granted D summary judgment on the ground that there was no duty to warn in a foreign language. The court of appeal reversed, holding that the adequacy of the warning is a question of fact. The California Supreme Court granted review.

b. **Issue.** May a manufacturer of nonprescription drugs be held liable in tort for distributing its products with warnings in English only, where that is all the law requires?

c. **Held.** No. Judgment affirmed.

1) D clearly had a duty to warn purchasers about dangers in its products, including a duty to warn users of SJAC about the reported association between aspirin use and Reye's syndrome.

2) A statute may be used to define a standard of care in a civil suit. Usually a plaintiff uses a statutory standard of conduct to establish

a breach of duty, but here D seeks to use compliance to establish that no breach of duty occurred. A statute creates a minimum standard, and does not preclude a requirement for greater care in some situations. But where the evidence shows no unusual circumstances, the law's minimum standard may be adequate to establish the applicable standard of conduct.

3) The FDA has adopted detailed regulations to implement federal law regarding labeling, including warnings against unsafe use, side effects, and adverse reactions. The FDA encourages labeling to meet the needs of non-English speaking populations, but only requires full English labeling. California labeling laws are parallel to the FDA rules.

4) The California legislature has adopted statutes requiring the use of languages other than English under specified conditions, such as for public information materials. This suggests that the legislature has deliberately chosen not to require that drug labels be in foreign languages. The FDA also has discontinued a previous requirement to put labels in Spanish. In light of this legislative approach, it would be impractical to have various juries determine what an appropriate drug warning would consist of or to have the court give precise guidance. Instead, the existing legislative and administrative standard of care on this issue should be adopted for tort purposes.

D. JUDICIAL AND LEGISLATIVE CONTROL OVER TORT LAW

Bower v. Westinghouse Corp.

1. Judicial Recognition of New Cause of Action for Medical Monitoring--Bower v. Westinghouse Corp., 522 S.E.2d 424 (W.Va. 1999).

a. **Facts.** Bower and others (Ps) were exposed to toxic substances from a cullet pile maintained by Westinghouse Corporation (D) that contained debris from the manufacture of light bulbs. The pile covered two acres and was 42 feet deep in certain areas. Ps did not exhibit symptoms of any disease related to the exposure, but sued in state court under various theories, including negligence, trespass, and intentional disregard for the health and safety of Ps. Ps sought medical monitoring expenses. The case was removed to federal court and D moved to dismiss based on a previous court's interpretation of West Virginia law that held there was no basis for a claim of medical monitoring without an accompanying physical injury. The federal court certified the question to the West Virginia Supreme Court.

b. **Issue.** Is there a common law cause of action for recovery of anticipated medical monitoring costs where the plaintiffs have been tortiously exposed to toxic substances but do not presently exhibit symptoms of any resulting disease?

c. **Held.** Yes.

1) A number of courts had recognized a cause of action for medical monitoring necessary to detect latent diseases that may develop as a result of tortious exposure to toxic substances. These claims reflect the significant economic harm that may be inflicted on those exposed to toxic substances, even where the physical harm resulting from the exposure is latent.

2) There is no reason to require present physical harm to support a claim for future medical expenses. The injury that underlies a claim for medical monitoring is the invasion of a legally protected interest, not a physical injury. Ps do not need to demonstrate the probable likelihood of developing a serious disease, but only whether medical monitoring is reasonably necessary to properly diagnose the warning signs of disease.

3) To sustain this type of action, Ps must show that:

a) They were exposed to a hazardous substance;

b) There is a probable link between exposure to the substance and human disease;

c) D was at fault in exposing Ps to the substance;

d) As a result Ps have a significantly increased risk of contracting a particular disease;

e) The diagnostic testing is reasonably necessary; and

f) The appropriate medical monitoring procedures exist. (Ps could also take advantage of relevant diagnostic tests that become available in the future.)

d. **Dissent.** The majority has violated the constitutional separation of powers doctrine by usurping the legislatures' authority to enact laws. The state constitution does not allow the courts to create causes of action. Even if it did have that power, plaintiffs may not recover damages unless they have a present injury. The cause of action announced today allows a recovery based on a speculative and amorphous showing of "increased risk."

Williams v. Wilson

2. **Limit on Legislature's Power to Modify Punitive Damages--Williams v. Wilson,** 972 S.W.2d 260 (Ky. 1998).

a. **Facts.** Wilson (P) was on her way to work when she was struck by a vehicle driven by Williams (D), who was intoxicated. D pled guilty to DUI. P sued for compensatory and punitive damages. The trial court refused to give an instruction on punitive damages under the state statute on punitive damages. The Kentucky General Assembly had adopted a statute that modified Kentucky law regarding punitive damages. The traditional common law standard permitted a jury to impose punitive damages upon a finding of gross negligence as measured by an objective standard. The statute required a determination that the defendant acted with "flagrant indifference to the rights to the plaintiff and with a subjective awareness that such conduct will result in human death or bodily harm," and required proof by clear and convincing evidence. P claimed the statute was unconstitutional and that she was entitled to an instruction on common law punitive damages. The court found the statute unconstitutional and gave an instruction on the common law standard. The Kentucky Supreme Court granted discretionary review.

b. **Issue.** May the state legislature change the common law on punitive damages by creating a new standard?

c. **Held.** No. Judgment reversed and remanded.

1) Case law prior to 1891, when the Kentucky Constitution was adopted, allowed punitive damages for negligent conduct that exceeded ordinary negligence, whether such conduct was expressed as gross negligence, recklessness, or wantonness. It is clear that unintentional conduct amounting to gross negligence was sufficient to authorize recovery of punitive damages. The new statute, by requiring proof of a subjective awareness that harm will result, is a vastly elevated standard for the recovery of punitive damages and a clear departure from the common law.

2) In this case, there was no way for P to prove essential elements of the statute since D did not participate and her testimony could not be taken. The statute could therefore lead to a new litigation strategy of having a defendant forego any participation, thereby awarding any risk of punitive damages.

3) The doctrine of jural rights places certain rights of recovery of damages for death or personal injury off-limits to legislative abolishment. It has been followed in Kentucky since 1932, although the concept existed prior to that. Punitive damages fall within the jural rights doctrine, and the legislature does not have the authority to change the law in this area.

d. **Concurrence.** The majority reaches the correct result, although it has extended the jural rights doctrine far beyond its original scope. Still, the doctrine of stare decisis supports the majority's ruling.

e. **Dissent.** The court need not address the jural rights doctrine in this case because the statute does not abolish the common law right to punitive damages. The statute merely established standards to guide the jury in its determination of whether such damages are appropriate and the amount to be awarded. The fallacy is the assumption that the element of "subjective awareness" can be proven only by the direct testimony of the person against whom punitive damages are sought. Even in a criminal case, mens rea may be inferred from the act itself and/or the surrounding circumstances. The jury should have been instructed in accordance with the statute. The jural rights doctrine is a judicial usurpation of a traditional legislative prerogative and the legislature is better suited than the courts to formulate broad public policy.

3. **Cap on Medical Malpractice Awards--Pulliam v. Coastal Emergency Services,** 509 S.E.2d 307 (Va. 1999).

Pulliam v. Coastal Emergency Services

a. **Facts.** Mrs. Pulliam arrived at an emergency room complaining of aching legs. She was examined by a doctor who had been retained by Coastal Emergency Services (D) to staff the emergency room. The doctor discharged her after prescribing a muscle relaxant. A few hours later, she returned to the emergency room and was examined by another physician who put her in intensive care. She died later that night from bacterial pneumonia. D was found vicariously liable for medical malpractice and the jury awarded Pulliam's husband (P) $2,045,000. The trial court reduced the verdict to $1 million pursuant to a state statute that limited medical malpractice awards to $1 million. P appeals, claiming the statute is unconstitutional.

b. **Issue.** May a state legislature impose a hard cap on the amount of damages that can be awarded in a medical malpractice case for injury or death to a patient?

c. **Held.** Yes. Judgment affirmed.

1) Actions of the legislature are presumed to be constitutional. Any reasonable doubt regarding a statute's constitutionality must be resolved in favor of its validity. A previous case, *Etheridge v. Medical Center Hospitals*, 376 S.E.2d 525 (Va. 1989), has already upheld the statute.

2) Stare decisis plays an important role in the orderly administration of justice by assuring consistent, predictable, and balanced application of legal principles. *Etheridge* can only be reversed if there was a flagrant error or mistake in that decision.

3) P claims that the statutory cap violates P's right to receive the amount of damages awarded by a jury. The cap comes into effect after P has had the benefit of a proper jury trial, so it is not like remittitur. P is not entitled to a new trial after the cap is applied. It is not the role of the jury but of the legislature to determine the legal consequences of the jury's factual findings.

4) A legislature may completely abolish a cause of action, or limit its availability with a statute of limitations, without violating the right of trial by jury, so it may also limit damages recoverable for a cause of action.

5) In enacting the cap, the legislature was responding to the difficulty faced by health care providers in obtaining affordable malpractice insurance. The cap has a reasonable and substantial relation to the legislature's objective to protect the public's health, safety, and welfare by insuring the availability of health care providers in Virginia.

6) P claims that the cap is an unconstitutional taking of property because P has a property interest in the full measure of the verdict. However, a right is subject to due process protection only when it has accrued, and there is no vested right in the continuance of common law rule. P's cause of action had not accrued when the cap statute was adopted, and nothing prohibited the legislature from capping remedies on unaccrued causes of action.

7) There was no violation of the separation of powers because the legislature has the constitutional power to determine the original and appellate jurisdiction of the courts. The legislature is not restricted from acting in the area of common law, and can provide, modify, or repeal a remedy.

d. **Concurrence.** The cap creates an unwarranted injustice in certain situations and creates the greatest hardship on those individuals who are most severely injured by medical malpractice. Yet this is a matter for legislative concern.

XXIV. ALTERNATIVE COMPENSATION SYSTEMS

A. OCCUPATIONAL INJURIES AND WORKERS' COMPENSATION

1. **Introduction.** Employer liability for employees injured at work was the field in which liability insurance first developed. Shortly thereafter, legislation was passed (now every state has such a system) to provide employer contributions to a state fund to compensate injured employees, regardless of fault (known as "workers' compensation" statutes). Benefits are limited in amount and duration. In most states, employers can insure against these risks or employees may choose to be governed by traditional fault principles.

2. **Scope of Coverage.** Workers' compensation covers accidents "arising out of and in the course of employment." Typically, workers' compensation is the sole remedy an employee has against his employer. Further, accidents occurring in commuting to and from work are not covered (the "coming and going" rule).

3. **Compensation Benefits.**

   a. **Statutory.** All workers' compensation benefits have a statutory basis. The statutes typically set a formula for the determination of the allowable benefit.

   b. **Amounts.** Using the formula to determine the amount of recovery requires reference to the statutes of the jurisdiction involved. Most states, however, consider the seriousness of the injury, expected length of incapacity, and average weekly wage of the worker. This provides lost wages. States also set a maximum amount allowable.

4. **Exclusive Remedy—Policy Grounds.** The workers' compensation statutes provide prompt, certain recovery for injured workers. The worker does not have to prove fault and does not risk losing benefits due to contributory negligence, assumption of risk, or other defenses. The employer gains the benefit that the compensation benefits are limited in amount and are the exclusive remedy available to the injured employee.

5. **Intentional Torts--Blankenship v. Cincinnati Milacron Chemicals, Inc.,** 433 N.E.2d 572 (Ohio), *cert. denied*, 459 U.S. 857 (1982).

Blankenship v. Cincinnati Milacron Chemicals, Inc.

   a. **Facts.** Blankenship, an employee of Cincinnati Milacron Chemicals, Inc. (D), was exposed to chemical fumes that caused permanent disability. Blankenship and other employees (Ps) brought suit, claiming D knew of the health hazards but failed to correct the problems, failed to warn Ps, failed to report them to government agencies as required by law, and failed to provide proper medical treatment. Ps claimed D's acts were intentional. The trial court, holding that Ps' suit was barred by the state Workers' Compensation Act, dismissed. The appellate court affirmed and the state supreme court granted certification.

b. **Issue.** Does the Workers' Compensation Act prevent employees from suing their employer for intentional torts?

c. **Held.** No. Judgment reversed.

1) The Ohio Constitution permits workers' compensation acts for injuries, death, and diseases arising "in the course of such [worker's] employment." However, when an employee alleges an intentional tort, the claim is not for an injury arising out of the course of his employment. Consequently, an intentional tort is not covered by the Workers' Compensation Act.

2) The Workers' Compensation Act was intended to assist workers by insuring a recovery for work-related injuries. In return for this greater assurance of recovery, employees gave up their ordinary tort remedies. However, if the Act applied to intentional torts, it would have the effect of encouraging such conduct, contrary to the purpose of the Act of protecting workers.

3) The compensation scheme provides less than full compensation for injured employees. It does not include pain and suffering or punitive damages. An employer should not be able to avoid these damages for its intentional torts.

B. "NO-FAULT" AUTO INSURANCE

Some states have adopted statutes changing the handling of auto accident claims through so-called "no-fault" insurance plans.

1. **Advantages to Adopting "No-Fault" Plans.** Eliminating "fault" as the basis for liability in auto accident cases alleviates the following objectionable features of negligence actions:

a. **"All or nothing" recoveries.** The plaintiff gets nothing unless she can convince the jury that the defendant was "at fault"; likewise, if the defendant can convince the jury that the plaintiff was contributorily negligent or had assumed the risk (prior to states adopting comparative negligence standards).

b. **Delays and expenses of litigation.** Proving "fault" requires litigation with attendant expenses and attorneys' fees for both parties. Until a judgment is returned (or settlement made), an injured plaintiff gets nothing (even though it is in the interim that she needs help the most); and the increasing burden of such litigation has congested court calendars so that plaintiffs frequently have to wait years for a trial.

c. **Inaccurate compensation.** There has also been concern that the settlement process has led to the overcompensation of small cases and the undercompensation of large cases.

d. **Cost of insurance.** Insurance premiums have soared due to the costs of litigation and high verdicts.

2. **Operation of "No-Fault" Plans.** Although the plans enacted vary considerably, the following are the essential provisions:

a. **Mandatory insurance.** All car owners are required to obtain (and keep in effect) insurance covering claims arising out of the operation of their cars. Failure to do so usually results in forfeiture of auto registration and/or driver's license. This policy would cover both liability and no-fault claims.

b. **Scope of coverage.** The insurance extends to all claims arising out of operation of any motor vehicle, without regard to fault.

1) Generally, this includes claims allowed under traditional tort concepts, as well as certain claims not currently allowed; *e.g.*, claims by an injured "guest" in an auto and by the driver who hurts herself by her own fault.

2) But the insurance does ***not*** apply to claims arising out of defects in the vehicle itself (*i.e.*, products liability claims, *supra*).

c. **Claims handled on "first-party" basis.** Any driver injured in an auto accident would make a claim against her own insurer (*i.e.*, the policy covering the car that the injured party was riding in), so that in the typical two-car crash, the occupants of each car would claim against the insurance covering that car.

1) Under the present "third-party" insurance system, the injured party usually makes a claim against the insurer of the other car.

2) The "third-party" procedure would be retained only when the accident is not covered by first-party insurance; *e.g.*, a pedestrian injured by an auto would still make a claim against the insurer covering the car that struck her. (Under a few plans, however, if the pedestrian owned a car, she would claim against her own insurer.)

3) Since "fault" would be immaterial, the claims procedure is relatively simple; any disagreement between the policyholder and her

insurance company as to the amount recoverable (below) is subject to arbitration.

d. **Damages recoverable.** None of the major plans provide insurance coverage for pain and suffering or disfigurement. Coverage is limited to economic losses (lost wages, medical bills, etc.). However, the plans vary considerably as to the amount of such coverage.

3. **Impact of "No-Fault" Plans.**

a. **Curtailment of tort litigation.** The plans vary concerning the extent to which traditional negligence actions (with traditional "fault" principles) would still be permitted.

1) **"Pure" no fault.** A few proposals would abolish tort actions altogether (*e.g.*, the American Insurance Association proposal). However, no state has adopted such a plan.

2) **"Partial" no fault.** All existing plans currently allow at least certain actions.

a) Under some plans, tort actions can still be maintained for all but relatively minor cases: for example, under one statute, the plaintiff can sue for pain and suffering whenever the medical expenses exceed $500, or when any permanent or disabling injury (*e.g.*, bone fracture) is involved.

b) Under other plans, however, only severe cases could ever be pursued in court; *e.g.*, a tort action could be maintained for economic losses not covered by the injured party's own insurance, and for general damages in excess of $5,000, but only if the accident caused death, permanent injury or disfigurement, or inability to work for more than six consecutive months.

C. OTHER NO-FAULT SYSTEMS

1. **Reasons for Expansion.** With the initial success of automobile no-fault insurance, suggestions have been made to use the principles in other areas.

2. **Defective Products.** Use of a form of no-fault liability has been suggested for the products liability area. It has been suggested that an "enterprise" could be liable for all injuries caused.

3. **Medical Malpractice.** If no-fault coverage were enacted for medical malpractice, several benefits would be gained. Patients would not have to prove fault but would give up other tort recovery.

D. COMPREHENSIVE NO-FAULT

1. **New Zealand.** The New Zealand Compensation Act provides a complete no-fault scheme. All personal injuries due to accidents are covered by insurance. Most tort claims have, therefore, been abolished.

2. **Social Insurance.**

   a. **Basic purpose.** Welfare programs are designed to compensate people who fall within specific criteria. The plans are not necessarily intended to cover accident victims, but such victims may fit within the scheme.

   b. **Available funds.** The funds available may take several forms. Recipients may be entitled to cash or benefits in kind.

TABLE OF CASES

(Page numbers of briefed cases in bold)

NOTES

NOTES

NOTES

NOTES